A Lost Love

ELEANOR LEE GUSTAW

CONTENTS

DEDICATION

To God, Who brought this story into my heart as I was considering writing another novel, and by showing me a vision of a thick, black-covered book, well-worn, and yellowed with age, high upon a shelf.

Within this slivered, yet clearly defined glimpse of an image, I seriously began to ponder its essence, where it eventually began to come together in such an amazing way, and was more than enough, aplenty, in creating this unique story!

Always, thank you for these extraordinary, wondrous moments of opportunity awaiting in inspiring my heart to reach for the moon and the highest stars of excellence, and the strength through its worth to keep moving forward in your Divine calling!

And to my beautiful mother, Bernice, who has always shared my heart's passion within my heart as an author and a poet. You always give of your love to me: faithfully, strong, and true, as a flower's exquisite beauty that fragrances my soul in the depths of its riches, which means the world to me!

And Miss Marty Cooper, a friend I have long since lost in correspondence and shall always miss but hold ever dearest to my heart in the gift of the sweetness we shared in friendship as close sisters. You are forever this special blessing to me; a beloved friend and a treasured gift, and I shall love you always!

And to Ian West, a beloved friend I shall forever cherish, who helped to bring this story to the forefront for publication.

ACKNOWLEDGEMENTS

In honor of a very dear friend, Bill Johnson, who inspired this story and always encouraged me in my work. May every blessing be yours as you follow your heart no matter to what we do in serving the Lord, our God Most High. You shall always hold a very special place within my heart; you and Harry both, on which the gift of the children's series of *Hope's Lantern*, written under the pseudonym of Lee H. Johnson, is based on fact, where God led us softly unawares upon this path.

A special thanks of appreciation to Ian West for everything he gave in this project with me as my Advertising Manager.

PREFACE

Although I have incorporated a flair of definitively unique and distinctive word structures within my scenes that are partially based on fact, and are threaded throughout the novel, this story is otherwise purely fictitious.

All characters and incidents relating to context are likewise, strictly fictional, and penned solely from the author's imagination. Any similarities of personalities and scenes are duly incidental.

The poems, *A Lost Rose*, *June's Gift*, and *My Wild Rose*, were written by the author.

The poem in Chapter 21: Christmas Blessings, which appears at the close of the chapter, is used by permission of the poet, Raya Hill, who created this lovely piece for my birthday. It is untitled. My deepest appreciation for this amazingly exquisite expression in honor of me, dear Raya!

– Eleanor Lee Gustaw

AUTHOR'S NOTE

There are stories of lost love that are found, but this is a story of a love lost forever, based partially on fact, until . . .

Other Book Titles by Author Eleanor Lee Gustaw

Fictional romance novels: Youth to Adult
A Lost Love
A Chord of Melody
Victoria's House (Upcoming)

The Stranger Saga: A fictional romance series: Youth to Adult
The Stranger
A Rookie's Daughter
A Rookie's Son (Upcoming)
And Then There Were Four (Upcoming)

Hope's Lantern series: Children to Adult under Author's Pen Name: Lee H. Johnson
Hope's Lantern
Hope's Lantern Lives (Upcoming)
A Gift of Hope (Upcoming)
Harry's Apple Tree (Upcoming)
A New Christmas (Upcoming)

The Sundog Snow Adventure Trilogy: Children to Adult
The Sundog Snow Adventure
A Cherry Pie and Mr. Crumble (Upcoming)
The Threesome Adventure (Upcoming)

Fictional Children's Novel
The Mysterious Man With the Lantern (Upcoming)

Fictional Children's Books: The Color Series
Mr. Yellow Saves the Day (Upcoming)
Mr. Lopez and the Red Apple (Upcoming)
The Mystery of Robby's Blue Shoe (Upcoming)

CHAPTER 1

Reflective Memories

Yellowed and well-worn with age, I reached for the thick, black-covered book high upon the shelf in the Drawing Room. Going back in time, my grandmother, Maggie Hanes-Danes, had written the story of her life in *A Lost Love*, that still mesmerized me to this day. It came through the turning leaves of the pages about the handsome man who came unexpectedly into her life, and Blossom, the little child who came as her beloved daughter in time.

Sitting on her lap, I asked, "Grandmother, can you show me the pictures, please?"

Smiling, with a slight laugh, I nodded, hugging her close. "Yes, my dear. You may not understand this for a while, Emily," I softly spoke. "But this is a story about *A Lost Love*, which has its own uniquely special scenes of a book's pages, that your grandfather and I have lived through the years. Let's begin now, shall we?" I asked.

Nodding, I turned the first page as she sat mesmerized, and my words drifted in and out as she peered at the opening picture. Depicted in the scene was a young woman in an underground garage speaking to the handsome man behind the wheel. The overhead light in the garage momentarily caught the beautiful blue of his car, causing it to brightly shimmer against the bleak surroundings. He would come to be her grandfather, Daniel Danes. Her grandmother, Maggie Danes, me, always a spirited woman, held my smiling eyes at attention as they twinkled while I stood by Dan's car.

Turning to the following page, the story began.

> The glow of the lantern filled my heart with warmth, I'd written, as I sat by the hearth, warming my cold hands. I turned toward the window as the wind howled, and the flame in the lamp on the table flickered. Shivering, I drew the soft, blue blanket closer about me, sitting in front of the stone structure.

My mind wandered to the day when I'd met my beloved, twice, in fact! Such a unique gift I could never have expected because of my overly busy and forgetful mind that morning.

The well-worn pages began to come to life as Emily sat contentedly on my lap.

> I had a wonderful dream, the story began to unfold with narrative intrigue, of a handsome man who helped me find my way. I didn't know how wonderfully it would come to change my life despite the storms that buffeted for a time. As I paused at an intersection in an underground garage, I couldn't remember where I'd parked my car. At that moment, a sleek car slowed to a stop, and I inquired of the stranger as he offered his help.

> "We'll find it in a jiffy," he smiled, as his eyes sparkled.

> I never took rides with strangers, but somehow, an inexplicable peace filled my soul as he leaned over and opened the door for me to get into his car. I was so grateful to him that I kissed him. Imagine that! He didn't seem to think anything of it and put his car in 'drive' as we made the search together. Shortly afterwards, we found my car tucked between two huge vans, nestled like a butterfly between two ravens, I laughed to myself!

This became the story of a young writer and a publisher, where they're still living their dreams in the love they found in time.

Thanking the stranger, I stepped out of his car, and offered him a bill for his kindness. Refusing profusely, he suddenly said, "Perhaps, we'll meet again one day, Miss."

"Perhaps," I replied. "Thank you again, Mister."

"I must be off now," he smiled. "I have an appointment and I don't want to keep my client waiting."

It was a perplexing dream, I thought upon awakening, as I drew the blankets aside and soon felt my feet on the cold floor. I reached for my housecoat hanging on the back of the bedpost, at the same time, stepping into my slippers. I knew that God still spoke in dreams sometimes, and I pondered whether this could be one such time, where it held a significant meaning to it, that I didn't quite understand. As the day moved on, it continued to come to my mind and the feeling held. While I didn't hold much to dreams as such, somehow, just perhaps, God was indeed speaking and would reveal it in His time and way.

Glancing at the clock on my bedside night table, I was a little perturbed, realizing that I had slightly overslept, and my alarm had malfunctioned. Peering out the window, the sun greeted me with its welcoming warmth. With all the tasks set out for me today, I had a lot to accomplish, because today, as well as tomorrow, were especially important. I hurried through my breakfast, not wanting to be late for any of them!

As my day began, around the bend, in time, how little did I know that my life was about to change. In fact, it already had, in a manner of speaking. I just didn't know it. In Time's journal, that mere encounter within this strange dream was leading me on a path to an incredible journey that had already begun to come alive, where I found God's heart close to it within mine.

Exiting my boarding house, I hummed softly, breathing in the fresh air, and listening to the melodic songs of the birds that uplifted my soul in praise just to be alive. This was the last day on the job for me as a secretary for a railway company. They were moving the firm to another city, and I wanted it to be a special day. I soon entered the premises, and with a deep breath, exhaled as I greeted my boss. Such a lovely man, I thought. I'd miss my colleagues, too, but it would give me more time for what I really loved – writing. I wondered what new adventures awaited me!

The following morning, I hurried to get my errands done before I was to meet up with my appointment. I was terrible at remembering even the simplest of matters some days, mainly because of my hectic schedule, and giving it proper attention, like where I'd parked my car. Underground garages, like this one, effused an almost eerie, closed-in feeling, and was much too dark to suit me, let alone trying to find one's vehicle in a maze of countless vehicles of varied sizes.

Pausing at the exact intersection that had been revealed in my dream, I was feeling a little disconcerted that I couldn't recall where I'd parked my car. Just then, a lovely, white sports car emerged from around a corner, slowing to a stop as I hesitated.

"What seems to be the matter?" the driver congenially asked.

Walking forward, I sighed. "I don't remember where I parked, Mister, and I need to get to a certain place - an appointment - straight away," I replied, in a bit of a dither.

"I see," he replied, rubbing his chin. "Well, perhaps I might be of service to you. If you like, I'll drive you around and you can tell me when we get to your vehicle."

A feeling of perfect peace rested in my heart. "That's very kind of you, sir. Thank you." I got into his vehicle and said, "It shouldn't be too far away, but I always get turned around in this place."

"It's no trouble and I'm glad to help."

Minutes later, I cried, "There it is! The blue convertible." I opened my purse and offered him a large bill.

"Oh, no!" he exclaimed. "It was my pleasure to help you. Just have a great day, Miss."

"But" I said, as I opened the car door and stepped back, but he wouldn't hear of it.

"I need to run. It was a pleasure meeting you." Pulling away from where I stood, his car slowly moved forward, and in a few moments, was soon lost to view. There was nothing more I could do but to tuck the bill back into my purse.

Minutes later, I reached my destination, parking in a beautifully spacious lot at a publishing house. Getting out of my vehicle, I closed the door, breathing in the lovely scents of the flowers that lilted in the sunshine along the pleasant walkway.

Entering the building, I approached the Reception Desk in a lovely wide and spacious area just off the foyer, but the secretary wasn't present. After ten minutes, I concluded that she was obviously busy elsewhere.

Cautiously, shyly, peering around a corner, I wandered along a considerably lengthy corridor. Without too much trouble, I found the person I was seeking as I quietly hesitated, momentarily, in front of a door. It indicated that it was the Editor's office with his name engraved on the glass plated window. Lightly knocking on the door, I took a deep breath as a slightly muffled voice invited me in and I softly entered, gently closing the door behind me. I turned around and looked across the desk where the editor was busy writing.

Studying him, his lovely, dark hair was beautifully cut, and the contours of his face, long and lean. He almost seemed familiar to me.

As he laid down his pen, I was just as startled as he was when his eyes met mine.

"Well, this is a surprise," he said, rising in his chair, reaching his hand to welcome me as we shook hands.

My legs felt shaky, but I answered with a strength I didn't feel. "Indeed!"

"You must be Maggie Hanes."

"Yes," I said. "I am."

"Please . . . take a seat," he kindly offered, sitting back down in his chair. "I'm Daniel Danes. 'Dan' for short." Looking deep into my eyes, he teased, "I'm so glad you could make it! I suppose I didn't need to hurry as quickly as I did, but you see, I was expecting a client, although I never would have suspected my client to be you! I hope you'll forgive me?" he mischievously said.

"Oh, I understand . . . perfectly," I exulted. "I don't know how long it might have taken me if you hadn't come along and helped me locate my car."

"No worries there. I must admit, that's happened once or twice to me, too." Becoming serious, he commented, "I think we may have a slight problem with your manuscript." As Dan paused, I tried to remain calm. "It's simply wonderful!" he burst out. "Maggie, I'm just wondering how you ever came up with such an impeccable plot that made the elements of your novel so amazing?"

"Oh, goodness!" I exclaimed. "You liked it?" I asked, stunned.

"Absolutely! You need to go on the radio and television, too – for interviews," he emphasized. "We want to also consider producing this book with the finest people in the movie industry."

Taken aback, I didn't know what to say. Tears welled in my eyes. "But you said there was a problem."

"Maggie," he said, "I understand your emotion. We want a sequel as soon as you can write one. Our team is most eager to begin working on your project – preparing the manuscript to galley as soon as possible. I'm just wondering if you have any ideas for the book cover?"

Drying my tears and composing myself, I replied, "No, I'm afraid I haven't any, but I'll know what I like – and I don't," I replied, trying to hide a smile, "when I see the options."

"I'll see what might inspire me and the design team," the editor promptly replied. "In the meantime, please relax. I'll call you when the galley is ready." Rising, he said, "Have a great day, Maggie, and thank you for stopping by."

"Sure," I said, rising from my chair and walking towards the door. "My pleasure. Thank you, Mr. Danes." As I was about to open the door, I turned and inquisitively asked, as he stared across the room at me with a hint of a smile, "Mr. Danes, just what is the problem with my manuscript, may I ask?"

Laughing, he smiled and replied, "University seems to have made a fair genius out of you, and as to the problem, I'm wondering what will follow."

Frowning, his words left me feeling unsure. "Forgive me," I quietly said.

Explaining it more concisely, his tone was soft and light, and almost sweet, as he said, "I'd love to see a sequel, Maggie! I thought I made that clear?"

"I see." Pausing, it struck me full force. "You do? Really? But I'll need to think about that," I cheerily exclaimed. "I've been rather considering that very same thing!" I grinned. Then, addressing his educated assumption, I confessed, "By the way, Mr. Danes," I braved, "I've never so much as stepped foot on the grounds of any university. I write from my heart and –" I hesitated, "with God's guidance. I don't know what I'd ever do without Him. Well, goodbye," I said, "and thank you!" Turning, I hesitated, contemplating as I glanced back, noticing his bewildered expression, seemingly speechless in the moment. Rushing down the long corridor, I hurriedly moved on, feeling the flush of my face against the cool of the morning as I exited the building, and found the freshness I longed for again, gratefully taking in deep breaths of the morning air as my soul sang its praise to God Almighty!

That night, I pondered how a country girl had come so far with no university education. I'd always relied on my heart to guide me. And without God to lead me on the path, I'd never have come to such special moments as I had now.

Within two months, the manuscript was approved and submitted to the printer. I was so excited! It wasn't long when the day came that Dan called, requesting me to meet him at his office. I could hardly wait, hurrying out the door, my heart all aflutter! When I was seated in his office twenty minutes after our conversation, he observed that sometimes, university is for the dogs. I kept my laughter in and couldn't help but smile at that! "You're so amazing," he said. "I can hardly believe what you've done all on your own."

"Well, I had help . . . from God," I smiled. "Remember?"

Laughing, he said, "Yes, of course. From God. You did mention that Maggie." Reaching in his desk drawer, he pulled out a book and momentarily held it in his hands. Then he looked up into my eyes and smiling, said, "We're so happy you came aboard our company, Maggie. I trust that the published result will be most satisfactory with you." Rising from his chair and coming around his desk, he gently placed the book within my hands.

I was so astonished that my heart's dream was now realized as I gazed upon the beautiful book cover, thinking of what to say. Then, gently running my hand over it, tears misted in my eyes, and I softly said, "Thank you, Dan! It's just beautiful! I didn't expect it be published this soon."

Dan pressed a hand to my shoulder. "We consider this book to be exceptional, Maggie, and we're anticipating the sequel shortly. Your book is absolutely superb! I wish that all my authors would take the same care you have in presenting an almost flawless manuscript. Just keep writing from your heart, and oh," he considered with significant meaning, "and with God's help, for sure! I believe you already have shared with me that you're working on creating the sequel. Might I ask how far along your writing is?"

"It's coming along considerably well, Mr. Danes. I'm presently refining the last details, so it should soon be ready for the initial galley. Perhaps, another month or so," I smiled.

"Well," he said, releasing his hand from my shoulder, "do take care and enjoy your newly published novel! And of course, I shall look forward to being in touch with you shortly."

"Yes. Thank you!" I replied with a happy lilt. "So am I! This is truly a very special day for me."

"As it is for me," he said, with such feeling as his beautiful, blue eyes sparkled, looking into mine momentarily, that it almost sounded personal. And it wasn't until I exited the premises that I realized I'd addressed him as "Dan," and not "Mr. Danes!" I hoped he hadn't noticed any!

Chapter 2

If Ever Dreams Came True

I didn't tell Dan Danes that I suspected that there were some days when I was certain mice ate better than me. Something had to change, and fast.

I leisurely browsed through a newspaper in the days ahead that someone in the nearby park had left on a bench. To my surprise, it was current. Idly, I leafed through the paper, and paused midway, when a dog came out of nowhere, chasing a cat, and rudely disrupting the quietude all around me. Outwitting the determined brute, I laughed as the cat scampered up the tree closest to me, leaving the dog staring in momentary dismay. The feline stared him down; unyielding; fiercely hissing; its eyes intense and focused, but the tenacious creature stood its ground, contemplating.

Although I was absorbed in the newspaper, the persistent clickity-clack of a woman's high heels, as she gingerly ran as fast as she dared along the path, briefly drew my eyes to her, then back to the naughty, inquisitive dog still trying to have his fun. Her lovely, long black hair was noticeably disheveled in the wind, but she didn't appear concerned about it at the moment.

The slender, young woman; mid-twenty or so, was very pretty. She was dressed more for an office setting rather than a morning stroll in the park, I thought to myself, observing her. It was obvious that her dear cat had somehow gotten away from her. Perhaps, she had been unexpectedly detained on the walkway, and slackened her hold on the leash, unaware, as her cat stealthily slipped away. Whatever the reason, she hurried right past me, without so much as a glance. Pausing a few feet from where I was seated, she leaned against the tree, getting her breath back.

The feline stayed glued to a broad, sturdy branch it was hiding out of; camouflaged against its beautiful black fur; its green eyes unwavering, and tensely alert to every tiny movement. Moments afterward, the woman stepped away from the tree. Regarding his intolerable behavior with stern disapproval, she attempted to shoo the dog away, loudly shouting, and flailing her arms every which way.

I leaned forward, and the newspaper suddenly shifted in my hands, as the wind picked up, fluttering the pages. I continued curiously watching the confrontational scene playing out before me, and the element of intrigue that held me there. Even though I didn't know the woman, I was both shocked at the strength by which she governed the situation, and at the same time, very proud of her! She assuredly had handled similar incidents, not indicating a jot of fear now, either, to the four-footed animal trying to hold her beloved cat hostage!

The dog grumbled; bewildered, rumbling deep in his throat, testing his next tentative move, but the woman remained firm. After a few minutes, however, he didn't press the matter further, and quietly dashed off, as if to say, That's that!

The woman's gruffness immediately vanished, and sweetness instantly was on her lips again, as she turned her attention to her cat, and lovingly looked into her face. Her tone was wonderfully kind and soft, as she gently reassured her feline. "It's alright now, my darling Violet," she said. She briefly placed her hands on her hips, making it more dramatic than it really was at this point, and I chuckled to myself!

Fortunately, her cat had climbed the tree high enough not to have been reached by the annoying dog, but she was still too far for her owner to grasp her from her leafy prison. It wasn't so easily persuaded, however, until she offered it a tempting treat. Drawing out a small package from an adorably small shoulder purse, and opening the package, the woman reached her arms towards the tree, where her feline remained hidden, still indecisive. She looked for her tormenting adversary, meowing, but he was long gone. The cat was finally convinced, albeit warily cautious, as it slowly, and carefully, descended; her eyes totally focused on the treat, and alert. Gently grasping her beloved Violet moments later, I found tears misting my eyes. Safe in the woman's arms now, she lovingly kissed her cat, holding her close in a firm, yet tender embrace.

Retracing her steps with Violet snuggled on her neck, the woman turned to me moments later, and sheepishly beamed, saying, 'How do you do?' Without waiting for an answer, she hurried along the path with her precious bundle, and I quickly lost sight of them as they disappeared around the bend, where trees obscured my view. Drying my happy tears, I laughed and turned my attention back to the paper. What an adventure, I exclaimed in my thoughts, turning the page. Giggling to myself, I didn't suppose that the dog would wander around the park any time soon! At that precise moment, I was completely startled when a masculine voice gently said, "Good day to you, Miss!" as he tipped his hat, and continued on his way. Even though he'd seemingly come out of nowhere, like that brute dog, I didn't suppose for one iota that the well-groomed, older gentleman, could possibly be that terrible creature's owner! Shaking my head at my own silliness, I concentrated on the newspaper, wondering if there was anything of value I might find within its bedraggled pages.

At that moment, the wind fiercely increased, nearly ripping the newspaper from my hands, making a tear, nonetheless, on the page it finally settled on. I was about to abandon it, when the *Want Ads* suddenly caught my eyes, and I drew in my breath. Perhaps, it was worth taking note of after all, I decided.

That very afternoon I called up the agency and the lady told me to come right in. Much to my surprise, she said I'd do just fine. "The client is a very nice man, and as I understand, a widower, and he needs help with his huge house. He has a hired cook, so perhaps, you might put a little more meat on your bones," she smiled, with a bit of arrogance, looking me over. "The address isn't far from where you live, and it's in a lovely part of the neighborhood. Have you ever been that way?" she inquired.

"No, ma'am, I haven't. But it sounds fine." Much to my chagrin and unorthodox way of thinking, I looked her over, too, trying hard not to laugh, and decided that with a few less pounds on her, she'd be quite the pretty lady!

"The job is yours if you like that kind of work. I hear the owner is a considerately reasonable man, so you should do very well." She lifted the telephone receiver and talked so low into it; I couldn't make out a single word. Replacing the receiver moments later, she said with a tinge of relief in her words as her smile met my eyes, "The Mr. has agreed to take you on this very afternoon. It's been about three weeks since anyone has cleaned his home, so you'd better not dillydally." I felt for a second like I was in a daze and seemed unable to move. Gently, with twinkling eyes, she said, "Off with you now, young lady! Time waits for no one!"

I immediately snapped out of my reverie and thanked her for her kindness.

"No need," she gaily said. "I've met the master of the house a few times myself, and I'm quite sure that he will be more than pleased with you!" Handing me his address, I noted it assured that I could easily find the place, and I hurried on my way.

The client lived in a beautiful neighborhood, just as the agency woman had stated. His home was like it had been drawn out of a fairytale book, and a wondrous dream before my eyes, that I could scarcely take it in. A gorgeous mansion was set back from the road with a massive yard, and beautiful maples surrounding it in a very charming and welcoming, yet pleasingly elegant and captivatingly familiar vogue signature in the area. The homes along the street were widely spread out, invoking a sense of perfect privacy and an enchantingly idyllic feeling. Leisurely striding carefree down the long, winding drive, I loved it already! I drank of its beauty; lingering longer than I intended.

An avenue of beautiful trees, parallel to the drive, bordered the extensive walkway, and was so wonderfully entrancing as I adored the pleasure of each footstep. Its quaint eloquence made for a fun walk beneath the shading branches.

When I reached the house, the chime of the doorbell immediately brought a beautiful, young woman to the door, inviting me in, and warmly welcoming me with a lovely, yet somewhat, shy smile. She ran her hand along the side of her flowered, lacy apron, dusting off a patch of flour, then closing the door, led me down a hallway to a magnificently spacious kitchen. She introduced herself as the mister's cook, Ethel Rodriguez. There seemed an especially fascinating intrigue about her that I'd never met in anyone else, and I liked her at once as her sparkling black eyes held my attention.

Ethel indicated for me to be seated at the table, offering me a lemon drink that was delightfully quenching, and an irresistibly tempting plate of cinnamon buns topped with a cream cheese icing, of which both were delicious. Across the table from her, I began to relax in her pleasant company. Twenty minutes later, she gathered the dishes from the table and placed them in the kitchen sink. Then, with a gentle grace, she gave me a tour of the large mansion, talking with such expressive animation, I was truly impressed.

Everything was so wonderfully enchanting and adoring, that it took my breath away. The uniqueness of the architecture, with its superbly delightful airy rooms, was truly like a picture right out of a book! Peace overwhelmed my heart amidst the aura and beauty of my surroundings, and I believed I would truly enjoy my work within this lovely abode.

"Tomorrow," she was saying, "you can begin work. My Mr. said not to mind what the agency might have told you, and he asked me to welcome you this afternoon to get you comfortable, Miss, and then you can begin fresh in the morning. He'll also take your time today into consideration and plus to your pay."

I had to think a moment what she meant, then laughed. While I didn't want to be rude, I couldn't take his money for just an hour or more, "plus" or "no plus" added on. "Oh, no!" I exclaimed. "He mustn't expect to pay me for this bit of time today," I said.

"He's decided, Miss, to reimburse you for the whole day just to have you," she insisted, "especially since his home hasn't had a proper cleaning for some time, you see, because you'll have a lot of extra work. So, if you kindly would, I wouldn't argue anything about it."

While I better understood his reasoning, I still felt uncomfortable with it. But I politely smiled and said, "That's most kind and appreciated and I intend to do my best for him."

Ethel smiled, and it seemed there was a pleasure in it that I couldn't quite put my finger on. I wondered if she'd had to take on any of that responsibility after the previous housekeeper had suddenly left.

How extraordinary and unusual his kind gesture was, I smiled to myself. The Mr. surely must be a very special man to express such a length of thoughtful and caring consideration. As I left the premises minutes later, my heart was deep in thought, unaware that my life was literally on the pinnacle of changing again.

As the days turned into weeks, this was one of my favorite places; wandering along the lovely avenue and sitting on a bench where the final curve at the back of the mansion met a beautifully intriguing yard with trees surrounding flowerbeds of wondrous beauty. A pleasant, white picket fence bordered the property line, almost completely obscuring the neighboring, far-spread house a quarter of a mile away, on the west side. With the overhanging branches of the trees obscuring this lovely paradise within its walls, it certainly held a captivating charm all its own.

The house next door was located at the edge of a thick wood, and no houses were adjacent on the eastern side to the elderly gentleman Ethel said lived there, providing greater privacy and an incredibly awesome view. A gurgling brook broke the woods near the center, adding to the lovely picturesque and cheerful portrait of this delightfully exquisite scene.

Mr. West, the closest neighbor, was retired, and I oftentimes caught a glimpse of him from the Mr.'s upstairs bedroom balcony. It was no secret that he loved his daily walks, and I surely couldn't blame him any for that! It was such a good feeling that Mr. West appreciated the beauty of the land, like me! I was over the moon when he invited me to enjoy his land whenever I had the notion! Ethel thought that quite funny and I wondered why.

"Oh," she confessed, "he called me up one day and asked me who the pretty lady was that turned into the Mr.'s avenue every day. He said he saw you walking often, and thought you'd enjoy the view up close."

I laughed and admitted that I would! I also found that Mr. West had a wonderful sense of humor and was very interesting company. I just didn't tell Ethel that his cook, Anna Snow, served the most delectable desserts I've ever eaten apart from hers!

I giggled and replied, "He's lovely, Ethel. You should come and walk with me over to his mysterious mansion!" I challenged.

"Oh, tosh, Miss!" she shyly answered. Then, a smile slowly came across her lovely face. "Really? I'd love to, Miss Maggie!"

"Then, how about tomorrow?"

"Okay," she replied, "but mysterious? No! No! He's much too nice!" she assured, with a lovely smile, and I smiled with her.

I knew Mr. West would enjoy Ethel's company with me, nary a doubt! With the trees obscuring the greater portion of his mansion, I chuckled to myself, I couldn't fool Ethel any about its mysterious beauty!

A beautifully elaborate bower at the entrance to the back of the Mr.'s property was a welcome joy within this delightful paradise, where he surely appreciated the gifts offered within its vast expanse of tranquil beauty. I was especially captivated by the lush roses which trailed over the arbor in a pleasing profusion, filling the air with enticing scents, soft and spicy, that wafted gently upon the winds. To every flowerbed, my heart exulted a praise to God for every petal and every blade of grass in awe to the goodness that filled this place within its sacred bliss of wondrous measure. Here, my heart drank in the richness of its solace within my soul, admiring the flowers and trees adorned within this priceless worth of hidden treasure, where I walked, lost for a time, along the paths bordering the flowerbeds, or upon the lush carpet of grass contrasting to its elusive aura.

The Mr. held a posture of being very private, I considered seriously, as I strolled along the well-tended paths later that day. The woman at the agency had neglected to tell me that he had a groundskeeper, Tom Wafer, who was a congenial gentleman: strong, young, and handsome, about twenty-seven, I surmised, with a lean figure. He began his days early, usually working until the early afternoon. Tom always had a ready smile and a kind word whenever we crossed paths in this extravaganza I was privileged to freely share and walk within its beauty. For Tom, as it was for me, it must have also fitted this astounding premise without saying!

This entrancing niche, although it was far more than that, was an oasis, breathtaking within my heart every time I visited my Mr.'s garden. I was wholly intrigued, certain that he had a heart of gold, even though we'd never met. I wondered if I might contrive to discover the reason behind his rigid policy in never meeting his housekeeper since he apparently conversed with his cook face-to-face. I supposed he'd have to, considering that she boarded under his roof.

I'd have to talk with Ethel, I determinedly decided. I just wasn't sure how to come up with a plan that would fit without a hint of a devious ploy, I smiled to myself! And in this instance, I hoped she'd reveal more than she might intend to!

On cold, rainy days, I took my breaks wandering the massive hallways of the mansion or sitting in front of the welcoming hearth that held an inviting aura in the spacious sitting room. Crystal chandeliers lit the room with glowing pleasure as well as two, huge lamps set upon the night tables alongside deeply plush, comfortable chairs, and two Victorian-style loveseats positioned off-side of a huge library that wholly intrigued me! An 18th century period desk flanked the hearth a short distance away with its simplicity and grace that Ethel and I both adored, and surely had had many a letter or story written by its master with a feather pen and inkwell! Sometimes, I thought that it was a pity, that, gone were those days from that era of a much slower pace in life, but I was also very grateful that inkwells were a thing of the past and I could write whenever it pleased my disposition, not having to bother with feather pens and such! Imagine writing beneath a tree with that!

The room was truly beautiful, with floor to ceiling windows. Entrancing French doors to the far side of the room opened onto a patio, where the picturesque aura drew my heart to it, like raindrops of iridescent colors shimmering in the dew. It held me to a feeling of explicit warmth, almost as though I belonged here, where my heart felt a place of both reassurance of care and joy.

Like a footstool that rested in the laurel of its exquisite fashion, I loved to bide my time within this wondrous splendor, and dream dreams of myriad fancy. Here, my soul drank in every niche of this blessed aura like bees to a flower's nectar, and such joy was never-ending!

Upon the open window in warm weather, feeling the welcoming breeze as the branches gently swayed upon the lilting wind gathered like a lullaby, it soothed my soul. But I also loved when the heightened winds rose in fury, and I peered through this same window as the branches thrashed so near, yet out of harm's way,

16

where I was thankful to be safely inside from its folly; Ethel and I, together. Yet, I also loved its spellbound wonder to experience firsthand within my yearning soul, where I could not resist such an enchanting temptation to be a part of this immense pleasure!

Much to Ethel's chagrin, I oftentimes insisted on the windows being open to feel the strong breezes furiously fluttering the curtains, or upon my face as I sat on the window seat, my heart full of inspiring dreams and whimsical joy. I also loved to dance carefree within the garden, or along the avenue of trees as the branches swayed in fury, and my heart found a solace there like nowhere else it could be found as the winds buffeted the windowpanes, and like a child lost in play for a time, I twirled and swirled within the beauty of the flowers and the trees to my delight! I tried to coax Ethel to dance with me, but she would have no part of it.

"Whatever will the Mr. think if he should come home and see me twirling in the wind with you?" she inquisitively asked. "I couldn't, Maggie! Why, he might make me leave this beautiful place forever!"

Laughing, I assured her that that was not so. "Your Mr. and mine seems to be quite the adoring man," I soothed. "I think that he may even be convinced to join us in such passion of childhood joy that will never leave my heart!"

"Maybe, for you, Maggie, he would," she said, unconvinced. "But for me? No! No! I dare not even think on it!"

"I wonder . . ." I challenged, with a twinkle in my eye.

"Wonder, what?" she asked, puzzled, crinkling her brow.

"Oh, just wondering, my dear Ethel, is all . . ." I left the sentence unfinished, but I didn't need to wonder for long!

When the next windstorm came, not finding me in the mansion, Ethel had come to tell me that lunch was ready. A trifle impatiently, she mused, "Maggie!" I was so intent on enjoying the moment with the full brunt of the wind in my face, I didn't hear her at first. Then, much to my amusement, Ethel grabbed a hold of my hand to get my attention, twirling with me! Between gasps, she said, "Lunch is ready, Maggie! It's about time that you put away this foolishness, for a while, at least!" she implored, her beautiful eyes staring into mine.

When I realized she was dancing with me, I burst out laughing. "Oh, what a thrill!" I squealed.

Ethel was about to retort when she gently caught my other hand in hers, and gaily exclaimed, "Oh, Maggie! It is! It is!"

We laughed and cried together until we felt dizzy and stopped.

"Whew!" she said, "I guess I was wrong about this, Maggie. It really is a lot of fun and now I understand your heart!"

We walked back to the mansion, arm in arm, where a beautiful lunch awaited us that she'd prepared. In between bites, I said, "I can't wait until the next windy day, Ethel!"

Shyly looking back at me with sparkling eyes, she sheepishly said, "Me, too, Maggie!"

I fancied the autumn with its beautiful colors and the snow shimmering on the large, glass panes in winter. I was sure that Ethel would love to dance in them with me, too! There, within my imagination, there was no denying the splendor of these beautiful scenes as I contemplated the glory of the turning seasons, each thriving in wondrous splendor to its own!

I thought that the owner must like reading, for the shelves were filled with rows of interesting books, such as mysteries and science fiction, and most notably, books on flowers. He had quite the range of taste, and it suited my own for the most part, except for the science fiction books.

I came across a shelf that held childhood stories, and I pondered, wondering if they had been his, for no names were inscribed in any of them. I suspected that his childhood surely must have lent many hours of pleasure drawn from these tales by the looks of the tattered corners of the pages, and it brought me back to my own. Somehow, it made me feel close to him.

When I mentioned this offhandedly to the cook, she said, "The Mr., he has good taste, yes. And" she smiled, her eyes suddenly shy, yet sparkling, "he's as gentle as a lamb and, what you say, dovelike?"

Taken aback, I thought that Ethel didn't quite understand the inference of the latter. Amused, I merely smiled. But she did arouse my curiosity in that!

The homeowner left cash with Ethel every Friday, and always with a receipt enclosed in a neatly typed envelope with but two words, *Personal Housekeeper*. I appreciated the consideration of being paid every week, even though it was a bit unusual. But I had to admit that I liked his way of handling business affairs with his employees!

"There's no photographs of him," I confided to the cook one afternoon. "What does he look like?" I innocently asked, curious to the answer.

Giggling, Ethel offered me a chair in the spacious kitchen at the table, simultaneously pulling out a chair for herself across from me. Setting just-out-of-the-oven cinnamon buns in the middle of the table that were richly dripping with a delicious cream cheese icing, she then placed a hot lemon drink, plate, and knife in front of me, and told me to help myself. Just like our first time, I mused! I sliced the bun and reached for the butter.

Settling down, she looked into my eyes and answered, "He don't want his worker to know." Ethel, I repeated to myself from our initial visit, was a beautiful Hispanic woman, neat and slim with lovely, long, black hair that fell in gentle, natural waves halfway down her back, but sometimes her English was faulty. Her features were delicate and refined with a high brow and a mouth like a rosebud. She must have a small mixture of Asian ancestry apart from her apparent Spanish, and perhaps a droplet of white blood as well, I decided. Maybe even a little more! Her face was long, yet a trifle rounded. No matter how one thought of her, she was truly gorgeous! Her spirit radiated a joy that was poignantly becoming and sincere.

"Not know?" I inquisitively asked, furrowing my brow. "Oh, dear!" I fretted. "Is there something wrong with him?"

Taking my bait, she slapped her sides, amused, and answered, "With the Mr.? Oh, no, ma'am. Now, that's a lark!"

Taking a bite from my bun, I sweetly smiled. "Then, what?"

"He don't want, what you call it? Helpers swooning over him."

"I see," I said matter-of-factly. "Then, he can't be as ugly as I was thinking." As I gathered my thoughts, I was drawn to the conviction that her Mr. was a man of grace, honor, and integrity. Perhaps, he'd had a bad experience, from what Ethel was telling me. Maybe, one too many. I was assured he held high standards and lived from that place every day. That tested my longing of curiosity even more, and I was most intrigued to meet him! Before my thoughts could go any farther, Ethel continued.

Looking straight at me, she said, a bit flustered, "I'd think that would be quite apparent."

"Well, *I* haven't seen him," I said, indignant. "Either he's super ugly, or reasonably handsome."

"Well, he ain't ugly!" she said, her voice slightly rising. "I'd think that would be quite enough for you!"

"Not for me!" I gleefully teased. "He must be a real doll!"

My persuasion finally resolved as her shyness vanished and she firmly insisted, reaching for a bun, "Oh, he is! A real doll!" she let slip, playing right into my hands. Then she filled her mouth with a huge bite of the cinnamon bun that was dripping icing from her hands. Picking up her serviette, she wiped her hands, as I watched, amused. Waiting for her to continue, she swallowed the food, took a few sips of her lemon drink, and considered further. A faraway look crossed over her face as Ethel dreamily spoke as in a whisper. "His eyes," she paused, drinking in the reverie, "so beautiful and blue like the ocean, and so captivating and alluring, and him very handsome, indeed!" she triumphed, her eyes shining with delight. Looking at me moments later, after indulging in the delicious lemon drink and another bite of the bun, her black eyes rested on mine, her face aflush. I laughed heartily, and when she had swallowed her food and taken another sip from her drink, she laughed right along with me. In the months I'd worked for her Mr., I knew that there was only goodness in the kindness of Ethel's heart for him, and quite assuredly, not anything personal.

Her description almost sounded like someone I'd recently met – my editor. But, what a crazy thought, I proposed. Still, truth is oftentimes stranger than fiction. Tossing my hair, I let the thought drop, and quickly finished my bun, and drank a few sips of my lemon drink. Anyway, my editor was of half Japanese origin, and I suspected Spanish, so it surely was mere coincidence.

Hmm. Captivating and alluring. I'd never thought of Dan's eyes that way, but sitting up straight in my chair, I nearly swallowed wrong as I took the last sip of lemonade. While I'd never met my boss at his estate here, and Ethel had never met my editor, it was startlingly surprising when I suddenly realized that she could still very well be describing Daniel Danes! I don't know how I ever missed that perfectly fitting description of perception she unwittingly noted in her Mr. As for Mr. Danes, he *was* very handsome, indeed! Relief instantly settled over me.

Composing myself, I looked into Ethel's gentle eyes. "I see," I said in contemplation, trying to hide the unexpected feelings stirring inside of me. "Perhaps, you are interested a little, *personally?*" I questioned, needing to know her answer for some inexplicable reason, while trying not to be in the least bit obvious or prying.

When Ethel realized what the connotation denoted, she vigorously shook her head in disagreement and assured, "Me? Oh, Maggie! No! Not even a little bit. He's just very nice to work for, and one simply can't help noticing his intriguing features. He's, what you say, so strikingly handsome, as I said, he takes one's breath away." Suddenly, Ethel looked puzzled and asked in her innocent, charming way, "I wonder where one's breath is taken?"

Laughing, I answered, "I believe it's safe to say that it's taken away in lots of joy!"

"I see. I'm supposing you're right, Maggie."

"Well, I hope that one day I can see for myself," I wistfully commented.

"Oh, I don't know . . . he's so, so careful and insistent on no face-to-face with his housekeeper," she said. Ethel's serious expression sent me into a tirade of giggles. She seemed a bit perturbed at that, then sighed and added, "If I can, only for you, Maggie, maybe I might help you with that."

"Oh, no, Ethel! That's very sweet of you, but I wouldn't want to be the cause of any troubles between you and your Mr. What if he never forgave you?"

"Then, I suppose I'd have to find work elsewhere," she sadly answered.

"I was only teasing," I said. "You don't need to worry any about that." Glancing at the clock in the kitchen, I pushed back my chair.

"That was wonderful," I said appreciatively. "You're a great baker as much as you are a cook," I complimented. "Thank you very much!"

21

Ethel settled to her own and merely smiled in that shy way I had come to be familiar with as she likewise arose and began to clear the table.

"I'll do it," I offered, feeling a little guilty for my bit of interfering and wanting to make amends for testing out Ethel's feelings with her Mr., even though I would have offered my help just the same without the guilt, my thoughts attested to. "The Mr. won't be back for a while, and I'd like to help. You've been on your feet all day, and soon will need to prepare his supper. I'm ahead of schedule with my work, so you take a few moments to rest while I wash up these dishes."

"Thanks, Maggie," she said, making no protests.

Ethel was dozing by the time I'd washed and wiped the dishes, including the baking utensils, and I tucked them away in the cupboard. I wiped the table and moments later, folded the towels I'd washed as I'd waited for them to dry in the dryer while Ethel and I'd enjoyed our snack.

Slipping on my jacket minutes later, I quietly tiptoed to check on Ethel. Ethel was still sleeping, and I decided not to awaken her. Surely, she wouldn't sleep too long.

I exited the home, locking the door quietly behind me, where the fresh air greeted me like a song. Cheerfully walking along the beautiful avenue of trees as I came to the street, I suddenly felt a tinge of guilt. Perhaps, I should have awakened the cook after all. Well, guess I'll find out tomorrow, I told myself, grinning with a chuckle, hoping that Ethel's nap was not jeopardizing her meal preparations! The Mr. seemed quite a patient man, according to Ethel, and hopefully he'd take his late supper in stride, should it not be ready the moment he entered his home as his expectation was accustomed to.

The wind picked up, but I felt unexpectedly exhilarated and happy. Then, I remembered our conversation together at the table this afternoon. So . . ., I slowly considered, the Mr. *was* handsome, I smiled to myself, with joy infiltrating my heart! I dared not meet him without the privilege of his invitation, but curiosity aroused my mind to the many possibilities I might contrive to meet him, or at least catch a glimpse of him. How could I pull that off, I pondered? I'd have to think long and hard, I decided, and the sooner the better.

For some reason, meeting him made that joy feel light and free and bubbly, I decided. Whatever could that feeling be?

Furrowing my brow, a startling thought momentarily had my mind on alert as I wondered if he'd feel the same about me, and I paused in my tracks on the sidewalk. The warm breeze felt delightfully exhilarating as it swirled about me, touching my face in play.

A car suddenly honked at a truck that raced right by it, passing me in a blur. As the car slowly passed me, I caught the female driver's expression staring straight ahead, still looking upset and rigidly stern behind the wheel, that I burst out laughing, completely forgetting about my worry in meeting Ethel's Mr.!

Loftily shaking my head, my mood lightened, and I laughed at myself and the thoughts that trailed in so many different directions as I came to my destination and walked up the path to my boarding house. Perhaps, that was all foolish thinking, or perhaps, just perhaps, it was worthy a thought for another day.

CHAPTER 3

Meeting the Mr.

The long summer days gradually transformed into a stunningly, gorgeous autumn in a wealth of beautiful shades of apricot, wine, and yellows splashing their hues in pleasing tones. Walking through the avenue of maples, birches, and elms, it held an intrinsic beauty that endeared my soul in awe of praise to the everchanging hues upon the turning days.

One afternoon, I was longer than I intended to be on my break. The air was balmy and fresh, and the trees aflame with colors that held me in their spell. Wandering, first along the avenue, and then through the garden, I didn't realize how much time had passed.

Entering the house, I glanced at the clock and hurried to my boss' bedroom to finish my duties. Right behind me was Ethel, all a fluster.

"You're late," she gently chided. "You must hurry and then call a taxi quick," she pleaded, her eyes wide with worry. "The Mr. will soon be home, and he won't like to meet you at the door."

"But I'm almost done," I assured her. "And I must finish."

"Okay, okay," she said, her anxiety rising. "Maybe, I could help you?"

"That's sweet, but I'm fine," I softly answered. "Please let me be to get it done."

"Alright," she relented. "I will do as you like, but please do hurry."

My car hadn't started this morning, and it was a long walk home. Keeping my mind on my work, I was a little anxious about calling up a taxi and shooing out the door without the Mr. meeting me.

I was returning the last ornament on his dresser when I suddenly heard the crunch of tires on the drive. Peering out the bedroom window, I paused long enough to realize that he'd returned earlier than usual, or more likely, I was running behind time, because of my unintentional, extended break. I supposed I should have had Ethel help me after all, I told myself. Lingering but an instant more, a blurred figure with black hair seemed to rush right past me down below as his vehicle slowed and disappearing, entered the garage from off the driveway.

Without a moment to lose, I hurried down the steps along the long corridor to the main floor. Grabbing my purse from off of the living room coffee table, I hoped to quickly sneak out the alternate door unnoticed, which led away from the garage. Much to my dismay, however, I heard his car door promptly slam shut and the sound of footsteps growing louder. And on top of this, Ethel had partly stepped into the hallway at the entrance to the secondary door and was blocking my exit! There was no way past him now. I hadn't even had time to call for a taxi. The walk wouldn't hurt me any, but I was tired and hungry. I didn't even have the time to consider the consequences of meeting the Mr. without his invitation or the unwarranted outcome it might create for Ethel. I was in a quandary, alright!

Ethel stood in an unnatural posture with her hands on her hips and disconcertingly staring in worrisome dismay, which was totally contrary to her personality, and preventing me to pass. If I said anything, the Mr. would surely hear, and it was my feeling that Ethel was presently too excitable if she answered me. That clearly left no alternative but to hurry past the Mr. where the foyer led to the garage, as Ethel seemed totally bewildered at the unexpected dilemma.

Remaining calm, as I reached for the door, hoping to keep my head down and slip past him, it suddenly pulled open from the other side. Trying to avert his eyes, I kept my head low, but was shocked to note that it was none other than Daniel Danes himself! My heart nearly stopped! Maintaining my composure, however, I said, "Excuse me, please, Mr. Danes."

Blocking my way, he gently said, "Maggie!" Such tenderness emanated in his voice, that I was momentarily at a loss for words. Diplomatically, he reached an arm out to me to keep me at his side. "You're not visiting my cook, are you?"

"No, sir."

"Then, . . ." A look of sheer astonishment suddenly crossed his face.

"Yes," I softly said, as the truth of that one word hit home.

"Maggie!" he repeated. Ethel was now standing at the door, wringing her hands worriedly. He momentarily turned his attention to her as he softly lisped, "Hello, Ethel. I believe I forgot all about my supper date with my client." Looking into my eyes, he gently said, "Forgive me, Maggie, I'll be with you in a minute."

Dan strode down the hall, with Ethel promptly following, but her direction changed, entering the kitchen, while he continued down the corridor, leaving me to myself. It wasn't like Ethel to ignore me, but I could understand why.

I didn't wait to see what surely would transpire, as I turned, running out the doorway as fast as I could when he reappeared, calling out to me. I trembled as I told my legs to move, but they somehow stopped short. I expected the worst and was very relieved that Dan didn't give me a good tongue lashing, but rather, seemed to take it all in stride!

"Maggie. Please . . . wait." Catching up to me, he said, "I'd like to have supper with you. I think we need to talk, too." His eyes were kind and gentle, yet questioning, but my heart was pounding. "I meant that *you're* my supper date, Maggie dear, and Ethel never needs to know our little secret."

"Oh, no, Dan," I protested, using his Christian name for the second time without thinking. "Really. That's all right. I understand. I didn't mean to put you in an awkward position with Ethel. Forgive me?"

Softly laughing, he said, "Maggie. There's nothing to forgive. I could use some company tonight and we wouldn't want to give our secret away to Ethel, now, would we?"

"Putting it that way, I suppose not. Okay, Mr. Danes."

"I'd love to hear you call me Dan from on now," he said. Taking my arm, we walked back the short distance to his home. "Would you mind waiting in the foyer while I tell Ethel that she need not concern herself about my supper tonight, please?"

"Certainly not, Dan. Take your time."

I felt nervous about the turn of events, but excitement also arose just knowing that I was going to have Dan to myself for a little while! He appeared almost as quickly as he'd left, and taking my arm, walked out the door with me. I felt exhilarated! He opened the passenger side door for me, then walked around the front of his car to his driver's side, and seconds later, was seated next to me.

I couldn't help but glance at the kitchen window when Dan backed out of the garage. Just as I suspected, Ethel was trying her best to discreetly peer out, thinking that she was invisible behind the shadow of the curtain. But at this time of the day, the sunlight caught the panes, splashing its glow where she plainly stood out in silhouette. Pointing that out, I saw Dan's eyes light up with an unmistakable, mischievous expression.

"We need to avoid unsolicited gossip as much as possible, my dear," he laughed. "I think we satisfied her curiosity at that!" he chortled. "I believe Ethel won't say a word about it – to you – or me, and most certainly – to no one else!"

Smiling, I wondered what dear Ethel was thinking, and I wished that I could somehow comfort her and let her know that all was truly well. But Dan had surely already assured her of that. Anyway, I told myself, I supposed it wouldn't be long before she'd learn both the secret and the truth, and not be disappointed, because somehow, I hoped that it would be better than we both could ever have imagined!

When we were seated at the table in the restaurant, Dan chuckled as he said, "I'll let Ethel in on our little secret tonight that I'm your editor to help put this incident in perspective. I'm truly your editor, after all," he smiled, looking into my eyes. The tender way in which Dan voiced his thoughts sent goose bumps up my back. But I scarcely minded as he seemed eager to talk, and I was enjoying his company. The waitress came, and we ordered, and our meals came shortly. Enjoying the food, I was happy to listen to Dan and allowed him to do most of the talking. His voice was sweet and musical just like his good looks, I silently told myself as I listened to him.

Changing the subject, he continued, "I'd no idea you were the one taking such wonderful care of my home. Your dedication is exemplary. And I'm sure you're wondering and too polite to ask, but my secretary, Pam, takes care of your weekly cheque, so I've never seen your name since she has the authority for that."

"I see," I said. "Well, I need the job, Dan, and I want to thank you for hiring me, although I'm not quite sure I'm what you expected," I said.

"Maggie, you're far more than I've ever expected or had in a housekeeper, I assure you," he said, his eyes twinkling. "But you're much too gifted a writer to be catering to such menial tasks."

"I don't mind. It takes time to get royalties. My book's hardly been out there," I pointed out. "Do you know something, Dan?" I sweetly smiled. "Although God provides in nature, and squirrels store food," I mischievously, teasingly considered, "I most certainly won't be running after them, like a thief in the night! Not even for a morsel!" I concluded.

Laughing heartily, Dan leaned back in his chair. "I think I've a more suitable solution. I've been looking for a good assistant, and a proofreader who has an editor's eye. It's a better paying position. Would this interest you?" he asked, his eyes so gentle, they suddenly fluttered my heart, and I truly had no idea why.

Stunned, I could hardly think, then I found myself reply, "Oh, it would!"

"That's the most wonderful news I've heard all day!" he smiled.

"What about housekeeping? Your socks won't pair themselves," I joked.

"Oh, no worries!" he laughed. "Ethel can take over until I get suitable help."

"I don't know. It's kind of fun matching your socks," I said.

"Is it?" he asked mischievously. "But, Maggie, I think you could be put to better use. Seriously, I would love to have you at my side." Dan's eyes were pleading and teasing and imploring, all at the same time, as they penetrated my heart with startling emotion.

"I'd like that, too," I smiled. "Very much," I added, as I looked into his eyes, and felt a tremor go down my back.

Reaching across the table to hold my hand, my heart shivered to the thrill as his met mine in a soft embrace. I felt something come alive within my heart in that moment, melting to his gentle touch. I sensed he felt something, too.

It was unpredictably in that moment that my thoughts randomly went back to Dan telling me that he intended for me to be his supper date, and he had called me, dear. I found my face flushing, hoping that he wasn't noticing, and wondering whatever this could be about, and if it held any significance. Composing myself, I glanced at Dan, and his eyes were sparkling as he offered me another bun, picking up the wicker basket, with his eyes still on me. As I reached for a bun with my hand and arm extended toward it, his hands suddenly slipped as the basket unexpectedly shifted, knocking hard against my hand and arm as the buns flew out, toppling onto the table, and falling onto the floor. A look of dismay crossed his face, and despite the pain I was experiencing, I burst out laughing. He blushed, and in what seemed but an instant, he deftly composed himself, his blue eyes sparkling again.

"I'm so sorry, Maggie," he graciously apologized. "You aren't hurt, are you?"

"My wrist and hand got the brunt of it, and my arm is also feeling a tinge sore, I'll admit." Seeing his concerned expression, I added, "But I'll be fine," I assured him.

"Let me have a look," he said. My hand was beginning to bruise and slightly swell, and he gently rubbed it. "I am truly so sorry, my dear. If I'd been more attentive to what I was doing . . ." He blushed and his words trailed.

"You were attentive," I sweetly said, smiling, "but not to the basket!"

"Please don't blame me for that observance, Maggie! You're much too lovely, and I promise to make it up to you!"

"You're more than a gentleman, Dan, and I appreciate your kindness. Really, I will be just fine," I affirmed.

Looking into my eyes, he softly said, "If I could but change what happened, I would. But perhaps, you might be my guest in my home and Ethel can wait on you?" he asked.

"Oh, no, Dan!"

"But Maggie, you need to rest your hand and arm, and I know that you're in pain. At least permit me to have Ethel bring you over meals until Monday, alright?"

His eyes were so loving and pleading, I finally relented. "Thank you, Dan."

He smiled and returned, "I'm going to make sure of that! Well then, are we ready to go, or would you still like a fresh bun?"

"I'm fine, thank you! It was a delicious meal, Dan!"

Dan made good on his promise, and I was truly grateful for the wonderful meals. Ethel even brought me nutritious snacks . . . ha, ha! as if cinnamon buns dripping with cream cheese icing fit that description, I smiled to myself! Her cookies and muffins were all delicious, and I wanted for nothing! Her baskets were also laden with fresh fruits and crackers, and I enjoyed it all! But what I treasured best was in her keeping me company and sharing those divine meals with me, too, which was just like the many times we'd shared around Dan's table.

Ethel tenderly and gently bathed my hand, and it noticeably improved. But when Sunday night came, Dan brought the meal instead of Ethel. "Maggie," he began, "I've decided to give you tomorrow off with pay just to be sure that your healing is complete."

"Oh, you mustn't," I began to protest.

"Yes, Maggie, and I don't want any argument from you!" he graciously said, insistent. A slight smile appeared on his handsome face, and he added, "One more day of rest, and then we'll see about Tuesday. Ethel will be by tomorrow with your meals." Patting my shoulder, he said goodbye, but I missed Ethel's company and I'd hoped that Dan would stay. It was lonely by myself with no one to talk to or enjoy a meal with. That may have been my routine, but then I never minded too much, because I didn't have pain. Well, I was much better, and I was equally determined as Dan, that come Tuesday, I would be at the office near his warm and welcoming presence!

With the unexpected incident at the restaurant, I suspected that life at the office may very well have its special and exciting moments with Daniel Danes at my side, or at the least, unrehearsed to breaking some dull moments in our workday! I could hardly wait to start, as I equally pondered if what I was feeling was merely nerves and the excitement of a new job working close with him, or if, just possibly, it could be something else . . .

When Ethel learned I'd resigned my position, her words to Dan were few as he privately reviewed the scene with me in his office the following Tuesday.

"Just like I thought all along," she grieved, sniffling, and shaking her head. "In Maggie, there was something extra special about her."

Trying not to show emotion, I politely listened as Dan merely nodded and choked for the words that would hardly come as he'd said to her, "That she was, but Ethel, she's come to work with me now."

Her eyes wide with surprise, she replied, "You, Mr.? Then perhaps, it twairn't be half so bad. Begging your pardon, I mean to say that maybe I can still see her sometime?"

"Of course, Ethel! I see no reason for you not to."

Dan and I couldn't help but laugh after he'd conveyed the scene, although I sensed something deeper, and my heart also broke a little. I was beginning to get used to Ethel and her ways, and a part of me would miss her and the beauty of his mansion, and the flowers that went right along with that. I'd miss Tom, too - his lovely morning smile and kind words. Somehow, when I thought about it, I couldn't help but sniffle a little myself, too. Until this very moment, this time had been a gift far more special and precious than I'd ever realized. And in *Meeting the Mr.*, I'd need to find what that dream was as I worked by Dan's side, trusting God to reveal His perfect plan in it all. If it wasn't here, then my heart was assured that God would lead me elsewhere.

I exited his office and tried to concentrate on my work. I bit my lip, knowing that it was going to take some getting used to before the empty places without Ethel's loving presence would wholly shift to Dan's. That alone sustained the loneliness creeping inside my heart as I continued the editing at hand. I was tempted to glance at Dan, where I could clearly see him behind his desk, but I knew the tears would surely come as my heart longed for her presence, wanting to share my heart in hers.

Then, for some odd reason, I recalled the day I'd pondered how her Mr. could afford such a lovely mansion. Murmuring softly to myself as I busied myself with the task at hand in ironing his shirts, I was deep in thought, wondering if I should pose my question to Ethel, momentarily oblivious to my surroundings. "Oh, that I can answer," she stated, startling me, entering the laundry room to call me for lunch. "He inherited it. Isn't it just so beautiful?" she said, smiling.

"It is!" I replied.

"Good thing he had such a marvelous grandfather who also provided fair money, or Maggie, you and I would never have met, and you are so special to me."

Choking on the words, I replied, "You're very special to me, too, Ethel!" I put the iron down, shut it off, and hung up the Mr.'s shirt, as my eyes misted. The sentiment I was feeling made the mansion that much more special, and I felt privileged and truly thankful for it, as I threw my arms about Ethel to the joy dancing in my heart. Then I composed myself and we shared a delicious lunch.

The gift of Dan's grandfather truly encompassed great love between them and had surely given him more than he would have thought, and in it, it blessed us all. Leaning back in my chair, I considered, then reached for my glass of milk.

I wanted to ask Dan so many things about his grandfather. When I did, he surprised me the following day with a book, titled: *A Man's Dream by Noel Danes*, that I deeply appreciated. I learned that he'd owned his own logging company as a young man, and done very well for himself, as was evident. But he'd always had a passion for criminal law, eventually opening his own practice in that strength to pursue his dream.

There was even a notation at the end of the book describing what a fair and honorable lawyer he'd been, always making every client his personal interest in his work. It read: "Noel Danes is the only lawyer this area has ever seen hold to such unique standards of personal understanding within the honor of his work. His conduct is exemplary, and we are all better lawyers for the immense blessing and gift his presence has given to us. He has defined something within each of us, whereto we have consequently become nobler persons ourselves, from which is often lacking in this profession, and that is the human element to every client whom we are sworn to serve. Because we're ultimately working for the Lord, He expects us, not only to do our very best, but to do it with the compassion that Jesus, therewith, taught His disciples. For this, our challenge has been redefined to a higher perspective that all of us here, as Noel's colleagues, are proud to serve in his footsteps with great humility and pleasure!"

What a beautiful way the final lines of Noel's book concluded in recognition of his vast contributions and unwavering honor of commitment! I felt like I was in the scene, experiencing every emotion that his colleagues had come to realize and experience, as Noel shone his light in an oftentimes dark world. It was a somber moment to also understand how valuable our lives are, and that one person can make a huge change for good in the lives of many just as one candle lit, can dispel the darkness, and fill a room with light.

Overwhelmed, the tears came, freely falling, to the joy of all Dan's grandfather had surrendered to the cross as a little boy, as the story noted. Tangibly creating such worthy influence and contributions to the people God entrusted as his clients, the fairness by which Noel measured the very heart of Him in everything he accomplished for a better world, was truly unprecedented in so beautifully walking in this straight and narrow way.

Noel Danes dared to rock the hardcore sentiment so often associated with lawyers and brand his own identifiable imprint of signature to the practice of law to a higher degree. In doing so, he lived by what matters most – living honorably, regardless of one's race or status, of which I came to see more and more each day, and to find this same lovely person in Noel's grandson I was privileged to know and work alongside, in Dan.

Good ground producing good by the Golden Rule that, in doing unto others as one would have them do unto themself, life offered so much more that came from the beauty out of the ashes, in every situation! Here, it wasn't hard to discover generational roots that had been planted in Dan's beautiful grandfather, and I suspected in his grandmother, Elizabeth, as well! What a glorious way to live, I happily said in my thoughts! It made me proud to know that I was working for the selfsame high ideals, that were characterized in Dan because he'd been a part, firsthand, of this unwavering example in his grandfather, and chose to live it out in his own life as well!

I also learned through talking with Ethel, that at the age of eighteen, just when Dan was preparing to go off to college, he inherited Noel's mansion. It must have been a grievous time for him, but I knew how very much Dan had loved his grandfather, and what it meant to honor that beautiful love.

When I asked Dan about his own thoughts, he was happy to share them with me. "It gave me so much peace to cherish his mansion, and to know that it would receive the care of which it was so deserving of," he tenderly said. "And every day, I still cherish everything from my childhood back then, that so fondly endeared this mansion to my heart as that little boy."

Dan smiled at the memory as he continued, "But bedtime was especially special, when my grandfather loved to read those wonderful tales to me!" His eyes glistened and I knew that as sweet as those memories were, he still missed his grandparents, and surely always would. "Whether sitting upon his knee or at my side in the big chair next to my bed, I will treasure every moment that we had. And although my grandmother died three years earlier than Noel, she was as much a part of that childhood love with me growing up, as he always was to me."

I never saw a broken man in Dan when he sometimes shared highlights of his grandfather with me, and I enjoyed and appreciated it as much he. It was more than evident that he would always treasure and wisely care for his mansion, as he did then as that young man, and still does today.

Personally, I felt honored in that closeness, somehow, in a way I couldn't so easily put into words, which was now a part of my life, and had always lovingly been known together, between Noel and my editor, Daniel Danes, his grandson.

In the warmth of Dan's lovely mansion, and the well-tended grounds by Tom Wafer, I was truly very happy, where peace seemed to fill every niche amidst the vast beauty, and I felt at home in a way I couldn't seem to find in words, but in my heart, that understood completely. I cherished this privilege, rereading the wonderful inscription inside the front cover before returning the book to Dan days later, grateful for his trust, and all it meant to me.

There, a distinctly bold and fine inscription written in his grandfather's lovely handwriting, left my heart breathless, which read: "This book belongs in my mansion, the mansion you've loved as a child, Dan. I know that God has special plans for you! Let His love be your constant stay as you serve Him with all your heart! Love, your grandfather, Noel Danes."

Little knowing just how much Noel's gift to Dan would impact my life, I looked to the new day, happy to have the gift of his wonderful presence close to me. Sitting behind my desk, I looked up from my work and across to his office. Dan was just placing the receiver of the telephone back in its cradle when he caught me looking at him. He smiled, and I smiled back, my face flushing as I went back to my work, concentrating on a poignant children's story, wholly captivating my heart in the moments after!

CHAPTER 4

Along the Journey

I'd done a considerable bit of editing in my days but being in Dan's presence made it so much more special. He was always warm and pleasant and didn't seem to mind it when I had a knot that I couldn't untie without his guidance.

In the days ahead, it took a little getting used to working in an office again, and at first, I missed Ethel a lot, especially our times of chatting on our breaks, sharing our hearts. She sometimes insisted on Dan bringing over her delicious cinnamon buns, dripping cream cheese, and all! But here, I felt a new purpose in my life as I looked forward to each day with our "Mr." in person, even though we didn't always see each other very much. But just knowing Dan was close by added joy within my work, and when opportunities availed themselves, I loved being near him within his endearing presence.

I came to lean on his opinions more than I should have, perhaps. Not that I didn't try my best to solve the problems that demanded strictest concentration before going to him. And when his work diverted his attention, he'd ever sweetly apologize telling me that he was sorry "for not being with me when I needed him!" Unless I had to meet the deadline on those days, I would mark the manuscript and approach him when he had some spare moments at a later time, where we worked on them together.

I especially loved editing children's books. Since my childhood, illustrations had always fascinated me, and had had a wondrous way of mesmerizing my heart, drawing me closer to the story from the time I was just a little girl. Like the words of an author perfected in a story, I loved to see the visually progressive scenes come alive – to life – within these treasured children's stories just waiting to hold the hearts of those who would come to turn the pages in future months.

"You know," Dan confided to me one morning, "I've always had this desire to create my own children's book. What do you think, Maggie?" he asked, his brow creased, deep in thought.

"A children's book! Why, Dan! I think that's a wonderful idea!" I burst out with joy filling my heart. My thoughts immediately flew back to the tattered children's books lining his bookshelf in the huge library. I was surer than ever that they belonged to him.

"Since you've been working on the interior text of *Autumn's Song,* he said, "I can't seem to get it out of my mind. Children's books have always been my favorites to work on," he admitted as he continued, "and I couldn't resist taking a peek, well," he softly laughed, "I should rather say that I took a look at how the story's progressing and it's simply wonderful! You have a very unique perspective at seeing everything in such a lovely light, and this will surely be a treasure when the interior text is approved along with the illustrator's work. If I were the author, I'd be very pleased with your work," he complimented, smiling, as his eyes looked into mine, "as I am with you as my Assistant Editor!" he gaily finished.

"Were you checking up on my editing skills?" I teased, my eyes twinkling.

Laughing, he shook his head. "Not a bit, my dear Maggie! Now, getting back to writing my own children's story, thank you, Maggie, for your kind faith in me. However, I don't know when I'd ever find the time to write, and I suppose I'm merely daydreaming."

That wouldn't do for an excuse one whit in my book, I told myself. "But Dan," I demurred, "if this has been a dream of yours, I think that you should really do it, and I won't let you give up on yourself so easily!" I encouraged. "You need to bring it from your heart to paper, because this definitely appears to be a special dream that God has given to you, and you shouldn't so quickly dismiss it. Have you thought of a title or what the storyline might be?"

"Hmm. A little."

Pausing, it gave me the opportunity to express my own sentiment. "Dan, I've thought of that, too. *For myself,*" I emphasized. "I worked some time ago, before I was employed with the Railway Company, at a publisher's house, and an executive asked me to write a book with him. We had a theme and I created quite a bit of the text, but he fell through on that, and I was very disappointed."

"About writing a children's book?" Dan asked in surprise, looking into my eyes.

"Yes."

Dan's expression took on new meaning. "Then, we should write one together, Maggie!" he enthused. "Would you consider writing a book with me?"

"Oh, yes! I would love to!"

In the weeks following, when Dan asked me if I had any ideas for our children's story, I shook my head, but the excitement of collaborating with him never left my heart. "Not a thing, Dan. Not even a title." But I believed with all my heart that there was a book with our names on it with blank pages invitingly waiting for God to fill it with everything our hearts could possibly give to it, so I kept on believing – and praying! How little could my heart have known the avenue by which it would come, but when it did, I would give it everything I had inside of me.

The call came a week later. Dan's sister, Julia, had taken considerably ill. The caller, his younger brother, Cole, wondered if Dan could take care of his sister's daughter, Blossom. "Sis told me that you're selected to be her guardian anyway. I think it'll be good for both of you, and you know how much Blossom adores you."

"I suppose," Dan replied. "For now, Ethel can care for her until I find a suitable nanny while I'm working."

Daniel Danes was a very private man, and although we worked well together from the time he'd hired me as his Assistant Editor, he had very sparingly only given me a few words that his sister, Julia, wasn't well. It took him a while to reveal that she had a daughter, and that her husband seemed to be unresponsive in his responsibilities to them. In fact, he added that his sister and her husband had been separated for some time.

"Their relationship is complicated," he confided, but that was all he said. And oddly enough, he never spoke about it again.

It took weeks before Dan even revealed to me what Julia's daughter's name and age were. I couldn't understand why that was so private to him, or was he merely being cautious in telling me those details?

Julia had eventually made her own way for herself and her daughter, and I was smitten by the gumption it surely must have taken for her to accomplish everything she had in her independence.

I met Blossom a few days later. She was a darling, energetic seven-year-old. Dan had invited me over for supper to meet both his sister and niece, although I learned from Julia that when Dan had asked if he might bring his Assistant Editor, she insisted on warmly extending the invitation to me as his supper companion for the evening.

"You'll love Julia," he said, smiling as he met me at my door later on that evening, "and I know she'll love you, too. As well as her daughter, my niece."

I felt a bit awkward, but I did enjoy Dan's company. But what I loved most of all was his courtesy to link arms with me as we came up to his sister's long walkway. I was feeling nervous, like an outsider peeking in a window I shouldn't, but out of respect to Dan and our professional relationship, I wanted to honor him with my support. And, as childish and silly as the notion was, I felt exhilarated with the secret longing of hope that everyone on her street were peering out their windows and noticing me at his side, this handsome Japanese!

Ethel's eyes opened wide with pleasure when we entered the large foyer, and she spontaneously hugged me. "Oh, Maggie!" she cried, taking my coat. "It's such a pleasure to have you back! I mean," she said, stumbling over her thoughts, "to have you here with the Mr."

"I'm happy to be here," I said, embracing her welcome, "and if I'm not mistaken, Ethel, you have spent many hours in your day preparing a feast for us."

"Oh!" she shyly said. "That 'twairn't nothing," she softly spoke, her eyes smiling, and her word misspoken. "I just loved every moment to give you this pleasure."

"Well, Dan is very fortunate to have someone like yourself who's willing to attend to his sister's needs at her residence. I hope we didn't put you to too much trouble and I'm anxiously awaiting to meet Julia."

"For you, dear Maggie, no pleasure is work in my book," Ethel lovingly said, as she gave me an extra hug.

Understanding her misuse of English at times, I smiled. "That's so sweet, Ethel," I said, "and Dan and I want to thank you for everything you've done on our behalf tonight."

"Yes," Dan added. "We do thank you, Ethel, and appreciate it very much."

Ethel smiled, nodding in understanding, not saying another word.

Dan took my arm again and politely excused us, ushering me into the living room where his sister was sitting in a lovely, Victorian-style chair, and Ethel went back to finish supper preparations. The moment my eyes met hers, I adored Julia, and I just knew that we would be very close friends.

Reaching out her hand in welcome, Julia's voice was soft-spoken and musical as she greeted us. "Dan, it's so good of you to come and bring Maggie. Maggie, this is truly an honor for me. Please make yourselves comfortable. I believe that Ethel has everything prepared and is almost ready to serve the meal." Then she turned to Dan and said, "Why don't you get Blossom? She's reading a story and waiting for her uncle, and to meet his lovely escort."

Dan momentarily left my side, and I didn't know what to say, feeling awkward in new surroundings, as lovely as they were. It seemed like forever, but moments later, a pretty girl entered the room. She curtsied and said, "Hello, ma'am. A pleasure to meet you." Blossom was wearing a pink dress that beautifully swirled a trifle in the front, and had tiny pink beads over the whole dress, which sparkled in the light.

"I'm pleased to meet you, too," I said.

We were interrupted by Ethel, who said that supper was ready and on the table.

"It smells delicious," I said, as Dan led me to a chair and then assisted his sister.

"I'm fine," she complained good naturedly. "I can still walk, Dan." Blushing, Dan hurried to my side, then, we bowed our heads, and he gave thanks. A beautiful bouquet of carnations was set at the center of the table, and their delightful fragrance wafted on the air. The place settings were lovely, each with Delftware that reminded me of an earlier era, and I adored them!

Ethel served us in her gracious way, and was unusually quiet, which didn't help me any. Polite and ready to please, by the time the evening was over, I was tired and glad to go home. When we departed, she hugged me close and whispered, "You and Dan look like the perfect couple, Maggie!" and then she suddenly released me. I stared briefly into her eyes, wondering what had made her say such a thing as that. Nodding, however, I thanked her and waved goodbye as we exited Julia and Blossom's home.

Dan didn't say much the following Monday, so I felt ill at ease, concentrating on my work, avoiding him. Ethel's strange comment came back to me, and I hoped that would be the end of it. While I was very fond of Dan, I had no other personal feelings toward him, at least, not that I knew of. I bit my lip, trying to put it out of my mind. I went back to my work, determining to accomplish more than I was feeling at the moment.

About ten-thirty in the morning, Dan asked me to finish work on another author's project, which was not very much in line with the endearing narrative in the children's book I had to put aside for now. While children's books could be tricky, there was no apparent deadline with *Autumn's Song*, so I didn't feel that it was my place to question his decision.

At once, I longed to go back to the children's title, and struggled with a paragraph on detective methods that needed work. The author had used poor English, leaving important words out, of which I wasn't very familiar with this particular subject. My research left it dangling with no clear answer to the content needing attention, and I finally put it aside, moving on to the next chapter, hoping that Dan would have a clearer perspective when I went back to it.

My telephone immediately kept me busy, and when noon arrived, he brusquely disappeared without saying a word other than, "Excuse me, please, Maggie." It wasn't like him and I immediately worried, feeling a bit disconcerted, wondering what he was keeping from me. I was also exhausted trying to figure out the demands of proofreading and didn't have much interest to continue my work when I returned from lunch. I suddenly felt lonely without Dan and in despair. In this moment of weary frustration, I wished he'd never involved me with his family.

When he called me at two o'clock that afternoon, he only said that something had come up and he wouldn't be back into the office. I felt both concern and relief. I wished I could close the office and take the rest of the day off like him, but there were too many demands and deadlines looming up ahead. I had to be responsible, but I didn't have to like it, I stormed in my thoughts! The following chapter involved another knot, and I struggled with it until I'd had all I could take of it, too, just like the difficult paragraph that had relentlessly imposed on my morning, and I moved on to the next pages until I could consult with Dan.

Dan hadn't even considered to telephone me again, and I almost wished that I'd left the office right after his two o'clock call. Maybe one day, I wickedly said in my thoughts, I might just do the same to him! His line was always, "I hope you understand, Maggie," whenever something unexpected hadn't fit into his day. Most times that was quite acceptable and it didn't bother me any, and I was more than happy to understand. But this time seemed different. Well, what made him think it always fitted into *mine*? I ruefully blustered.

Dan telephoned me at my home just when I was ready to go to bed that night. "I'm sorry, Maggie. My sister needed extensive tests today, and I spent most of the day at the hospital with her. I only arrived home about an hour ago. The lab results aren't pleasing." I heard a tremor in his voice, then a long pause, as his words came like a chill on a cold winter's day. He sounded like a broken man as he quietly spoke the words. "She has stage four cancer."

"Oh, Dan!" I exclaimed, feeling guilty for my earlier thoughts in the day, repenting in my heart without delay.

Choking up, but braving his heart, Dan composed himself. "I needed you, Maggie, but I didn't know how to ask or what you'd think. My thoughts continually went back to you, and I missed your sweet presence."

I could hardly believe his words! I was happy to know that I counted as someone he missed.

"I'm so sorry, Dan," I meaningfully said. "I would have dropped everything and come to be with you," I gently replied, trying to amend my foiled mindset earlier. "Is there something I may still do for you and Blossom now?" I kindly asked.

"Not tonight, thank you, Maggie. But if you'd stay with Blossom tomorrow at my sister's, I'd appreciate it, and I'll pay you well. Then, when Ethel takes her lunch break, I wonder, could you be with me? Ethel can keep an eye on her for the remainder of the day. I'll send a taxi for you at about 11:45 a.m."

"Of course, Dan. I'd be happy to."

"Oh," he added, "and of course, you'll be very well compensated for your time with me out of the office."

I understood Dan well enough to know that it was pointless to argue with him about his insistence of compensating me, especially when he was having a hard time with Julia's situation. I wasn't so cold that I wouldn't do this as a special favor for him, with or without pay, and in such moments as these, I really wondered if he truly held any personal feelings to me after all as it sometimes seemed, and perhaps, I was foolishly naïve to believe.

Furthermore, I thought he could see it my way a little, too. None of this was easy for me, and I looked at it as being a support, and truly a friend, to him during this trying time in his life. Anything to help, it was my pleasure and my honor.

I didn't exactly express the truth in looking after Blossom, but I did want to help Dan. I supposed that there was enough truth in that respect. I knew it was surely difficult for Blossom as well, and I did so want to please her.

I considered how quickly things can deteriorate; it had only been a few days before, Friday, to be precise, when Julia had graciously invited me for supper with her brother. But I suspected that cancer didn't care anything about time in that respect. I hoped and prayed that she'd be feeling better when Dan and I spent time with her the following afternoon at the hospital.

The next morning was certainly different than I expected. Ethel gave me a tour of Julia's home before Blossom awoke, and just as she was serving me biscuits with fresh cranberries and raisins in them, Blossom sleepily entered the kitchen and nudged Ethel, rubbing her eyes, and leaning on the chair where Ethel was standing. Blossom kept looking at me, her eyes studying my every move, making me feel uncomfortable. When she'd had her breakfast and was dressed, she insisted on me indulging her by building a house with her blocks, then skipping rope, and lastly, playing hide-and-seek, next.

Julia's home was lovely, and she certainly had excellent taste in colors and furnishings, some of which were reflected in her Japanese and Mexican heritage, most intriguing, while sustaining a modern flair in its delightful ambience!

I was particularly smitten with a painting of horses running free across a plain that had the most enchanting style of frame designed by a Japanese artist, in her living room, where Blossom and I spent our morning.

I hadn't seen a coloring book since my childhood, and I was taken with her pleasure of flipping through the pages. Pausing midway, Blossom grabbed a coloring pencil from where a small box sat nearby. Her hand swiftly filled in the portrait of a young girl on a swing. A boy was standing at her side; a smile as wide as could be. One could almost hear the wind in the trees as the girl's upswept hair was blown all awry!

Moments later, Blossom insisted that I color with her; her beautiful blue eyes, both questioning and hopeful. I seated myself beside her, shading in the trees surrounding the swing, becoming lost in it with her.

"Oh, it's lovely, Miss Hanes!" she said appreciatively, clapping her hands. "May I?"

"Certainly!" I said, allowing her to complete the picture.

Blossom filled in the clouds and a slow, satisfying smile appeared on her face. Abruptly turning to me, she gave me an impulsive hug. "Thank you!" she impetuously exclaimed.

Taken aback, it was wonderful to feel Blossom's arms about me as she momentarily held me close in a gentle hug. The scent of her hair was pretty, too, reminding me of wildflowers. I replied, "It was fun, Blossom, and I enjoyed it, just like you!"

Still, as much as I wanted to please Blossom, I realized she also needed to please me. When I asked her if she had any children's movies we might watch, she clapped her hands, then hurried to a beautiful cabinet designed, Julia later told me, by a Mexican she employed in her dress shop, across from where Blossom and I were sitting.

"The Spanish influence in this piece is remarkable," Julia later shared, and I marveled at the care and exquisite details that went into this unique work that was highly treasured in her home.

Opening the cabinet door, Blossom exclaimed, "We have lots! Come see!" Eagerly, I joined her and drew in my breath.

"Why, Blossom!" I gasped, almost in disbelief as I pulled out several classics. "Are all these movies yours?"

"Mmm hmm. All mine!"

"Why, it's simply wonderful! You know, I never had any children's movies growing up," I said, reminiscing.

Looking puzzled, Blossom asked, "You didn't? How come?"

"Because, dear Blossom," I explained, "television wasn't yet available until I was much older and these movies weren't, either."

"Ohhh," she drawled out the word, furrowing her brow. "What did you do for fun?"

Laughing, I said, "Well, I played outdoor games with my friends and read a lot. I also cut the grass and enjoyed that, too!"

"Hmm. I guess I'm pretty lucky, aren't I?"

"You certainly are!"

"Would you like to watch something with me?"

"Oh, yes!" I replied.

Noticing my hands were full as I gathered several to peruse, Blossom suddenly asked, "Maybe you want to choose one you like?"

My heart filled with immeasurable happiness and a love I never thought possible, as I began to feel the joy of this little girl's heart in mine. "Oh, I would!" I declared. "Thank you, Blossom," I gratefully said. Rifling through the movies, my hands stopped at *Cinderella*. "If you don't mind," I pondered, "I'd like to watch *Cinderella* with you," I said, offering it to her. "All right?"

"It's my favorite!" she enthused. I replaced my handful of movies in the cabinet as Blossom put the movie on and moments later it began to come alive on the screen. I joined her on the divan, getting into a comfortable position. Blossom sat close beside me, cuddling against my side as we were drawn into the story. About halfway through Blossom fell asleep with her head on my shoulder, and when I looked at my watch, I gasped. The taxi would soon be arriving.

As if reading my thoughts, Ethel peeked into the living room, telling me to hurry. "I just assumed you'd be watching the clock," she said, a bit surprised. "Well, never mind that now, but please do hurry, Maggie, and have a bite before the taximan gets here. I have a place setting all prepared for you."

Carefully moving Blossom so she would rest against the edge of the divan as I arose, letting her sleep, I gently covered her with a light blanket, then scurried into the kitchen behind Ethel's bustling apron. She disappeared for a few minutes, and I pulled out a chair and sat down, quickly eating the sandwich with a glass of milk and a dish of freshly cut banana and cream for dessert that Ethel had kindly prepared for me.

Ethel came down the long corridor just when I heard the taxi in the drive. She grabbed my hand and stuffed a large denomination of bills into it. "The Mr. left this for you this morning. I almost forgot to give it to you."

"That wasn't necessary," I replied. "But thank you, Ethel."

Tears welled in her eyes, and she replied, "The Mr. is a mighty blessed man to have someone as special as you to care for him and his family."

I said goodbye and opened the door as Ethel said, "It was so good to see you, Maggie. I'll be back at the Mr.'s house tomorrow."

"It was good to see you, too! Please say goodbye to Blossom and now I shall say goodbye to you again," I said, as I exited Julia's home, closing the door softly behind me.

The taxi was a bit late. The driver apologized, explaining that it was due to the wait the train posed in making its way along the tracks at the last intersection, and I hoped that I'd still arrive on time. I didn't want Dan pacing, wondering what the delay might be.

As the taxi pulled out of Julia's circular driveway, thoughts began to compound my mind and I wondered how Dan was faring . . . and his beautiful sister, Julia. It seemed as though the drive would never end. On top of that, it seemed as though most of the town had the same idea, and traffic was becoming congested. But it was noon and well expected, I supposed. Anxious, I almost asked the taximan to put on more speed when I suddenly saw the large hospital building looming up ahead.

Dan met me in the lobby and much to my surprise, gently embraced me. I felt awkward and hoped no one had seen us. I'd long since dreamed of such a special moment with him, but in a serene setting, quiet and private, just the two of us longing to share our hearts and the closeness we felt. But I understood his heart in the moment, and I didn't take it personally.

"How's Julia?" I asked with concern.

"She's resting comfortably. I think the doctor will release her tomorrow. Her housekeeper will be back from her trip tomorrow, and I think that Ethel has already told you that she's back at my home then as well?" he asked with a question mark behind his words. Nodding, I didn't know what to say until he softly spoke, referring to his sister. "She's waiting for you . . ." Tears misted in his eyes and his thought went unfinished. Dan wanted to speak with the doctor, and after showing me to her hospital room, he briefly left me.

Julia was extraordinarily beautiful. When I entered her room, her Japanese eyes smiled as she warmly greeted me. She appeared more alert and looking well.

"Maggie," she softly said, "it's wonderful to see you again! Dan never stops talking about you."

Taken aback, I was stunned at her words, and didn't know what to say. Finally, I returned, "It's very nice to see you again, Julia."

"How's Blossom?" she asked. "I suppose she kept you moving from one activity to another." Dimples showed as she smiled.

Laughing, I said, "She's just fine. We kept busy playing games, drawing and coloring, and then she fell asleep while we were watching *Cinderella*."

"Oh!" Julia enthused. "That's her favorite movie!"

"It was wonderful!" I agreed. "I never had any of these movies growing up as a child, and she offered that I choose one that I liked. I'm so glad I did! We really enjoyed it together."

"I can see that you did, and I do appreciate your care over her. And Dan," she paused, "he's quite taken with you!"

"He is?" I asked, surprise emanating in my words.

"He says you have fun together!" Julia coyly let the words drop in her musical tone, but they were as a bomb to me.

Stumbling for words, I found myself reply, "Fun? Well, if untangling knots in the editing process is fun, he never mentioned it to me," I said offhandedly.

Chuckling, she replied, "No! No!" she exclaimed, pausing. "Maggie, I didn't mean that at all." As her eyes held mine, somehow, I had the distinct feeling that her definition of the word, fun, held a deeper implication that she was not dissuaded from.

Blushing, I said nothing, knowing that Julia's inference in this regard had somehow made it to her heart within a personal meaning between Dan and I as she blithely continued, "But I'm wondering, I hope Dan treats you well?"

"He's very considerate in our work," I answered.

"Do sit down beside me," Julia quietly invited. "I think Dan will be gone a bit longer and I'd love the opportunity to chat a little more with you."

Pulling up the chair against the wall next to her bed, I furrowed my brow and merely nodded. I waited for Julia to continue, knowing that something specific must be on her mind.

"I'm glad to hear that he's considerate. He's always been special to me in the way he's thoughtfully kind and loving. I think Dan should take you out for supper tonight to thank you for all your kindness," she gently remarked, her lovely eyes penetrating mine.

"Oh, no! I couldn't," I fumbled. "I mean, I'm here to help in any way I may."

"But you could, Maggie!" she firmly stated.

"I'm just doing my job - out of courtesy to Dan," I stressed.

A hurt expression came into her pretty eyes. "He looks forward to seeing you every day and it would be as a favor to me."

Choked with emotion, I found no recourse to what I was feeling. I was relieved to hear Dan's footsteps, and within seconds, he stepped into the room, so I needn't answer. Our stay with Julia wasn't long and I let Dan and her take most of the conversation between them.

About twenty minutes later we arose, promising to return soon. We said goodbye and I wiped away telltale tears that insisted on breaking through my deep emotion. I asked Dan if he minded taking me home.

"I hope your car is fixed soon," he dryly commented. "I need my lovely assistant rested in the mornings," he brightened, smiling, his tone changing and taking my hand. "I'd like to pick you up tomorrow if I may, please, so you don't have that long walk to the office, Maggie."

"My car should be ready by six tonight, and the walk is not a worry," I answered. "I'm sorry for this extra bother."

"Don't be silly," he kindly assured. "I'm happy to accommodate you anytime. Should you change your mind then and need a ride tomorrow, please call me."

I thought the taxi ride had been long, but this seemed endless. Silence hung between us as we got into Dan's car, and he turned out of the hospital parking lot. I was relieved when my boarding house appeared, and Dan made the turn onto my street.

Taking my hands in his, he paused, then said, "I hope you know how much it means to me and Julia that you care so much."

"It's my pleasure, Dan."

He relinquished my hands, and I opened the door to step out. Saying goodnight, my emotions rose like a burning flame inside my heart. Thinking over what Julia had said, I burst into tears as soon as I closed the door to my room. I had so many thoughts tangled all together that I didn't even know how or where to begin to sort them out. Did Julia really suspect my feelings for her brother? Were my feelings that obvious?

Suddenly, I shuddered as a cold shiver ran down my spine. "Oh, no!" I cried, placing my hand over my mouth. "Did Dan know my heart in this, too?" I asked myself as the full import hit me like a ton of bricks. I could almost be sure that Julia shared perhaps, a little more than was necessary with her brother, Dan.

In that moment, I realized that the only one who may be able to answer my many questions was Ethel, and I knew that I could trust her explicitly to keep this between ourselves. It was not at the top of my list to involve her any more than I sometimes wanted to be involved where it concerned Dan's personal family affairs. But I needed to know if he might have hinted to Ethel any of his feelings toward me, or if Julia had likewise confided any confidence in this regard, as well.

That was the trouble, I said, continuing my thoughts. I cared so much. Too much. Dan and I were good friends, that I could see, and he depended on me. But love me? That was so far off, I had to hold my feelings to myself. I never meant to be more than a trusted employee, but I found myself caring for him more than my heart wanted to, and I didn't ever want to lose the precious gift of friendship we shared as colleagues.

In that instant, my dream suddenly came into focus. I had kissed the man in my dream several times as a way of thanking him for helping me to find my car. But this wasn't a dream. Could it be that that was symbolic in some way? Whatever was I going to do about it all, I wondered?

My heart was stricken with pain and the reality that love had come so softly, unawares, I hadn't even noticed how much I loved Dan until Julia had brought it to my attention. In that moment, I felt hot tears fill my eyes and tumble without recourse down my face until I could cry no more.

CHAPTER 5

Moments of Grace

Blossom was thrilled to be at home with her mother again the following day. When Dan and I stopped by for a few minutes to visit her, we were greeted by Julia's housekeeper, Olga Olson. Her face brightened when she opened the door and saw who it was, ready to please like Ethel, and taking our coats.

Blossom bounded happily into the room, running into Dan's arms. She smiled at me as though she had a secret she could barely keep in! I was pleased to see that her mother, Julia, looked as lovely as ever when we were seated in the living room. Although I realized how sick she really was with her cancer, no one would never have known she'd recently had any need for a medical stay in the hospital.

Dan and I visited them every few days, and I hardly noticed anything astray with my heart as we laughed and filled our visits with joy in Julia's delightful presence.

Over the next couple of months, Julia was well enough to still work in her dress shop. And while I could see at times that it was harder on her than she was willing to admit, I was really happy that she had this wonderful diversion. I think she needed it more than any of us realized.

I loved helping Julia out, and Dan insisted that I take some time off from the office to be this support to her.

"Maggie," he said, "I know how much you and Julia adore each other. I think it's only fair that you and my sister have some time with each other. You needn't worry about losing any pay cheque; I am more than happy to keep you on the payroll. I think this will do you and Julia a world of good. What do you say?"

I loved the idea and spontaneously threw my arms about him without thinking. "Oh, Dan! This is really thoughtful of you! I would love to have this pleasure with your sister!"

"Then it's all settled!" he gently said. "When can you start? Tomorrow? I mentioned this to Julia and she is thrilled at my suggestion, too! I know she'll take you on as soon as you say the word!"

"Tomorrow?" Suddenly I was missing not being with Dan at the office. "Are you sure?" I asked.

Dan looked inquisitively into my eyes. "Is that too soon, Maggie?"

I didn't know how to express my feelings without letting Dan know how much I'd miss his lovely presence. Biting my bottom lip, tears began to mist my eyes and I softly whispered, "Tomorrow, Dan. It'll be just fine. Thank you so much for this wonderful gift with your sister."

"It's my pleasure!" he meaningfully replied. "I know that a change will be good for you and that Julia will really love having you at her side. I'd like the honor of picking you up tomorrow morning, along with my sister. I'll give you a call sometime in the afternoon. I asked Ethel to prepare a lovely meal for us all, so I hope that is okay with you," he asked.

"Oh, Ethel! Yes, Dan! Thank you very much! I shall look forward to my day tomorrow. With Julia, Ethel, and you," I added. "What about Blossom?"

"A school chum has invited her over, so it'll be just the three of us, as you have already mentioned."

The day with Julia was wonderful and we sold a lot of clothing. I was very appreciative that Dan had invited us to his mansion for supper. When it was over, and we'd said goodbye to Ethel, he drove me and Julia home, dropping her off first.

When we arrived at my boarding house, Dan said, "I've been wanting to ask you all day, Maggie; How did everything go at the boutique?"

I knew there was more behind his question than this, and that he was curiously interested in knowing how Julia was holding up.

"Everything was terrific," I said, "and Julia looked rested and happy."

"I could see that," he said. "You know something, my dear Maggie, I think this is the finest idea that I've had for a long time. What I am trying to say is, that you are good for my family, including me. Thank you for giving us this joy in you!"

Tears rolled down his cheeks, and I gently patted his hand. "It's my honor, Dan. Any way I may be of help, I will be happy to."

"I am very grateful for that," he said. He hesitated before continuing, and surprised me by admitting what was on my own heart. "I missed you at the office, Maggie. Every time I glanced out my window or walked by your desk, I expected you to be there. Well," he finished, "I'm happy that you're giving Julia this special time. I know it means everything to her as it does to me. Please kindly let me know if you or Julia need anything, and I'll do my very best about it. Please promise?" he asked.

"That's very sweet and considerate of you, Dan. I shall, I promise!" I laughed. His ocean-blue eyes twinkled with that beautiful smile I so loved in a way that always warmed my heart.

In the days following, it was not only a wonderful experience, but I felt a part of this special woman's life in Julia, and the sister-in-law I hoped to one day be with her. I still missed Dan's presence every day, but being with his sister was something so extraordinarily special, I hardly noticed anymore.

Every week he invited me, along with his sister and niece, to his mansion to sit at the extravagantly laden table Ethel so lovingly prepared for us. Listening to the chatter around the table, when my eyes caught Dan focused on me, joy filled my soul, and I smiled at his pleasure.

What I loved best of all, however, was when Dan graciously drove me home those nights we all dined together at his mansion, and we were alone to these moments in sharing our hearts before we bid goodnight. I knew that my heart deeply loved Dan, but I tried not to show it. I was satisfied with his companionship as good friends, as we got to know each other on those special evenings. I knew that he was, too.

Enjoying the warmth of Julia's delightfully charming presence, and simply being with each other; sharing our hearts, was a gift of immense treasure. I found that I cherished it far more deeply than I truly realized, and which we otherwise wouldn't have had together as time moved forward.

"One day soon," she sweetly smiled when her illness was worsening, "I want you to own this boutique with my brother, Dan. You will, won't you, darling Maggie? I will get everything in order legally that it may be so for you and my dear brother. He's been a silent partner from the beginning, and we can keep it to this direction, if you desire." Her voice was tender as Julia's lovely Japanese eyes looked into mine. I felt an emotion within me rising so strongly, that I could not stop it, knowing that we already were sisters-in-law.

I assured her that I would be thrilled to honor her request in every way I could. "You know I shall, dearest Julia! It's simply divine, and I promise to do my very best in continuing your legacy. You have a most beautiful creative talent enough to see the generations through! And I'm certain that one day, Blossom will love being a part of it, carrying on your name, and the integrity by which it stands!"

"Aren't you the sweetest?" she teasingly said, taking my arm. "I wonder, now, dear sister, what you may think of this addition to my boutique?"

Julia led me halfway down the center of the shop. When she paused, I gasped with pleasure. A rack of new styles of dresses; trendy and beautifully fashionable, were gorgeous. "Oh, Julia! How enchantingly lovely! But when did you have time for this breathtaking creation I see before my eyes right now?" The rack was plumb full with similar chic styles and colors; all breathlessly enchanting, but my heart was most smitten with a blue dress that had immediately caught my attention.

Julia laughed in that musical way I'd always adored, and answered, "I had an idea for this some months ago, and I'd almost forgotten about it. Last night as I was enjoying the moon from my terrace, I suddenly remembered about these dresses. They were all finished, except for the blue dress. I had almost completed it before my hospital stay. I particularly remembered it, because I called it *'Moon's Pleasure,'* and I wanted it to be especially special. It is quite lovely, isn't it, Maggie? For a romantic walk, don't you agree?"

"Oh, my, indeed!" Admiring the blue dress with puffed sleeves and lace on the bodice, it was a beauty. It was exquisitely vogue right to the tailored waistline that naturally fell in a soft fluency to the lace that finished it off, trimming it like a delicate flower, but aspiring, as the moonbeams, I'd have to say. At that moment, I truly realized what a gift I was inheriting in the dress shop, and I would treasure every creation that Julia had designed with the whole of her heart and her soul.

"Just so know, dear Maggie," she lovingly whispered, "you'll find my patterns locked away in my kitchen cupboard on the top shelf above the pantry. The key is in the pantry cupboard under my tea towels. You'll see. I want you to keep the ideas I have designed my fashions from." Then, slipping the blue dress off the hanger, she looked into my eyes and handed it to me. "Would you please give me the honor of trying the dress on so that I may see how it fits and if the title reflects the blissful joy of a *Moon's Pleasure?*"

Curiously, I looked intently into her eyes, and smiled. "Yes, Julia. As you like. It shall be my delight."

When I came out of the dressing room, Julia's hands flew to her heart, and she gasped. "Oh, my dearest Maggie! It's exquisite on you! Just as I thought, and your favorite color, too! Now, I want you to wear this dress on a special night when you and my dear brother, Dan, take a walk beneath the moon. Really, Maggie, it is wonderfully elegant, delightful, and perfectly beautiful on you, just like you!"

Taken aback, I didn't know what to say. My eyes misted and I hugged her close and softly whispered my heart's deepest passion. "I shall wear this beautiful creation in honor of you always, my dearest Julia! Beneath the moon some night . . . with Dan, I pray. Thank you, sister dearest!"

"That is all I ask," she whispered back. "You and Dan. I know that it shall come to pass one day when he shall know this love you hold within your heart for him. I think he does already," she wisely said.

I threw my arms about her and cried. "Oh, Julia!" I said. Then, I turned and changed back into my clothes. When I came out of the dressing room, Julia wrapped the dress in tissue and placed it in a flowered bag, and gave it to me. Peace filled my heart, and we exited the boutique together.

Dan had just pulled up outside the shop and was waiting for us. I locked the door for Julia, and we stepped into his car. Ethel's supper would be on the table when we arrived in a few minutes. I couldn't wait to see her, but I didn't know how I'd ever face Dan, and the emotions that were bursting inside of me to what I was feeling for Julia's love, and the love I hoped to know one day in him. I dared not catch his eyes on me across his table . . . not even for a moment.

Julia taught me so much about her Spanish and Japanese heritage, and countless things. I laughed at her stories about her three brothers, and loved her passionate joy in sharing of her beloved daughter. I didn't know exactly how I'd come to have this privilege, but I was deeply moved, and cherished every moment that was mine in it. I supposed I could say that it all began with my joy to write, and the day I met Daniel Danes, her beloved brother. He really changed my life and made it so much better!

I was also growing fond of her daughter, Blossom, and found the same sweetness spilling over in her as Julia held, as we got to know each other better.

It also didn't take a poor man to recognize how very much Blossom loved her uncle Dan, and that it was more than mutual! Here, I saw a different side to Dan, and it brought me back to those childhood books I'd seen upon his shelf in his library. I suddenly could see him as a little boy, his hands eagerly holding onto the pages as his parents read him countless stories, and through that love, the pages tattered in that joyful wonder of his boyhood years!

We often played games together or took turns reading stories as Julia looked on, enjoying the activity, and Blossom's eyes lit with joy in our presence. It was so beautiful to see her feeling free and happy! Although very little was ever spoken about Dan's childhood, Ethel did admit that his love for reading had always been a huge part of it. "His parents read to him every evening," she recollected. "That's what Mr. West told me one time when he visited with my Mr. here. I'd forgotten all about it until this very moment, Maggie."

"'Dan most likely won't ever tell you,' he chuckled, as I gave him a tour of the Mr.'s flower garden," Ethel related, "'but the beauty here and the books of his youth, were invariably the loveliest and most special moments and memories he's cherished most of all. His grandfather, Noel, loved to also read to him and take on the role of the characters, changing his voice, as well as sometimes dressing the part! Dan squealed in delight, begging for more!'"

I was astounded, but it certainly answered my silent questions. It also helped me to better understand Blossom's identical love of reading, and it gave my heart a beautiful feeling to know how much joy Dan had known in that boyhood time, just as his niece was experiencing in hers. Clapping her hands and jumping up and down in her moments of glee, nothing was more lovely than this, I thought, as I turned to Dan, and he smiled, looking deep into my eyes, and I felt my face flushing.

But I loved it best when Julia felt strong enough and participated with us. Her musical voice accentuated the characters in the storybooks, as we both did, too, Dan and I, to the thrill of this darling child! Reading such books as *Little Red Riding Hood*, Blossom was attentively focused on the storyline, until the scene shifted, and she screeched in fearful terror as the big, bad wolf was about to eat the grandmother!

At times such as these, I wondered how the author could have come up with such a dire plot, I asked myself. We made sure we balanced the books between the good and the bad characters in this, although there was always that tug-of-war between these worlds, as there always would be.

Blossom particularly adored her favorite story of *Cinderella*, and I shared her same enthusiasm. We selected character parts, and sometimes assumed more than one role, and Blossom was thoroughly smitten! But as the months flew by, I began to see that Julia was failing more than I wanted to admit. By the middle of the summer, however, I realized that Julia's time on earth was short, and I couldn't imagine how difficult this would be for her little girl, as well as for Dan and me.

To the days following, Dan had work that couldn't be avoided, so on this particular day, he dropped me off at the hospital when

Julia became too sick to stay at home, with the promise to pick me up just after four o'clock in the afternoon.

Through the weeks, I enjoyed spending time with his sister and found myself drawn to her so softly, as I was to her brother, that it was like we'd known each other all our lives.

"You love Dan," she gently said, the moment I sat next to her bed. "I can see it in your eyes, and your heart is sure in it with him."

Tears filled my eyes, and I knew that I couldn't keep it from Julia any longer. "I do," I began to weep, "but I don't know what Dan's true feelings are for me. Sometimes he talks like we're strangers, even though we're very close friends. From almost the very beginning when we first met, he always said I was his Dearest, and that he'd waited his whole life for me. He also shared that he'd never tire of calling me his Dearest. To ponder the thought, as he sometimes says, that we are like strangers or that I'm his breather, is mystifying to me, and I don't understand that at all." Looking into her eyes, the tears were unrelenting as I said, "I've never considered him that way for a moment, and I could never entertain the thought that Dan is my breather or like the stranger he seems to see me as at times. And it makes me wonder what is wrong with me," I cried.

Julia's expression was serious, yet ever loving in her eloquently and exquisitely passionate way I'd come to appreciate over time. She so delicately and beautifully took my hands in hers and gently said, "I think that my beloved brother just is lost in all of this, and in such defining moments in how he truly feels about you, Maggie. But I'm convinced he loves you, and no one else. The way he looks at you and confides to me, why, there's just no mistaking it in my mind that your heart has long since been his. He often says that there's no one ever like you he wants to be with. Coming from Dan, that is very deep and personal, dear Maggie."

The tears continued and feeling overwhelmed, I couldn't speak. Then I just had to tell her. "The way he shares with me like married couples do, and the words he speaks, I think his heart knows, too, Julia, just as you said, but that it needs more time. But does it, Julia? Why would his heart still struggle so?"

"I cannot see that far into his heart, but I will pray," she said, lovingly holding my hands. "And Maggie, I've very seriously considered this from the day we first met that you're the one I want my daughter to grow up with as her second mother, and I'm so sure of you and Dan marrying, that I changed my will to accommodate this impression that my heart knows is truest true. Dan can be slow to know his heart at times, but when he does, he never changes his mind, so we will have to trust the good Lord to direct him!"

Looking to me, I was taken aback at her deeply serious sentiment. "Oh, Julia," I said, tears streaming down my face. "You'll always be Blossom's mother. And I am truly overwhelmed by this extraordinary love and trust from you. I love her so, and I'll love her always, but Blossom shall always know that you're her mother forever. I do believe that Dan knows – perhaps, he needs that time to know it's sure, yet for me, it's a very hard place to wait in."

Julia's eyes misted as she gently squeezed my hands. "I know that Dan loves you, my dearest Maggie. I know! You're a gift of rarest joy and blessing, and I want to thank you for being a wonderfully special part of our lives. You will marry my brother . . . I know it! Just think! We'll be sisters-in-law, Maggie! And together, you and Dan will raise Blossom to be the lovely woman she'll be one day that lives inside of her, not merely as her guardians, but as the little girl today I know you both love and cherish in her so."

Julia cried with me as we hugged in a lovingly long embrace as I whispered with deepest passion and love for her, "What a wonderful gift! A wonderful joy!" I exhorted. "You and I, sisters-in-law! But I can honestly tell you that we are much more than this already, for we are truly sisters!"

"Oh, yes, Maggie! Sisters in every sense of the word, and I love and adore you so!"

"Me, too!" I lovingly admitted. Going back to her thought, I proposed, "Dan and I are going to be more than Blossom's guardians, Julia! We have since loved her as our own daughter and I am honored for her love," I cried. Like a dagger thrust into my heart in the pain that would soon take Julia from us, and the pain that her daughter, Blossom, would soon know without her, the hurt was almost unbearable.

Without question, I wanted to be with Dan when he called me early the next morning. "I'd like to pick you up at your boarding house right away, Maggie, if you please. The doctor just called, and he doesn't expect my sister to live more than a few hours. Would you . . .?" he left his sentence unfinished.

As Dan began to cry, I quickly affirmed, "Yes, my dearest Dan. I'm ready and here for you in but a moment. Please do come for me. I want to share these last special, precious moments with you and Julia." Olga Olson had resigned her position with Julia to study, and I understood fully that this was a hard place for both Julia and Dan at this time. But I was assured without even asking, that Ethel was caring for Blossom, and my heart wondered what they were feeling, too.

Julia was looking pale and could barely talk, and when we slipped out for a quick lunch, I felt fidgety. "I have this disconcerting feeling," I began.

He arose and I put down my coffee mug. When we got outside the café, Dan paused, and turning to me, threw his arms about me. Weeping, I held my beloved as he held me close, and I cried with him, neither of us speaking a word, for we didn't need to, and I wondered if the tears would ever stop. Then we walked arm in arm to his car and back to the hospital.

Julia was still with us, I thankfully said in my thoughts, but it was apparent that she soon would have her mansion in Heaven. I believed that the angels were almost finished with completing the final touches. A curiosity of immense joy welled up in my spirit as I wondered just what it would look like, and how soon I might visit her when I went to Heaven, too!

Sitting on the bed beside her, Dan and I cried together in the love we had known with this incredibly wonderful woman, and the woman who had come to mean so much to me, once a stranger. And I pondered whether Dan would get past his brokenness and see us not as mere strangers, but as the "perfect couple" that Ethel had observed, and especially, his sister, Julia.

When Julia took her last breath, the room filled with an amazing peace and explicit perfume of beauty, and it was hard for us to leave her behind, but we knew her soul was now in Heaven with the Jesus we all loved.

I didn't know exactly how to comfort my Dan, but he didn't seem to need it in the moment for the grief and comfort we'd shared shortly before. In time, our hearts would heal, and for this gift I had come to find, not only in him, but in his beloved sister, through the deep sorrow of my own heart, I would be ever thankful.

My thoughts shifted as I suddenly realized what faith it must have taken for Dan to lovingly invite, and welcome me, into his family throughout these wonderfully incredible months. Such extraordinary joy had become truly very precious and touching, that it momentarily took my breath away!

I looked into his beautiful eyes, and for the first time, I saw his heart in a new light. As private and personal as Dan was, he passionately shared this deep place from his heart with me, never wavering. That was an immense privilege and honor, where I'd enjoyed a wealth of blessings in countless ways: from working alongside of him, and falling in love with him, to loving his niece, Blossom, and becoming sisters in every sense of the word with our beautiful Julia.

Through my tears, I lovingly reached for his hand to meet all that God still had for us, aside from this difficult time. Dan held me close, and I knew that God would not fail us as we walked hand in hand, together, venturing onto a new journey more beautiful than we could ever have imagined or planned; all, in its time!

That night as I lay upon my pillow, I prayed with all of my being that our beloved Blossom would surely always be a cherished part of both of our lives, as I prayed the same for me with her beloved uncle, Daniel Danes. I couldn't imagine my life without them; not even for a moment.

Perfect peace settled over me as I drifted off to sleep, like God was right beside me, and I surely knew He was!

Julia died that afternoon, and my heart was broken, and I didn't know how it could ever be mended again. How little did I perceive the abundance of gifts that God had blessed within our last conversation in this the day afore, or in the honor I'd been so privileged to be a part of with this wonderful family who had so warmly welcomed me as theirs. Julia's kindness was so extraordinarily beautiful, and I recalled a day when we were sitting on her patio, enjoying the beauty all about us.

"It's so beautiful here," I expressed. "Peaceful. God gave you such a special gift within this lovely oasis."

Looking into my eyes, she softly said, "Yes, that's true, Maggie. But you are the gift that God brought as the lovely fragrance of the flowers to me and Dan and Blossom."

In that moment, the title of our book came into my mind. Sharing it later with Dan, he was ecstatic! We couldn't wait to begin the story!

Julia's Song was all I could think about. But much to my dismay, days later, Dan approached the subject.

"I've given it considerable thought," he began, "and I've decided that I want you to write the story, Maggie. This is something special I'd love to share with you as a once in a lifetime opportunity, but I need you to do it without me. You're a fine writer, and I want the publisher to know that every word has come from your heart alone; for you to get all the credit. That will be more than enough for me."

I was thunderstruck! I respected his wishes, but I suddenly felt that depth of loneliness that I had been struggling with over the months, with no idea of what to write within the pages of the title.

Then, unexpectedly one morning, the story took form in my mind from the moment I'd awakened. God wouldn't even let me have breakfast first, I teased Dan later! It was Saturday, and I spent most of the day creating the content. I emailed it to Dan hours later, anxious to know what he would think about it.

Dan was absent from the office the following Monday, but shortly after eleven o'clock, he posted me an email that made my heart jump with joy.

"It's perfect," he wrote, "and I can never thank you enough!"

Julia's Song would hopefully grow in popularity. Julia died, never seeing the story, but the legacy of her life would live on through the pages, and in the heart of her daughter, and all who were privileged to know this amazing woman. I didn't have the finances to publish the book, and so it remained dormant in my files.

Dan and I were becoming closer, where our relationship was based on the rock of Christ. He took my breath away when he revealed that it was because of my desire to hold Christ high when we'd initially met, in giving God the glory for the novel I'd published with his company, that he knew I was in his plan for his life as well.

"You always put God first," he said, "and I like that. I also gave my heart to Him many years ago, and I should have told you long ago, but I'm sure that Julia shared that with you."

"She didn't need to," I smiled. "I knew that in my heart sometime after we met, Dan."

"But she did tell you?" he asked, his eyes twinkling.

"Yes, she did!"

As close as Dan and I were, both within our work and friendship, I don't know how our story ends.

Days later, slipping on his jacket, Dan confided to me that he was going to take a leave of absence from the office. "I have no idea when I'll be back, Maggie. I'm offering you my position as Senior Editor. You know as much as I do in this business, perhaps, more . . ."

"But, Dan," I protested.

"Maggie, please," he implored with tenderest feeling. "I need you to do this for me – as a special favor. Please tell me that you will." Tears misted in his eyes as he waited, pleading.

"Alright, Dan. I'll do my best. But just remember that I'm not totally cut out to filling your shoes, and . . ."

"Thank you, Maggie," he interrupted. "I won't soon forget this, and I'll pray for you," he said. He turned and walked out of his office before I could even wish him well or say goodbye. Not even a hug. My world began to crumble, and I wasn't even sure why.

In that very moment when I lost sight of him, Daniel Danes' presence impacted me more than I ever could have imagined. Amidst my pain, I felt a love so overwhelming in my heart, that I couldn't stop it, whilst at the same time, my life now seemed meaningless and empty, and I could barely think.

Why hadn't Dan taken the consideration to speak with me in a private setting? What was I going to do, my heart cried in agony, as the full import pierced my heart no less than if he'd driven a dagger right through it? I hastily ran to the bathroom and cried my heart out until I could get my emotions together. When I returned, I called in Kathy Stokes, who knew about as much as I did in this position.

"I'm leaving for the day," I announced, "and I'm asking you to take over. Dan has left indefinitely and put me in charge as Senior Editor and I'd like for you to be my Assistant Editor."

Before she could respond, I said good afternoon to her, grabbed my purse, and practically ran out of the building, leaving a surprised Kathy staring after me. Letting my tears now freely flow, blindly, I got into my car and cried until I could cry no more, after which I headed to the Mr.'s home, hoping against hope that I wouldn't meet him there. I rang the bell and a surprised Ethel answered.

"Ethel," I quickly asked. "Is Mr. Danes here?"

"No. He told me this morning that he had a lot of things to do and not to expect him until late tonight."

Blossom appeared, running into my arms.

"Please, Ethel, would you take Blossom and put on a movie for her," I asked, hugging her close, then letting her go. "I need to briefly talk with you in private."

"Sure. Blossom, come along. You can watch *Snow White* while Maggie and I chat a bit."

A few minutes later, Ethel reappeared, closing the door behind her. "What's wrong?" she asked, concerned. "You've had something terrible happen, dear Maggie, and your eyes, so red from crying, tell me you are very disturbed."

"Mr. Danes is taking a leave of absence at the office. But if he hasn't told you, don't let on that you know, please, Ethel."

Taken aback, Ethel said, "A leave of absence? No, Maggie, he hasn't told me anything, not one word. But don't you worry, I'll keep this troubling secret from the Mr.," she promised.

"I'm wondering, would it be all right if I wandered through the avenue of trees and the flower garden? I need to think."

"Of course, Maggie. You are welcome to come anytime."

"I don't know about that," I said. "Mr. Danes might not agree."

Laughing softly, she said, "Oh, believe me, Maggie, the Mr., he likes you a lot and he won't mind one bit!"

Ethel entered the house and left me to my reveries. Why was it that one day the world was so perfect and the next day, everything was black like the night, and nothing could be seen clearly? *Thick like mud. Mud thick* sometimes fit it better, I decided. That exactly said it. I wondered what had prompted the person who thought that phrase up to say such words, I mused. They certainly seemed to have their place, especially on a day like today.

As for myself, I never intended to love the man who hired me or kindly chose to help me locate my car that morning I was expected at his office. Where had that love began? Why was there so much torment associated with the lost love I momentarily felt within my heart?

Would I ever see Dan again or talk with him? Where was he planning on going? And why couldn't he have the respect to share this with me? He said his feelings for me were mutual, and countless times, how much he cared. Not that he had told me he loved me, except for a slip of misplaced words once when we were corresponding through letters, but wasn't that true just the same? Could I have so wrongly judged his heart in mine?

Within so precious these wonderful months, were we no more like strangers as he'd infrequently made a point of telling me? His sister had confirmed as much in that truth as I felt within my heart, that he loved me. But where was that love now if it had truly ever been?

As the days moved on into weeks, I lost interest in the publishing industry, grieving for Julia and the man I loved in her brother. While my heart truly wanted to honor Dan, his absence often left me in tears, as I took hold of my new position. Here, I felt comfortable enough to hold onto the memories Dan and I so lovingly had shared together within its walls, trusting God for what I could not see.

Dan remained as silent as the night and as quiet as a sleeping bird. His absence felt like a dark world without his wonderfully beautiful and loving presence. I missed his sense of humor . . . I missed everything about him in this special man of honor and integrity I had come to love and respect to the core of my being. Nothing I ever asked in our work was too much for him, and he always graciously lent his wisdom to me, side by side. He was the most wonderful man I'd ever met, and I deeply loved and cherished him altogether. My heart had never been so broken as I wept until I could weep no more.

Alongside my pain, I clearly felt his own feelings and pain, and wondered if he felt like a man lost to himself in the grief of losing his beloved sister. I understood that without question. But like him, my heart was broken, too. I'd come to love Julia like a dear sister, and the pain in losing her was almost more than I could bear at times. We should have shared this grief together.

Here, the spring seemed to leave my heart for a time, and the misery I felt, now without Dan's wondrous presence, held me in its wintery grip, and I'd no idea when the spring would come to me again, or if it even might venture to come again at all. It became a double death where my heart died a little more each day to all the beauty once so beloved within our friendship.

Moreover, Blossom was lost, too. In the initial weeks after her mother's death, she cried herself to sleep each night. The haunting of those tears in childhood grief tore at my heart until I felt like I was beaten, and had nothing more to give to her, or anyone around me. The torment and grief, like a fire uncontained, flared and roared as we tried our best to get through each day, lifting our hearts to God, and trusting Him ever still for our futures.

Ethel was lost in it with us, but somehow, she seemed to measure her pain with the love that was always waiting in that very heart of God's love. I marveled at such trust of faithful assurance sustained within that peace, and while I was deeply moved by her example, I was also deeply perplexed as to why I couldn't find that same trust of faithful assurance. I believed, like Ethel, so what was the matter with me? I asked myself time and again.

"She isn't lost, Maggie," Ethel shared one afternoon when I thought I could bear the pain no more. And in the days and weeks that followed, she would remind me again that "we shouldn't feel lost without her," she so tenderly explained. "She's with Jesus. How could she ever be lost to us when God has her beautiful soul in Heaven with Him? And how can we feel lost without her when her spirit is alive in Heaven more than it was on Earth? She's strolling the golden streets of Heaven, her arms outstretched to the gentle wind, admiring the acres and acres of beauty everywhere! Just imagine the waterfalls and the flowers . . . Oh, dear Maggie, I have to say it again that she's more alive than ever with Jesus forever!" Then tenderly placing her hands on her heart she'd say, "She's here – in our hearts, too, Maggie, and she shall be always."

I was very grateful that, for as many times as I needed to hear those wondrous words and be reassured, Ethel patiently opened her heart and shared it with me countless times over. And somehow, I had the feeling that it healed her heart a little more, too, as I drank in the comfort and gift of her wisdom, like the pearl of great worth that was lost, then found, which Jesus talked of in the Bible.

"You need to find Julia in your heart again, Maggie, and I know she's there, but you must look to find your peace. The love and memories will never be lost when we have loved and cherished one so. And" her words startled me, "you will also find a part of her alive in Blossom, more precious than all the jewels in the world."

Ethel had a wonderful revelation of insight there and I knew deep inside of me that I wouldn't want anything better for Julia than to be walking those golden streets of Heaven! Slowly, it became a part of my own heart, too, turning my grief to joy, where, one early evening, the spring unexpectedly came back to me. How beautiful and sweet it was upon its return, where I drank in the fragrance of this perfect healing which had found its way back to me out of the depth of darkness that had clung too long a time within my losses. Such a treasured gift this was . . .

I came to appreciate the goodness of all God gives to us in a new way as the waning light of the quiescent evening lifted my soul like wings of a butterfly, and the full, golden moon celebrated its own triumph as it streamed through my window, then I soon closed my eyes in sleep in perfect rest.

In time, my heart was able to forgive Dan, where it became as fresh as the day when we had unexpectedly met in the underground garage. And I prayed with all of my heart that the blessings which had come to me would come to him as well, and be a part of the perfect healing we have because of everything God gave to us on the cross, and the resurrection that sealed it in His immense love for the world He would always love.

For now, the pages go unwritten. The stranger at my side . . . gone. Forever, even so, Dan will be this unexpected, jeweled gift in my heart that loves him more each day and shall live forever in this special niche within my soul. A man I came to love so softly . . . without him even knowing, I murmured, as the tears tumbled down my cheeks, spilling onto my bare arms, as I cried through my pain until I could cry no more.

Herein, I was often reminded of Ethel's words of wisdom, and found myself holding onto them, where I sat at Jesus' feet, finding jeweled blessings within *Moments of Grace* in Him, and learned from Him, filling my soul to a broken wholeness that still wavered at times. But I knew that His grace was sufficient for my journey through it all, and that it would eventually come, where my heart would no longer be torn and broken, but restored to all my heart desired within that hopeful yearning, unless God's plan no longer fit Dan into mine.

That's when I suddenly remembered this verse, and it gave me comfort. The apostle Paul said in Romans 8:28 (KJV), "And we know that all things work together to them that love God." In those moments, I realized that God is the architect of love. In His great wisdom, He still guides hearts and lives in truth to all who truly seek Him.

Although it wouldn't always be easy, I'd made a promise to Dan, and I would keep it; continuing the work we had shared all these wonderful past months. It was just as Paul encouraged in 1 Corinthians 15:58 (KJV), "Be ye steadfast, unmovable, always abounding in the work of the Lord, forasmuch as ye know your labour is not in vain in the Lord." That was hard for me do at times when my heart was missing Dan so much. But knowing that we are really working for God, it was key towards realizing that my work had purpose, and it oftentimes helped to pull me through my day.

Still, I couldn't help myself expressing these words that carried my thoughts, softly embracing all that my soul was feeling.

> *Dan, my heart whispered, as the tears streamed down my face, you are my wild rose upon the vine. So lovely; so beautiful! My dearest darling and my beloved!*
>
> *I choose to trust God's plan, even when my dreams fall away, and I pray that you will soon find the purpose to that which He has called you.*
>
> *Somehow, someday, I know that our best is yet to come in Christ, and we shall stand tall on the mountaintop again.*
>
> *To whatever plan God brings, I am fully assured that it will be as perfect as that wild rose upon the vine; its enticing fragrance to embrace our lives in a wondrous way, and far beyond our human understanding! Like the beautiful fragrance of the rose, I shall adore and love you forever, my darling!*

CHAPTER 6

Remnants from the Past

Time could not erase the pain in my heart. Dan and I had journeyed together through the loss of his beautiful sister, and I knew how much he missed her. But my grief was no less than his. Sharing the pain and leaning on each other for support was surely a way of healing our mutual pain. I could never have imagined that he would abandon me in this time when we needed each other more than ever.

To honor Dan and the high position he entrusted to my care, my commitment remained strong, as I continued to strive for the highest excellence in my work that I was capable of. The company began to flourish, and we were temporarily overwhelmed with working toward publishing a huge volume of diversified books from our authors. Eventually, I hired two extra editors who lifted our burden, and did outstanding work. It was a choice I never regretted!

Having a daily routine helped to settle me more without Dan's sweet presence, and while Ethel was a wonderful support to me, I needed Dan. I didn't know how to cope with Blossom some days, completely understanding her broken and grieving heart. In these tempestuous times, I was thankful for Ethel's command and kindness as we helped her through this difficult time.

I rented out my apartment at the boarding house, while I stayed at the Mr.'s to be better able to assist Ethel, and the renter was more than gracious in accommodating me, as I may need my apartment back at any given moment since I couldn't predict Dan's return. Of course, if naught came to naught, I trusted that Dan would allow me to stay until my renter was gone, and I could return again.

In her deep grief, Blossom's tears fell as she cried herself to sleep at night, and I sometimes stayed with her to give Ethel the rest she needed. "I know your heart is broken," I cried with her, hugging her close. "But it's really only God who can heal our pain and bring back the wonderful, lovely memories from the remnants of the past that you shared with your mother."

Blossom liked me and Ethel to read to her, and oftentimes she fell asleep before the story was barely started. It bruised my heart that this little child had lost her mom, and the uncle, who should have given her every consideration in that.

"You need to get some rest," Ethel said to me one night after Blossom had fallen asleep, and we sat across from each other in the Victorian chairs in the Drawing Room. I arose from my chair as Ethel rose with me, and the tears began to fill my eyes.

"I can't," I cried. I threw my arms about her as we cried in each other's pain. "I miss Dan terribly, and I miss Julia's presence. And Blossom . . ."

"You love him!" Ethel exclaimed, letting go of me, wiping away her own tears as she searched my face. "I've seen this love between you for a long time."

"Yes, Ethel. I do. I love Dan very much."

"Well, let me make you a hot lemon drink and warm some biscuits to go with it," she gently offered.

"Alright. But I'd prefer a cold glass of milk over lemon tonight, Ethel. I admit I'm a little hungry."

"No wonder. You scarcely touched your supper. Why, the Mr. won't even recognize you, Maggie, if you don't get some meat on those bones of yours!"

Laughing, I dried my tears and sat at the table. In a few minutes, Ethel brought a plate of tempting cinnamon rolls, and another of her wonderful biscuits, as well as a glass of milk for me.

"Eat up now, child," she said. "I'm not letting you leave the table until every crumb is gone from your plate! Maybe, I'll just have one myself, too," she smiled, reaching for a cinnamon roll.

"You make the best of everything, Ethel," I praised, taking a bite of her delicious biscuits. "Where did you learn to cook and bake the way you do? Why, you could have your own restaurant with baking on the side!" I suddenly exclaimed.

"Ohhh," she drawled, shyly, pleasure shining in her eyes, "I taught myself. I tried this and that and it worked, and so I told myself to keep on trying."

"That's simply marvelous!"

"My fiancé, he liked it, too, but he found someone else's he liked better," she divulged, the memory clouding her face.

"Oh, Ethel! How awful! He didn't deserve you and I'm glad you didn't marry him."

"Well, fortunately, we weren't engaged too long," she said recollecting, "and I'm very glad that I found out the truth about his waywardness before we married. He played two sides, like a double agent, he did! Better, what you call? Riddance!" she exclaimed in a cheery tone finding the word she was searching for.

I couldn't help but laugh and said, "If I recall correctly, Ethel, I believe the whole saying is, 'Good riddance to bad rubbish!' And that's exactly what it is."

"Mmm hmm," she agreed, her eyes flashing in pleasure. "Riddance and rubbish!"

"Well, God will give you the perfect man and he will be deserving of you," I stoutly said. "Any man who doesn't appreciate you can get out, that's for sure!"

Smiling, she chuckled, heartily replying, "That's for sure, I'll say!"

I didn't know if Ethel really understood those words, but she would learn in time if she didn't. I laughed with her, and said, "Now, I suppose we should get to bed, Ethel. Blossom will be up before we know it!"

I turned to go to the guest room, but Ethel suddenly stopped me. "Oh, my! I completely forgot, Maggie. I wanted to surprise you and decided to do something special since I know how hard it's been on you, what with the Mr. gone and all. So, I'm cleaning the whole room and Blossom kept me extra busy today that I didn't get it quite done. Everything is, what you say? Topsy-turnvy," she informed me, "so this afternoon I made up the Mr.'s room for you."

Startled, I bit my lip, knowing her heart was in it, and I took a moment to lovingly correct her. "It's, topsy-turvy, Ethel," I softly said. "Not, topsy-turnvy. There's no 'n' in the last word."

Frowning, she brightened and said, "Oh, I see! Crazy English again!"

"Yes, Ethel. Crazy!" I laughed.

I walked down the long corridor leading to Dan's private bedroom. I wasn't very happy about having to intrude in this manner or even opening the door, for it was his private domain, but Ethel had left me no choice. That is, of course, except to sleep on the chesterfield, which wasn't much to my liking.

It was one thing to have cleaned his room when I served as his housekeeper, and quite another, I surmised, to take it temporarily as my own. But I took a deep breath and when I walked through the entrance, peace suddenly filled my heart. Ethel said goodnight, and I quickly changed into my pajamas that she'd thoughtfully placed at the foot of the bed along with my robe and slippers.

This had always been my favorite room to clean for the "Mr.," as Ethel called him. It was wonderfully large, spacious, and well-laid out.

The large, private bathroom was pleasantly wallpapered in a lovely shade of blue depicting soft mountains in the background, and a beautiful waterfall cascading in a white flurry as it tumbled down the mountain. From there, it continued flowing along a lovely and quaint stream. A picturesque meadow of daisies stood against the edge of a brook, mixed with unidentifiable red blossoms I didn't know the name of, as though oblivious to the rushing waterfall. I could almost hear the thundering noise, deafening beyond imagination!

The rest of the entire room was distinctly refined, drawing out the lovely features of the furnishings. The beautiful setting, pleasing to the eyes, impeccably drew out an exquisitely respective decorum, likewise painted in a powderpuff blue that filled my heart with joy.

But I loved the presence of the room most of all. It was the Mr.'s after all, and his graces and kindness filled the spaces with his warmth in sweet solitude of comfort, almost as though he was with me.

I adored the substantial window seat that overlooked the flower garden and the gentle wind that blew softly through the open screens of the magnificent French doors. I couldn't resist the curiosity to see beyond the room at this time of night, which I'd never had the privilege of seeing before, and eagerly walked toward the doors. Unlatching the lock, I stepped across the threshold momentarily, where, at the moment, the wind was playfully fluttering the white curtains trimmed in lace, and caught me unawares as they softly brushed against my face. Laughing, I pulled the curtain aside, where the most delightfully charming balcony gave me a wonderful view.

The sky was dark but for the myriads of twinkling stars, and it left my soul breathless in its beauty. The moon, full and lovely, bathed the garden below in a sheath of glory catching the Victorian posts in its path, where the lights seemed to shimmer against the unmistakable iridescence portrayed within its wonder. Such a scene might also be appreciated from this amazing vantage by relaxing around a small table and occupying one of the two chairs set to the side on such a night as this, or to just enjoy the beauty of the outdoors throughout the day. However, I was enthralled to glimpse such a magnificent stage on this wonderful evening by standing behind the fence that substantially encased the balcony.

The rustling wind in the trees, mellow and sweet, on this moonlit night, called my soul to the blissful solitude within its stunning beauty. For but a moment, I shut my eyes; smiling, as the wind lightly touched my face, and I drank in the rich sonnet singing in my heart. It were almost as though Dan was welcoming and inviting me within this wonderful aura to the wondrous peace that stole into my soul. I felt exhilarated and happy, and truly privileged to be blessed within this profoundly enchanting aura. Refreshed, I stepped back into Dan's bedroom, locking the doors behind me, my heart no longer disquieted within me.

I slipped out of my slippers and removed my robe, then contentedly drew aside the blankets and sheet, settling comfortably beneath the cozy coverings. I turned on my side and closed my eyes, falling asleep an instant or two after my head found the pillow, whilst the wind caressed my face like a feather in the warmth of the darkening night.

For a moment, I didn't know where I was when I awakened. It felt so cozy in the bed, I hardly wanted to get up. A gentle knock lightly tapped on the door, and I heard Ethel's sweet voice.

"Breakfast is ready, ma'am."

I realized that I was in Dan's bedroom, and quickly threw the blankets aside. Dressing, I washed my face and hands in his pleasant bathroom, wondering what he'd think if he suddenly appeared and found me there! Perish the thought! I told myself. Then, a voice softly spoke my name.

"Maggie!"

I nearly jumped and wondered if I was still dreaming.

Standing stark still with towel in hand, I heard the voice again. "Maggie! Good morning!"

I hung the towel on the bar, opened the bathroom door, and stared in disbelief.

"I understand you spent the night here," a man's pleasant voice said, stepping forward.

"Dan!"

"I didn't mean to startle you," he said.

"I . . . I . . ."

"It's quite alright, Maggie. Let's have breakfast together and then I'd appreciate it if you'd take the morning off and go to the lake with me. Ethel informed me of your new assistant, Kathy Stokes, and I've already made the arrangements for her to take over while you're detained, with me," he emphasized. Pausing, he continued, "A fine choice, indeed! Now," he said, looking into my eyes, "will you do me the honor?"

"Me?" I asked.

"Yes, only you. I think you're still sleeping, my dear Maggie! I need to talk with you about some things."

I nodded as he took my arm, and we walked out of his bedroom together. Stepping into the long corridor, which led down to the short flight of steps, we reached the dining room moments later. Dan graciously pulled out a chair for me and I sat down. He pulled up another, sitting across from me, while Ethel hastened to bring our breakfast to us.

I suddenly felt uncomfortable with Dan staring amused as Ethel fussed like a mother hen, trying to coax me to indulge in a second helping. "I told you last night," she flatly said. "You need some meat on those bones."

"Oh, Ethel!"

Dan laughed. "Ethel, if you don't mind, I like Maggie just the way she is."

That did it! I couldn't eat another bite. "Please excuse me," I said. I went to the bathroom to brush my teeth and get my belongings out of Dan's bedroom.

"There's no need, Maggie," he said, appearing so quietly behind me, I hadn't noticed. "I won't be staying. You just make yourself comfortable, please, Maggie. In fact, I insist on it. When you're ready, let's get going."

I was all too happy to get ready as fast as possible. Moments later, I appeared in the foyer where Dan was patiently waiting for me.

"I'll have her back shortly, Ethel," he said.

Dan and I wandered along the beach. The sand was always difficult for me to walk on, but by walking at the edge of the lake, the sand was sufficiently firmer, making walking easier. I felt awkward, not knowing what to say or think. I waited for Dan to begin and to tell me what was on his mind.

"Maggie, you mean so much to me and you have been my dearest ever since we met in that parking garage. I have been very blessed to work with you. I know that you might think that I'm shirking my responsibilities since my sister died, but I needed a new environment. I went to see a friend and visit her during this time." He paused and my heart nearly stopped. Oh, no, I thought. So, there was someone else . . . How could I have misjudged his intentions for me? "But" he continued, "it doesn't seem to have solved any of my problems."

"I see," I said.

"Life certainly can have its challenges, Maggie," Dan chuckled. "My friend has always been a good listener, but she was experiencing a bit of her own trouble with her husband. I always enjoyed sharing conversations with Mrs. Dillion, who was my

English tutor. I didn't wish to impose, and only had luncheon with her. I came to see that any future relationship with her would be futile, and I actually felt great relief about it. I thought about you and Ethel, and what you both mean to me; especially you," he tenderly said. "And Blossom, too."

I didn't mean to, but I couldn't help but laugh. "I'm really sorry, Dan," I apologized. Not wanting to pry, I simply encouraged, "I understand."

"I know you do, Maggie. That's why I came back. I wonder . . ."

"Yes, Dan?"

"I wonder if we might still stay in touch?"

Looking deep into his eyes, I paused, then softly said, "Of course, Dan. I'd like that very much," as hope gently arose within my heart. That English tutor didn't seem much to his liking after all, I smiled, and she certainly wasn't much of a liking with me! Somehow, I was able to forgive Dan's absence with this little bit of insight.

"I'm not staying, as I mentioned, Maggie, but I wonder, would you continue to work for me – in my position, please?"

"Of course, Dan. Nothing's changed, unless you want it to."

"Oh, not at all, Maggie. I didn't mean that. I just can't go back yet, and I am busy with other matters elsewhere for some time. I'm not sure for how long."

"Anything I may still do for you, Dan, you know that I will."

Tears filled his eyes, and he began to weep. Then, he hugged me close, and softly whispered, "One day, dear Maggie, I hope you'll allow me the grace to share my heart when it is free again."

I looked a long moment into his eyes before I spoke. "As long as I am still here, Dan, you may share your heart anytime with me. And just so you know, you needn't wait until your heart is free again," I tenderly said.

"Then, I shall write to you when I can. Now, I suppose we should get back. If you want the day off, Maggie, just for being with me now, you may have it with pay."

"I'll see," was all I could say.

We walked along the beach for some time, enjoying the beauty of its tranquility. We didn't speak a word. We didn't need to. Dan held my hand, and in some of those special moments, he put his arm about my waist, holding me close. Like two dear and kindred friends, we were content in each other's company, and the silence that moved within this lovely scene.

When we came back to the road, Dan drove me back to his estate, and he left moments later. I decided to take him up on the offer, and wandered through the garden, resting after lunch. I didn't know what to do with myself, and settled down with a book afterward, but I found it difficult concentrating.

My mind wandered to Dan and why he still kept everything so private between us in not sharing what was really on his mind. I was sure that he was still hurting from the loss of his sister, and quite honestly, I didn't know how I could go on at times without him. If he'd just come to the place where he could leave it all with God and unlock his feelings and deep emotions with me, I believed that his heart would truly be free again and he'd never have cause to look back, because he'd find his soul wholly restored in it all. I still also believed that we needed to share our grief together, and I prayed that, through our letters, we might find that freedom in grace to move forward.

Love carries one another through every valley and every hilltop to the peak of the mountain, I said in my thoughts. For only there is the beautiful tapestry of God's divine beauty seen within the panoramic splendor of the heart. I prayed with all my heart that Dan would see how much I loved him, if only he might love me, too.

Ethel insisted that I watch a movie with her and Blossom after supper, and after a while, I found myself enjoying it. But when I went to bed that night, my heart still missed Dan, that I tossed and turned all night, crying into my pillow. While I had that one promise of hope from him, anticipating hearing from Dan soon, the joy of the walk with him along the beach this morning, eased that pain, and my soul was filled with the joy of his lingering presence that I couldn't explain.

It was a lot longer than I expected when Dan's first letter arrived at the publishing firm for me. With trembling hands, I slit open the envelope and withdrew a single sheet of paper. My eyes fell on his words, and I began to read his letter.

Dearest Maggie,

I'm not sure where to begin, but let me first say that I miss you, and you'll always be this special gift to me and Blossom as you were to my sister, Julia. I'm doing fine, Maggie. Don't worry. Just keep on doing what you do so well. I know I didn't properly express my appreciation to you, but I do thank you for everything you're doing for me in my absence. You're something so extraordinary and beautiful, and ever shall amaze me. You have a heart so pure and lovely! I'm assured that God is looking after us. I'm still praying for you. We'll catch up later.

Sincerely,
Dan Danes

I expected letters to follow more frequently, but months passed, turning the seasons, and I finally couldn't take it anymore. It was then that I realized I needed a diversion, and I knew exactly what that was. The children's book I'd written on behalf of Dan and his sister, Julia, came back into focus. While my finances were still strained, I began to seriously consider putting my disappointments and feelings aside and doing something for Dan that I hoped would give him the pleasure he'd once been so excited about. I didn't know if he'd ever see the book, but at least I could try. For now, the money I'd put aside for another project would cover the illustrator's expense. I detailed my heart's expectations to Dan's company two weeks later at the following board meeting. Everyone was excited and surprised, and we began the process leading to publication without delay.

"Your book is very special," the editor confided. "I'm sure that Dan will see it and appreciate it in book form."

Tears welled in my eyes. "Yes, Mia. Perhaps. Thank you! I just feel like there's a loose string in my life and that I need to do something with this very special story that Dan entrusted to me. The rest will be up to God. There's nothing more I can do."

The illustrator took great care in visually creating the scenes. It was a joy to see the piece come to life, even from its meager beginning with the line art. Knowing that this was my book, this first step was very meaningful and precious to me. It was also very important, because it drafted the ideas in rough form to the vibrant illustrations of pictures that would hold the very essence to our story, as it does to any. The detail intricately expressive, would be a masterpiece, I was quite confident, when it was completed; a masterpiece I wanted so to share with Dan.

"We want to get this particular book out before Christmas," Mia said. "There's no other children's book like it on the market and its qualities are truly unique and distinctive, and most original. It will help to touch and heal broken little souls, like Blossom's, and help them make something beautiful out of their lives as they see their lives comparably similar through her eyes and relate with her, who lost her mom at such a delicate age."

Weeks later, capturing the essence of all I held in my heart, when the day arrived and I saw the initial galley, tears blinded my eyes as I wept to every detail so lovingly woven in the tapestry portrayed by the dedicated and skilled illustrator. It was just about perfect, I told myself, with only minor changes needed, and my heart rejoiced in my pain for the craft so intricately created in telling our story.

Leafing through the pages, Dan's past words echoed in my heart, and I gratefully expressed my own emotion. "It's just beautiful!" I exclaimed to myself.

The interior designer simultaneously worked on preparing the text. "You've simply done a marvelous job on this!" she exclaimed. "I can see why Mr. Danes chose you to take over his position. Your skill is absolutely astounding, and the fluency, breathtaking! What a wonderful gift you have to write in the unique and beautiful style you have portrayed in this story! I can't wait to see both the illustrations and text come together, and that will be in only a few more days, Miss Hanes!"

Greatly encouraged, I was overcome with joy to every word, and every illustration; so beautifully special, and almost there! By the afternoon, the illustrator had adjusted those few changes, and it was beyond any words I could say to what my heart was feeling. The interior was perfect, too, and the next day, after carefully reading through the tentative book, I approved the galley. It was then directed without delay to the printer, whose work completed the final stage of the book. It was only two days later when the book was printed, and I held our precious children's book in my hands for the first time.

Breathless with emotion as the tears filled my eyes, that night I packaged the book and sent it through a friend in the office, where it would eventually reach Dan.

I'd done all I could, and I wondered just what Dan would feel when he, too, would see the book for the first time as I had, and tenderly leafed through its pages. I hoped he'd recognize and understand how much I still truly cared. I hardly knew what to say to him or if I should say anything at all. But to honor our standing, and good relationship of friendship from the past, and his desire to remain in touch with me as he'd requested, and asked me to from his previous visit, I finally found the heart and courage to voice my sentiments. The words were simple, but meaningful, and I trusted that Dan would be as proud and honored as me to have this precious, treasured heirloom that it would become in time.

> Dearest Dan,
>
> I pray with all my heart that you are doing well. I know how much you looked forward to the day when *Julia's Song* would be published. I've enclosed the first copy for you.
>
> Dan, I miss you. We all do. I pray for the day when you will be back with us again. Blossom wonders if you're happy. I sometimes don't know how to calm her heart in telling her how very much you love her.
>
> Sincerely yours,
> Maggie Hanes

Silence continued to be Daniel Danes' present signature. What had I done that was so wrong? Where had I failed him so? The agony of those questions was oftentimes so tormenting, that I could hardly see my way to the days ahead.

Another year came and went. A literary agent called, wanting to rebrand the book. My emotions arose, missing Dan so much that it was like the breath of death had come to break me. I wanted so to die, feeling lost and alone, misunderstood, abandoned, and not knowing why, as I struggled to get my emotions out for the man who I still loved in Dan.

I wept and screamed, restless as I wandered through the avenue of trees in the changing seasons, where the breathless scenes should have revived my soul, but served to only deepen the pain inside my broken heart.

Memories of better days flooded my soul, where we were happy and at peace with ourselves and the world. I thought that writing his story would take all that away, but there were times I truly tested my purpose as an author, feeling that I had no place as a writer in the world at all. I worked until I felt like I would collapse, weak from hunger and exhaustion, hardly sleeping.

Then, one day in the late afternoon as I was going through my files, a calendar caught my eye. Although the calendar was for the upcoming year, I went through every month, pausing at the following October. To my astonishment, the Bible text from Psalm 62:5-6 KJV beneath the unusually, lovely photograph, inexplicably drew me to the words which read: "My soul, wait thou only upon God; for my expectation is from him. He only is my rock and my salvation: he is my defense; I shall not be moved." Stunned, I reread the verses, feeling the life flow back into my weary heart as God lifted me to Himself. And I was assured that He was leading me down the path, guiding my heart, where He would reveal His plan in His time. Trusting Him for it all, peace stirred my heart and my burdens melted away, where sweet rest gave refuge in my soul. He had the answer to it all and was working behind the scenes, where all God asked of me was to wait on Him. There, nothing would move me because He was fighting my battles; my defense in everything.

The days flew by as I felt a contentment that I hadn't felt in a long while. Then, the feelings came back, clouding my peace. The silence of Dan's heart to mine was too much to bear some days as I faithfully checked the mail. Struggling to leave it all at the cross, I felt like an absolute failure, not even being able to hold onto the peace that God had the power to impart to my heart to every breath I breathed. Here, the mirror of my soul seemed to shatter into a million pieces; more.

Daniel Danes would always be the man of God's choosing. My feelings didn't change for what we had come to mean to each other, both in our friendship and our work. As sure as I lived, Dan would be the one and only man for me.

I found peace in my work, especially in my own writing. I found myself creating a sequel to our book, a treasure that came from a heart that wholly cherished this beautiful man and his wonderful sister, and the daughter she'd left behind. Dan was as much a part of everything that had come to me, especially the children's book we had shared in *Julia's Song*, which became a bestseller. The sequel, *A Chord of Melody*, was an expression to the love held between Julia and her daughter, Blossom.

But what I missed most of all was our spiritual time of devotions that made him this extraordinarily strong and special man to the honor of everything in all he stood for. So, why then, I asked myself, was it difficult for Dan to recognize that nothing would ever change between us regardless of how long we were apart?

This question burned within my soul as I continued to struggle to find the answer that took him so abruptly away from me and everything we had dearly shared in the passion of our work. What was missing? And would I ever have the answers to the questions that so troubled the deepest depth of my soul for the man I loved with all my heart? If only Dan knew just how very much I loved him, my heart so cried.

Dan held the purest heart I'd ever known. It was that purity that I longed for, and which had first drawn him to me. And it was that very purity that set him apart from any other man I'd spent time with. There would always be that something special about him because it connected our souls to our Creator God. Like a jigsaw puzzle, would that missing piece ever return to me, and if it did, would it fit perfectly? And would Dan's heart still love me and cherish the sacred gift God had given to us in each other, where his heart once followed mine in everything we'd shared, and the dreams within all we loved within our work? Like a sea between us, I didn't have any answers to my troubled questions.

CHAPTER 7

Words That Lend Voice

Dan's silence was killing me inside. Some days my only comfort was in reading the Bible. In the darkness of those clouds, my heart turned back to its restless emotion, where I continued to hope for a word from him. Thoughts of abandonment tormented my soul and I wondered how he could be so seemingly cold in not considering his niece, at best.

I'd briefly met one of the senior executives that Dan had introduced to me when I initially joined the firm as an employee. Carlie was sweet and warm, and offered to send my letters to Dan when I offhandedly mentioned how much we all were missing him at the time I'd written him that first letter. Why I couldn't have his address was a mystery to me, and anything Dan sent to me in reply was posted to Carlie with no return address on the envelopes. To me, this was very unusual and tended to make me upset. After everything we'd journeyed through together with his sister, Dan could have respected our relationship and directed his letters to me personally.

I eventually received my answer in time, but it would be a long time in that coming. Moreover, I'd find that Dan was totally unaware of why Carlie had managed to keep us apart in this respect, although we were still able to correspond, but only through her as our liaison. In this hard place, I realized that to be really kind to him, I had to trust what I knew from our past, and pray that in everything, it still stood on firm ground.

While I didn't know his situation, I prayed, as always, for anything to indicate where, not only he stood with Blossom, but where he stood with me. I detailed a brief letter and posted it through Carlie without giving it a chance to dissuade my tormented brokenness, but there were nights that I still cried my heart out for him even now. If he didn't want me, the least he could do was to be man enough to tell me, I fumed. And surely, he wanted Blossom. Why, I couldn't imagine him not wanting her, because I knew how very much she loved him, just as he loved her!

Dearest Dan,

I pray that you are well. Everything is fine here. Blossom continues to shine, and Ethel and I are enjoying her companionship. She's the little girl I've come to love so; whose story I wrote. And the man I came to cherish with the little girl, in you. You've been the light of my life; a lantern burning brightly in the hearth of my soul. I cannot tell you enough how very much you mean to me, Dan, and how very much I miss you.

Your presence was truly a special gift that I shall cherish always in my heart. Please know that I am always here for you. We, Ethel and Blossom and I, hope that you will soon return. I found myself praying these words last night, and I trust that they will be a blessing to you.

Lord, always keep my heart open to hear
Your stillest, smallest whisper in Your voice.
To have a heart that forgives, blesses, works,
loves, shares, respects, and most of all,
a heart that lives for You in all I am and all I do.

Apart from this, Dan, I know of nothing else to say, but how I long for your presence and the pleasure in sharing our passion of work together. I hope you find your heart again . . . very soon.

My heart is with you always,

Maggie

The following week, I'd almost walked out of Dan's bedroom, heading out the door to the office, when a shadow suddenly fell across the walls. Startled, I expected to see Ethel, when a man appeared, nearly bumping into me. At first, I didn't recognize him. When he whispered my name, and gently placed his hand on my arm, I knew without a doubt that there was no mistaking that it was the Mr.

"Maggie!" he tenderly spoke. "Are you off to work?"

Taken off guard, I couldn't find a voice to the words that were choking my heart inside. Here he was at long last again, and now I wasn't sure that this was what I wanted after all. I felt weak in the knees as tears misted my eyes, and I felt helpless to say what my heart had long since hoped for and wanted all these broken months inside of me.

The Mr. seemed to perceive my anxious thoughts and led me to the far side of the bedroom where a blue brocaded, ornamental canopied drape was drawn, concealing a lovely window view, as well as a beautiful desk and Victorian chair. Across from it, a loveseat invitingly sought in welcome, the comfort to relax in total privacy.

Leading me to the loveseat, I sat down with the Mr. next to me.

"Maggie, first of all, I need to apologize for my silence. But there was never a moment that you weren't in my thoughts. And I want you to know that I missed you, too, as I know you missed me. Your letters meant everything to me." Taking my hand in his, he smiled, as tears threatened, looking deep into my eyes.

"Dan, I . . ." but my eyes blurred, and I couldn't help but cry, sobbing on his shoulder as he took me in his arms.

"I had a good reason for this long absence, Maggie, and I trust you will be able to forgive me, if not in this moment, in time."

"Oh, Dan," I cried. "You're back and that's all that matters."

Wiping the tears from my eyes, I couldn't have been more taken aback as his words pierced my heart. My soul trembled and that deep ache returned.

"I've decided to take Blossom with me to Europe. I have been studying abroad in Austria to intimately learn each facet of moviemaking and such. Later, I anticipate closely learning each department in the publishing business."

His words hardly touched my heart as I felt the agonizing torment of losing everyone I loved so. No Blossom? No Dan? my thoughts continued. I couldn't even begin to take in such a double loss. My feelings screamed inside of me as I pushed him away, and I could endure it no longer.

"Dan! How could you? I love her and I love you!" I burst out. Dan's eyes grew large, taken aback by my revelation, as I realized my blunder too late; and I rattled on. "I suppose you never stopped to think about what my feelings are for you and for your beautiful niece. You come and go like a spoiled schoolboy. Well, Mr. Danes, do what you please then, but I'm done with the publishing business. I won't have any part of it anymore! I quit, so perhaps you'd like to take back your job for the day until you can assign someone less stupid than me!" I tore away from him, grabbed my purse, and gave him no recourse for a rebuttal. Slamming the door behind me, I hurried out of his room, along the corridor and down the short flight of stairs leading to the main floor. Without pausing, I ran past Ethel, tears streaming down my face. Blossom poked her head out of the kitchen door, surprise and shock expressed in her eyes, crying after me.

"Miss Hanes! Where are going?" she cried.

My heart broke and I stopped in my tracks. Blossom ran into my arms, and I soothingly said, "I don't belong here, darling. But I will always love you."

Blossom's eyes filled with tears and began to spill down her cheeks. Trembling, she cried, "But I don't want you to go! Please, please don't leave me!" Clutching my leg, I was suddenly immobile.

"Blossom, please let go of my leg!" I spoke.

"No! I won't! I won't!"

Dan appeared, watching the scene. Gently, he took Blossom's hands away and picked her up in his arms. "Miss Hanes just needs some time, Blossom."

Looking into my eyes, my heart flared with anger. "Time? I've had that aplenty," I scorned. "Perhaps, it's something you will need to experience, to understand the heartbreak you have caused us all, Mr. Danes!"

Ethel's expression was dire as she watched the scene unfold before her eyes. Shocked at the upset between us, her voice was stricken, when out of nowhere she burst out, "My goodness!" she said, pausing briefly. "Such a perfect couple you make!" she suddenly exclaimed, with a little smile.

I barely heard what Ethel had just said, and I later thought hard on that.

Putting Blossom down, Dan came to stand in front of me. "I know you're upset with me, Maggie, and you have every right. But would you please consider what I've been going through? I have feelings, too, you know."

"Oh, is that so?" I flatly stated. "Where have you been keeping them?"

Ethel hung her head, wringing her hands. Her lips moved, but now, her words were quieted within her heart, and I imagined she was thinking all sorts of things in the moment. I hoped she wouldn't judge me too harshly and understand my point of view.

"Maggie! I am most sorry. I think we need to talk, and right now."

Fire raged like an explosion inside of me. "No, Dan. I've missed you and had to bear your silence. You abandoned everyone here as though you had no means to communicate. I believe that says it all." Perhaps, I was being selfish, but the pain in my heart from losing my beloved for so long, was something I couldn't deal with in the anguish my soul was feeling even now. Turning, I promptly stomped out of the house, not daring to look back for even an instant. My heart was sorely broken, and I questioned how I ever could have been so wrong to have believed in my love for him and that that love had come from God.

Minutes later, I turned the corner. Don't you suppose that car of mine just had to act up again, and I was back to walking! I was tired of taking taxis and putting up with the derogatory comments of some of the drivers.

I heard distinctive footsteps, knowing Dan had followed me outside, but I stubbornly refused to turn around and face him. Seconds later, a hand tenderly pressed against my shoulder and slowly turned me about. "I would appreciate the consideration of your presence, Maggie, because you mean so much to me," he said.

Fuming, his words caught me unaware, and I sighed, then nodded, knowing deep inside my heart that he deserved a second chance, even as many as it took to smooth the waves, like a storm, between us. After all, I seriously considered, if that were me, I'd appreciate the identical respect in that as well. With gentlest grace and kindness, I humbly replied, "All right, Dan. I'll give you that much. But I meant every word of what I said."

Amused, Dan smiled. "Are you sure about that, Maggie?"

"Quite!" I willfully returned, as a streak of stubbornness held on, but my words were soft and pliable.

"Point taken, but let's talk in the garden, shall we?"

Oh, no! I exclaimed in my thoughts. That wasn't my idea, for sure. What if Ethel should suddenly find us, or, or Tom, I asked in my thoughts, beside myself . . . but Dan was already taking my arm and leading me to the large garden I'd loved from the very first time I'd experienced its vast grounds.

We arrived a few minutes later with silence between us, and Dan still holding my arm. We passed Tom Wafer, who was heading out to the avenue of trees to trim the hedges set at the backdrop. He smiled, as if he knew a secret, winking at me. Such folly breathed inside most men, but I knew that Tom was an honorable, delightful gentleman, and his wink, harmless. Still, I wondered if he might not be thinking a thought or two, maybe even three, as we passed each other, Dan's arm linked in mine, holding me close to himself, nonetheless. I could feel myself blushing, and immediately looked away.

"I'd forgotten just how beautiful this idyllic spot is," he softly said. "Let's go all the way to the back of the garden, all right, Maggie?"

Nodding, my heart stopped pounding as I began to relax. I had to admit that it felt wonderful to be so near to Dan.

The apple trees were blossoming, their delicate perfume lilting on the air. Tom, the groundskeeper, usually worked full days in the spring and autumn to get the much-needed work done. It was mainly in the summer that he worked shorter hours.

Dan led us to the canopy of birches, their leaves filling out, and extending their branches over a lovely bench that I had sat at alone, enjoying this magnificent splendor through the years.

"You didn't allow me to finish," he tenderly said, his hand upon my face, drawing me to look into his lovely, blue eyes. "Yes, I need to take Blossom to Europe with me. I miss her and I want to keep my promise to my sister."

"But . . ." I interrupted.

"But" he gently said, the softness of his voice straining to make me understand, "I want to take you, too."

I couldn't have been more surprised, and the stubbornness took more force. "What? Dan! Why?" I burst out. "You haven't needed me all this time. Why ever would you need me now?"

"Because . . ." he faltered.

"Because . . .?" I repeated, with a questioning connotation, raising an eyebrow.

"Because . . ." he attempted again.

"Because, what?" I asked. "We've always been honest with each other. That hasn't changed, has it?" His expression was unmoving, focused only on me. He looked helplessly up at me. "You need to tell me, Dan, and right now!" I demanded.

Tears welled in his eyes as he fought for control of his emotions. "Because I love you!"

Stunned, I didn't know what to say whilst my heart danced with joy! Dan loved me, too? My heart was so full, I couldn't even answer him.

He waited expectantly, pulling me gently toward him seconds later. "I love you, Maggie," he tenderly whispered. His lips found mine, and my heart filled with the loveliest explicitness of joy and confusion all at the same time as I tried to put his words into perspective and fully comprehend the heartbeat of its profound significance within his desire.

I'd longed and hoped and prayed and cried for this moment. Now that it was here, my heart was filled to the immense beauty within the tangible presence of my beloved, and I was wonderfully assured, that it was real!

"Will you be my wife, my dearest Maggie?" His words held such depth of emotion; truth that had been bottled up within each of us far too long.

Like the poignant blossom of a flower, my soul rejoiced in the miracle that God was offering to me in this sacred moment. I had most assuredly come to know God's heart in Dan's absence, as I'd sought His answer in prayer; abiding in His Word, and faithfully sitting at the feet of Jesus each night. Now, that it was here, joy, more wonderful than I could ever have imagined, bubbled up inside of me, and I could scarcely think, for the amazing wonder filling my soul with joyful praise!

This moment was so special; I felt God's Peace; His Presence, as I looked into my beloved's face, and I couldn't wait a second longer to tell him just how very much I loved him, as the beauty of God's love touched my soul. I could not have asked God for anyone more wonderfully handsome or beautiful as I had found in this amazing man, Daniel Danes. Most importantly, he had a pure and lovely heart after God, that was by far worth more precious than all the gold or silver in the world. It wasn't wealth I sought with him, but his heart; the jeweled man I had found in him through Christ.

My emotions arose like a burning flame amidst the thorns of a wild rose, where its perfumed beauty held itself in tallest triumph to exclaim its glory. Then, I felt myself draw close to him, as I softly whispered, "Dan, I've loved you for a long, long time."

I paused to catch my breath as Dan softly murmured with the loveliest elegance, "I know, my darling Maggie. I've known for that very long time, too!" Dan gently swept me into his arms, and tenderly kissed me long and sweet.

I could no longer hold back all the love I held for him as he held me close, and the loveliness of his heart embraced my soul. I belonged to him now; completely, wholly; and together, we'd walk this life with God at the center of our lives. It wasn't hard to see that it already was much more wonderful than I ever dreamed! Dan kissed me with tenderest passion, and my heart was finally free to love this man that I'd respected and adored since that unexpected day when we'd first met.

"I've never felt like this in all my life," he softly said. "I know I never shall. Julia tried to tell me that, but I just didn't know how to express it to you when she was . . ." Tears welled in his eyes. Gently, I held him close. He tenderly lifted my face to his, breathlessly kissing me, my heart enthralled to his every word. "To marry you, my darling Maggie, will be a wonderful gift like none I've ever had," he softly whispered.

Momentarily speechless, I found my voice as I lovingly answered, "And your heart, Dan . . . is it free now, again?" I meaningfully asked.

"Yes, my Maggie! My heart is free again! Now, darling, will you marry me?" he tenderly asked, kissing me.

"Yes, Dan! Yes!" I said, kissing him. Such passionate joy would never leave my heart, and I knew that I'd always love Dan with all of my being. And it seemed like I hadn't been wrong after all, believing that, with God, Dan had always had my heart, too! "How I love you in these divine moments; every one, my darling!"

As Dan bent close, he whispered something so extraordinarily overwhelming, it took my breath away! "Love and kisses," he tenderly said, kissing me with deep emotion. Then he withdrew a beautiful ring from his pocket and lovingly placed it on my finger. It glittered in the light, holding all our love and dreams within its radiant beauty, just like our hearts, I thought!

Love and kisses. I'd never heard it said like this before, and I really loved the enchantment of it spoken in this prolifically beautiful way! In these wondrous moments, it perfectly defined my heart's content within the sacredly whimsical fairytale-like, and exquisite breath of all that I was feeling, too, as it did for him. In time, I came to deeply cherish it within my heart as this special signature expression where love had truly come to me!

We celebrated our engagement in the days to come. Ethel was beside herself. "I knew it!" she fussed as we shopped together for my trousseau. "I knew it, and the Mr., why he so adores and loves you, Maggie!"

"I know, Ethel. Isn't it grand? When we get back from our honeymoon in Europe, just think! I'll be living here in his mansion with you!"

We hugged a long moment, then with a quivering tone, Ethel's voice softly cried, "I . . . I'm so happy, Miss Hanes. We will see each other every day! Just imagine! What joy has soon to come to us!" she said.

Ethel rarely, no, she never addressed me as "Miss Hanes." I was surprised she even remembered that! And while her sentence was a little mixed up, I held it to my heart like a lovely, wild bouquet of flowers, full of spice and beauty. "I'm so looking forward to your presence every day, too, Ethel," I returned. "So very, very much! We'll be almost just like sisters!"

"Oh, we are already!" she spontaneously declared. "But now we'll be sisters, like close of heart, together, in home," she expressed.

"What a beautiful way to see that," I said, cherishing her lovely expression. Tears misted in my eyes, and I sometimes wondered whose English was faulty. I couldn't think of a sweeter or more endearing way to put it than how Ethel had just lovingly offered in her love to me. I couldn't help but reflect by adding my endearing feelings to hers as I lovingly returned, "Yes, Ethel, we be that already – sisters of heart – together!"

There was one thing that I wanted to know. "Ethel," I said one afternoon, looking into her shining eyes, "I've been wondering why you told me that first time I was with Dan in Julia's home for supper as we said goodbye, and you whispered to me that we were the perfect couple, and then when Dan returned from Austria, and I was furious with him?"

"Because you are!" she smiled, her eyes dancing. "I felt like I would burst if I didn't tell you so – both times at that!" she softly laughed. "And I hoped that you'd come to see just what a perfect couple you and Dan have always been in each other."

"Hmm," I replied, smiling. "Did Dan hold the same sentiment when I was so upset with him that day?"

"Oh, I knew he did, Maggie! And I did have a chance to remind him of that after you had left!"

"And . . .?"

"He merely smiled and patting me on the back said, 'I think that you know just how dear our Maggie is to me, Ethel, and you needn't have to tell me twice!'"

"Well, Dan could have been more open with me," I pouted a little. "It might not have hurt so much, him leaving for so long and all, if only I'd known his heart was in mine all along."

"I do understand, my friend, but now that he is truly yours, I think it's best to love him and forget the flaws within his bones. After all, he is a man!" she smiled, teasing. "Alright?" she lovingly said, as tears misted in her eyes.

"Yes, Ethel! I'm so happy, I can hardly believe it!" Tears misted in my eyes, too, and reaching toward Ethel, we cried in each other's arms for the joy of it all! But I couldn't help but whisper, "And what a wonderful man he is!"

She whispered back, "Oh, Maggie, he truly is!" Then, looking out the big window in the living room, she shyly challenged, "And there's that delightful, wild wind you love so well, Maggie! Why don't you dance amongst its pleasure for a while? I'll take care of things here and set a lovely table for a late afternoon lunch after your delight is done."

"Oh, it is tempting!" I exclaimed. "Well, why not?" I softly laughed. "I shall indulge to my heart and soul's every whim, but it won't be for long, I promise!"

Ethel and I enjoyed our special time together, and I was grateful to Dan for adding this joy to my day in granting me the afternoon off to spend some time away from the office to be with her. I'd always known that Dan was an exceptional man and that his heart truly was made of gold. "You've never failed to be here for me and my family," he tenderly said, "so if I can give you this little, extra pleasure, then it shall be a gift to me as well, my darling Maggie!"

Dancing in the wind had always lent that wondrous, carefree gift I loved so well as I'd serenaded the breezes, swift and bold and beautiful upon my face and arms. And I wondered how often I'd have this pleasure once Dan and I were married. I thought about it for a while, and I concluded that it wouldn't change a thing! The mansion would belong to me, too, then, and I'd be free to swirl to my heart's content! What a wonderful revelation that was that came to me this day!

Dan wanted to really enjoy being engaged for a while, and I loved his wonderfully enchanting idea. We didn't set a date for our wedding. Dan wanted to surprise me, he shared one evening, as we ambled along the avenue of trees. They were so breathtaking at this time of the year. Looking into my eyes, his shone with tenderest love as he gently remarked, "My dearest Maggie, I think that perhaps, we should wed beneath the arbor of the roses. What do you think, my love?"

"I love it, Dan!" I enthusiastically returned. "I love it to pieces just as I love you!"

He laughed at my words, kissing me passionately, adding his own response to mine. "Then we shall, my darling! We shall!"

I knew that the roses usually bloomed in June, but the roses cascading in wondrous beauty, like a waterfall, were a mixture of early-blooming varieties and other varieties, some a little later, even into July and August. My goodness, I chortled to myself, absentmindedly thinking about it one day. I wondered what season of blossoms Dan truly had in mind. Anticipation arose in my heart, as my inquisitive nature pondered when Dan would consider the perfect time for his roses to bloom as we wed beneath their glory.

Dan and I took long walks, usually every day, enjoying the new season as the spring turned into summer. Blossom was thrilled to have me in their company most afternoons after work, and although I still lived at the boarding house, I loved to share meals and evenings, and especially weekends with my soon-to-be real family, including Ethel, and even Tom!

One day, just after arriving at work, Dan asked me first thing, if I'd retrieve some important papers from his estate directly after lunch, then immediately deliver the required file to his office. I was more than happy to give him this consideration! He explained where I would find the material in question and said that he'd give me the key I would need at that time. I didn't question why we wouldn't share our lunch hour together, since he also informed me that he had a lot of work to accomplish, and this apparently was the answer.

"I'm sorry to disappoint you, darling," he said, "but this is really an important matter, and I appreciate this kind gesture that much the more."

Kissing him, I smiled, and replied, "You know that I'm here to help you any way I can, dear Dan, so please think nothing of it!"

Dan remained at his desk while the staff, including myself, had our lunch break. As soon as I returned from my tiffin, he immediately asked me to step into his office. He looked tired, but before I could ask him how he was, he broached the matter of the file. A half-eaten sandwich was on his desk, and I hoped he'd finish every bite before his expected conference meeting with the board, which would commence within the hour.

"I'd go myself," he said, "but I need to finish finalizing these papers. And my lunch," he sheepishly grinned. Looking into my eyes, he smiled, and sweetly complimented, "I don't trust anyone but you, Maggie, to do this special errand for me." Handing me the key to his cabinet, he kissed me, and I hurried off to fulfill his request.

On Dan's behalf, I'd already called Ethel, telling her when to expect me. As soon as he gave me the key, I briskly hurried out of his office, and moments later, I reached the front door, quickly making my way to the parking lot of the firm. Shortly afterward, I arrived at Dan's estate.

"I won't be but a few minutes, Ethel," I cheerily said, hugging her in greeting.

Entering Dan's bedroom, I paused before collecting the papers he'd entrusted me to gather for him. For all the times I'd been his housekeeper, I'd completely forgotten, that behind the love seat, a delightfully spacious niche quaintly opened to the loveliest, charming alcove. Carefully stepping behind the love seat, I took a moment to appreciate the beautiful, ornate cabinet up close. Concealed within its lower recess, and totally hidden from view, I supposed that it surely was a piece from Julia's. Of Japanese origin, it was exquisite. But knowing the importance of the file, I dared not linger. Dan assured me that the file in question would be here.

I took out the key from my purse, that he'd given to me, inserted it in the lock, and a moment later it clicked open, where a drawer held several file folders neatly in place. It was deep and the file he needed was near the bottom of the pile. Gently lifting them out, a couple of papers slipped from beneath it, falling to the floor. Not knowing whether they were significant to the papers in the file, I bent down, and picking them up off the floor, I innocently read a few lines, as pain slowly spread across my face. I felt suddenly sick and weak all over. Both a paper and a photograph, must have stuck together, adhering to the file until it loosened when I pulled it out.

Peering at the picture, a bitterly startling realization came to me, and my heart nearly stopped. For a long moment, I clasped them to my heart, my mind awhirl. I was so stunned and shocked, not wanting to confront the truth before me, that my hands trembled as I tucked the paper and photograph back in the drawer as I held the folder in my other hand, carefully closing it. My feelings battled within me like a tug-of-war as I fought to keep myself under control, rushing out of Dan's room, but it was all in vain. Choked with enormous emotion, I held one hand over my mouth as I cried, passing Ethel in the kitchen. Seeing my tears, she was bewildered as to what had just caused me such unexpected grief.

"What happened?" she asked with deep concern. "Please sit a moment, Maggie." I wanted to leave and run as quickly out the door as I could, but I knew that I was almost feeling too weak to even stand on my legs. I gratefully sat down, with Ethel sitting down beside me, consoling me as the tears fell unbidden.

"Oh, Ethel!" I cried. "He's . . . he's . . . already married!" I lamely burst out. "And a son . . . he has a son!"

Ethel's face turned chalk white. "The Mr.? Married? No, but that can't be, Maggie. You must be mistaken. He's never had another woman in his house but you!"

"Well, that paper is a picture and they, him and his wife, both have wedding rings on their fingers!" I curtly spoke in my anguish.

"There has to be an explanation. *There has to be!*" she emphasized. "I've known the Mr. a long, long time, and I've never found him to keep any secrets."

"He might not have had another woman here except me, Ethel, so how do you explain that picture? It's real! Go - see for yourself!"

"Oh, no, ma'am. I couldn't. That's private. Why, the Mr. would never forgive me."

"No? Well, here!" I stoutly declared. Tearing off my engagement ring, I threw it on the table. "Give that to the Mr. as something for him to think about! He's played me twice and I don't feel good about being played a fool twice over, I assure you, and you can give him that message!"

Storming out of the house, I headed back to the firm. Guilt crept in as I thought of Ethel having to take the brunt of Dan's indiscretions. I surmised another apology would be in order.

When I returned to the office, I wasn't going to let Dan see my tears, or have a hint that trouble was brewing between us, either. Gritting my teeth, I straightened my posture, and knocking on his door, entered. "The file is here, Dan," I announced, placing it on his desk.

Without even looking up from what he was concentrating on, he merely nodded, and fuming inside, I walked out, leaving him to himself. My heart was pounding, but I pulled myself together, concentrating on my own work. Half an hour later, he stood in the doorway of his office, asking me to come in.

"Thank you for bringing me the file, my dearest," he lovingly said. "I'll be needing this folder in just about ten minutes or so. I appreciate your help in my rush to finish my proposal. I won't be home until late tonight, so if you still wish to stop by, I just wanted you to know, as we'll be having another conference call. I didn't want to disturb you with another favor so soon, so I asked Myra, and she faxed it only minutes ago. I hope you don't mind?"

"No problem," I replied. "I believe I'll take the opportunity to have some quiet time at my boarding house."

"All right. Then, I'll see you tomorrow." His phone rang and he excused himself. I was relieved for the interruption, since normally he would have kissed me as a show of appreciation, and I wasn't sure how my heart could bear it at the moment. A part of me missed and longed for it still, but the other part of me was too hurt to have found the exquisite joy that was a part of it, and so much more.

I went back to my desk, wishing the afternoon would end, but it dragged on, and I was weary by the time I arrived back at my boarding house. I wondered if I'd burst, not knowing how to confront Dan, and what it meant to our future.

I'd hardly closed the door when the doorbell unexpectedly chimed. Katherine Brooks, my landlady, had prepared a lovely casserole dish, as well as a delicious dessert of fresh fruits, and homemade buns that we soon enjoyed together.

"I've been thinking about you all day, Maggie! I hope I'm not intruding?" she asked in that special way of hers.

"Not at all!" I smiled, inviting her in. Her friendship was like a coffer full of treasured gold to me, and I enjoyed our times together. As a parting gift, she drew a wrapped present from her purse, insisting that the good Lord had drawn her heart to purchase it for me.

Beneath the wrap, lay nestled an exquisitely lovely, blue shawl I'd admired when we'd shopped together a few days earlier, momentarily bringing it to my face. Thanking her, I carefully draped the shawl over my shoulders, admiring it in the mirror. Katherine exclaimed over it with me, delight shining in her eyes. "It's just perfect!" she gleefully said, a pleased expression on her face. We chatted a bit more, and moments later, she left.

I felt restless, thinking back to the scene that had played out earlier in the day. I reached for the book I'd started reading a few days earlier, trying to concentrate. My mind kept wandering, and I finally closed the book, and placed it back on my night table next to my Bible.

Lost in thought, I turned my attention to a pair of beautiful robins just outside my window as their clear tones filled my soul to the melodies of purest bliss. Curious, I wondered if they ever had any unresolved problems and if they did, what they did about them. Oh, I knew it was all just silly thinking, but what if that were true? I supposed it was true, that birds did have conflict. I reckoned they fought it out with flapping wings or swooping at each other, or perhaps stealing feathers and downy and sticks or twigs from another's nest! Goodness! I laughed. Where were my thoughts going? Still, at such times, suddenly feeling so alone and lost in the moment, when they flew across the street, I almost wished that I could fly away with them!

Later that evening as I prepared for bed, everything suddenly came flooding back . . . the joy of Dan's precious love and the heartbreak of his abandonment. I'd had enough of it all. I thought that the pain from the past was gone, but in this split second, it came flooding back, more real than I ever imagined. Absently taking my pen, I scrawled that deep torment in words so shocking, I hardly dared think what the future might still hold for us. Disturbed and astonished at my feelings, I cried myself to sleep. Where did the truth of it all really lie?

A Lost Rose

My Dearest Rose, come to me,
Entrancing moon of beauty see
The mist like filigree in meadow's span,
Where love once gently held my hand.

Whereto the petals of the rose doth fall,
Where my soul so mourns, my heart still calls
The one I love so sweet and fair,
And all my days, now empty, bear.

The joy of fragrance like a flower,
Once held our heart's in friendship's bower.
Alas, the silence of your wondrous love,
Holds tears in flight much like the dove.

The passage of our rose once fair –
Sweet note of signature so rare.
And 'though the moon still rules the night
Its haunting beauty nary does light
The hearth of once such sweet delight.

A future hope must surely be,
A hidden joy somewhere for me.
But I shall ever mourn your love,
And all we shared by God's great love.

I awoke in the night feeling thirsty, and when I switched on my lamp, my eyes were immediately drawn to the poem beside it on my night table; my heart, still torn and ragged. Brushing away telltale tears that insisted on misting my eyes, as I stared at the words, the relentless pain pierced the depth of my soul even now. For a mere instant, I felt as though I could not breathe.

Then I gathered my emotions, and held them out to God; my hands outstretched in total surrender. Peace filled my heart as I shifted my thoughts toward the cross, and all that Jesus had accomplished there for me; everything to bring abundant life into each corner of my wounded soul.

"God," I prayed, "You said in Your Word that You have good plans for our lives; an expected end. But right now, I cannot see that. Help me to stay on the highroad, and watch those plans unfold, more marvelous, than I can ever imagine in the brokenness within my heart; to Your time and way, most beautiful and free. For it is there where I yearn to be this special blessing to the one I hold dearest to my heart. Thank You, Lord! Amen."

In that stark moment of realization, I softly whispered the words my heart had longed to say: "I forgive you, Dan." I prayed my faith wouldn't falter, but even if it should, I still would always mean each one of these precious words, and the power they held to move forward, of that which Christ offered in His love to me.

I reached for my pen, and slowly, with resolved purpose, scrawled the word, *Forgiven*, across the poem, even though all too soon, this peace would but be forgotten, in these sacred moments, but still yielded in the forgiveness sanctified at the foot of the cross.

Forgetting all about my thirst, I crawled back beneath the warmth of the blankets, and soon was fast asleep.

CHAPTER 8

Portrait of Hope

Ethel's relative shyness still surprised me. She called me up bright and early the following day. "The Mr., he, what you call it, asked me to invite you for supper on Saturday. He said it was important and especially stressed that you be on time."

Annoyed, my good humor was quickly dissipating. "Tell him from me not to expect me. Who does he think he is, bossing me around on my day off?"

Patiently, Ethel expressed that it concerned the top management. "The Durifs will be attending as well, and I know how much you like the Mrs., Maggie. He also requested that you wear that lovely, blue dress you recently purchased. 'To match the stars with your eyes,' is how he put it. Please reconsider, dear sister. It's just for an evening, and I've been missing you."

"The Durifs? I wonder why?" I asked, more to myself than Ethel.

"He didn't say, but they're very influential in the industry. Perhaps, there's some special reason. Will you come, Maggie?" she coaxed in that loving tone of hers.

Having considered the "sister" part, when Ethel so lovingly put it that way, I agreed, although I pouted about it in my mind. "All right," I conceded. Then, my thought suddenly turned, and I exclaimed in dismay, "Ethel, my engagement ring! What do I do about that? I don't have it and Dan will be sure to mention our engagement to the Durifs, if not the entire management!" I blurted.

"Men don't have very keen eyes about such matters. I don't suppose he's noticed that your finger is, what you say, 'missing a stone,' now?"

Smiling to myself, I corrected Ethel's English. "I suppose that's one way to put it, Ethel. But I'd just say that my finger has no ring."

"Uh huh. I see that. Well, not to worry. I have it safe in my jewelry box. He won't be home until later tonight. I'll wrap it in paper and meet you at the avenue of trees. Can you come about 5:15 p.m.?"

"Yes, Ethel. I appreciate this gesture."

"Think nothing of it, Maggie. I'm happy to oblibe you," she misspoke.

I was relieved that Ethel's intuition had graciously kept our secret with my ring safely hidden from my fiancé. I could play the part, but I'd rather have embraced it and not deceive the one I loved. I was rather worried that Dan might unexpectedly appear before Ethel could pass the ring to me and I could slip it back on my finger. I quietly stole out of the office just before closing to ensure I wasn't late to meet her. Dan was still busy on the phone, and didn't notice. I breathed a sigh of relief, arriving at his estate a few minutes later.

Keeping within the tree line along the border, I hurried, hoping Ethel had not forgotten her promise of our brief appointment. But she was waiting for me by the avenue of trees just as we'd planned, and after it was done, I breathed a sigh of relief. We quickly hugged, and with tears in my eyes, I hurried back to the street, turning at the first intersection with long strides, where I came to my boarding house shortly afterward without meeting Dan.

Later that evening when I slipped beneath my blankets for the night, it struck me like an arrow piercing my heart as I laid upon my pillow, just how deeply love's bruise can hurt. Staring out the window as the darkness pervaded, and the stars began to peek out, the music of the birds faded upon the quieting eve to the stillness of the night.

A warm breeze lifted the curtains, playfully fluttering upon my face. It felt wonderful even though my heart was sad. I didn't know how much longer I could take part in any further charade to please the one I loved. Truth had always stood strong beside us, just like the beautiful trees along his avenue that I'd loved from the first time I had ever laid eyes on their glorious joy of loveliness.

How could Dan be so cruel as to expect me to attend his supper? How would I ever get through it? Fear tugged at my heart, and I cried myself to sleep. I awakened weary and deeply saddened upon the beauty of the dawn, and the pastel colors God's hand had gently sketched upon the sunrise, as a a reminder of His love for me, and the details of how very much He deeply cared for His creation.

I dressed after my shower the next morning, and my heart suddenly missed my dearest Ethel. I wanted to run to her and throw myself into her arms and cry my eyes out. But I braced up, and after a hasty breakfast, went out my door and walked to the office even though my car was fixed, and gleaming in the sunlight. I fidgeted with my engagement ring as it caught the rays, colors dancing, sparkling like a rainbow. How had my life become so complicated? I could lean on God for His support, and dear Ethel, who was like a true sister to me.

I was happy that the day at work was exceptionally busy, so it kept my mind off Dan, and I was left undisturbed, for the most part, as he was busy with his own affairs in his duties.

He met me at my office just before I arose to leave for the day and apologized for missing lunch with me. "I'm very tired," he said, "but if you wish to drop over for supper, you'd be welcome, Maggie."

I wasn't sure exactly how he felt on that, so I thanked him and told him that I needed to rest, which was true, and hoped to get to bed early. Understanding, he smiled, and said goodbye, and we parted ways.

Early the following day, the telephone's persistent ring surprised me to its caller. "Maggie," a voice whispered so low that I could barely catch the words. "This be Ethel. You forgot to lock that cabinet. Good thing I found that out before the Mr. noticed. I shouldn't have, but I quick-like took a peek at that paper and pickture," she said, excitedly, mispronouncing the word. "You were right. Maybe, could you come at your lunch break and meet me in the garden quick?"

"Yes, Ethel. I promise."

105

Now I'd have to have that on my mind along with everything else, I bemoaned. On top of that, I'd have to make an excuse to Dan because I couldn't join him for lunch. Well, surely, I could think of something! But it did have me drawn to a curiosity that I hoped might shed some light on it all. And I needed to honor my promise to Ethel, just as she had kept her promise to me. Men, I fumed inside. They sure could complicate matters in the direst of ways, I said.

Dan called me into his office the moment I arrived, and I didn't have time to brood about Ethel's telephone conversation. Hanging up my jacket, I immediately sat down in front of his desk, wondering what was on his mind.

"Good morning, Maggie. How was your walk?"

"My walk?"

"I noticed you coming up the walkway."

"Oh, fine. Just fine, thank you."

"Well, I wanted to discuss something of extreme confidentiality. As you're aware, the top management will be attending a special supper at my estate this Saturday. Most of my staff will also be in attendance, including the Durifs. I think you'll find everything to your liking, at least, I'm really counting on that, Maggie. For now, would you be willing to take Blossom to the park this afternoon? I have things to do and that would be greatly appreciated. I'd forgotten to mention that something needs my attention at noon, so if you'll excuse me today, I'll have to forgo lunch with you, my dearest."

"Sure, Dan. Do what you must at lunch. But, Ethel," I began.

"Ethel is the person I need to talk with and isn't available this afternoon," Dan almost spoke businesslike to me. "I can promise to be back by three o'clock this afternoon and you may have that extra hour off. With pay," he said in a matter-of-fact tone.

I supposed he'd lost his humor for the moment, and I didn't like that none, either. If this was going to be married life with him, but for a fleeting moment, I wasn't quite convinced I wanted this as my feelings tore at my heart, I stoutly declared in my hurt, and the deep ache of love that I held in him only made me feel that much more the worse for it.

He needn't talk businesslike to me; I scorned in my thoughts. After all, I was his fiancée, and long before that, his special friend.

I wouldn't ever have even considered the same attitude with him. *Never*, I couldn't help but emphasize, repeating myself. I didn't fuss, however, and kept it to myself. Especially his words, "With pay," as if I'd have cared, but for the pleasure just to be with Blossom. Surely, he knew how much I loved her and that that in itself, I was worth this much consideration of respect in not wanting anything other than the joy of her company. What was wrong with him? I asked myself. I sometimes felt like I was going crazy.

"Okay," I agreed, even though I felt as if Dan was brushing me off. I wasn't one bit happy to be coerced about it and even Ethel was apparently involved, somehow. Could I trust no one now, not even my dearest friend in this lovely woman? The torment was almost too much for me to bear. I called Ethel to change our plans.

Then I thought of Blossom and my spirits lifted. At least she would be respectful of my feelings, I encouraged my heart, or would she? Maybe Dan had wheedled his way into her heart and somehow turned her away from me, too, and I was sad again to think that he was tearing us apart after all we'd been through together, and how much we loved each other.

My soul found no rest in the moment, and I prayed that this little girl would never change – ever. Within this stark realization, I acutely became aware of just how very much I loved her. This love was so overwhelming that I could scarcely think of how very empty it would be without her darling presence. In that instant, Blossom truly became a beloved daughter to me from the love by which Julia had personally chosen to entrust her to me as her mother on her behalf. I now clearly understood every bit of it. Justifiably, my life would forever be changed, as it would be for both Blossom and her uncle, Dan. But if we never married, I'd never know her as this beloved daughter, and share this joy with Dan in raising his beautiful sister's daughter. I could scarcely think on it . . .

Part of me dreaded seeing Blossom, not knowing what her response to me would be, and Dan seemed oblivious to my dark thoughts stirring up countless scenarios. It was less than an hour before Dan would leave her in my care.

Dan ordered two taxis. One to bring me to the park and one to have his niece escorted with Ethel to meet us there. Ethel remained in the taxi until Blossom joined me, which struck me as very peculiar, but I merely waved to her, and she waved back. Surely, she could have escorted Blossom to where I was waiting at a picnic table and taken a moment to say a proper hello to me. But then again, her and Dan had a secret to which I obviously wasn't privy. Out of nowhere, I now suddenly recalled when she had so blithely agreed with me, and confessed that Dan was "a real doll," and that suspicion arose in me like a giant that, perhaps, there was something between them after all. Well, I said to myself, either he's mine or he isn't. I wouldn't be played for a fool, especially with my dearest friend. Unrealistic as it was, if Blossom hadn't appeared with Ethel when she did, I might well have run away! Getting my emotions under control, and wiping away an unbidden tear, I turned my attention to Blossom. The moment she saw me, she hurried, rushing into my open arms, hugging me tight, as my eyes filled with joyful tears.

"Oh, Blossom," I cried, "I'm so delighted to spend the afternoon with you!"

"But why are you crying?" she asked, puzzled as we held each other close.

"Because, dear child, I'm so happy to be with you; just the two of us!"

"Me, too!" she said in that musical way of hers, just like her mom.

"Well, darling, let's take a stroll amongst the trees and then we can go to the playground, and you can do whatever your heart desires, okay?" I kindly asked.

"Oh, goody!" Blossom said, as I took her wee hand in my mine.

She had questions aplenty about the names of the trees and the flowers that dotted the land along the trails. I knew most of them, but some were not familiar to me. The woodland, with its shady branches, was exhilarating, providing a cool experience of pleasure.

After our walk, we made our way to the lovely playground that had been created by the town in the park. Blossom wanted to experience everything: the swings, teeter-totter, and finally, the sandbox. I had so much fun with her that I forgot my worries, and my heart had found its joy again, and I loved participating just as much as Blossom did!

When Dan picked us up, he invited us out for supper with him, and I could hardly believe that the hours had melted away so quickly! He added that he needed to attend to some matters at the office, and would pick me up at 5:00 p.m., and presently dropped me off at my boarding house.

I rested until it was 4:30 p.m., then got ready so I'd be on time for Dan. He had waited to express his feelings about our afternoon, and began to relax, beginning the conversation after our orders were placed with the waitress.

"I can see you both had a wonderful afternoon," he noted, smiling.

Blossom began to share of our activities, and I merely grinned as she sat beside me, her fork held in midair. Dan and I knew there was no stopping her in her excitement, and I for one, didn't mind one iota!

When Blossom was done talking, Dan turned to me. "And you, Maggie. I can see it in your eyes and your heart speaks well. You enjoyed it, too?"

"Oh, I did, Dan!" I enthused. "It was one of the nicest afternoons I've ever spent. I guess that's because Blossom is so special to be with," I finished.

Laughing, and putting his coffee mug to his lips, he slowly took a sip and swallowed, before placing it back on the table next to his plate. He looked directly into my eyes and then Dan said, "I'm very pleased that both my girls had so much fun." Then he arose and us with him. Paying the bill, I thanked Dan for the meal.

"The pleasure's all mine, my dearest Maggie." I found myself blushing and was thankful for Blossom's immediate interruption so that Dan wouldn't notice it any. If only it had ended there!

Considering his words, Blossom softly measured her own in childish understanding, posing her thought in a question. "How come it's a pleasure, Uncle Dan?"

"Well, that means that I enjoyed being with Maggie. You, too!" he added.

"Ohhh," she drew out the word. "I see. You liked it!"

"Yes, Blossom. I liked it very much."

Blossom remained quiet on the way back, until she unexpectedly piped up, "Maggie's face turned red, Uncle, and I'd like to know why when you said it was a pleasure to be with her."

I nearly flipped and I found my face blushing again.

"I noticed, Blossom, but it's not polite to mention it, and as for my answer, I think you need to wait and ask me again when you're older."

I thought it best to address this head-on so that Blossom wouldn't keep wondering.

"Pardon my intrusion, Dan," I said, glancing at him, "but Blossom, I merely blushed because of your uncle's compliment and also because I like him. Does that settle your question, my dear?"

Thinking hard, and without finishing her sentence, she mischievously said, "I see that you like him a lot, Miss Hanes, and . . ." Giggles filled the air, and much to my joy, Dan did the most unexpected thing imaginable as Blossom held her head down while laughing. Leaning over, he put his right hand on my shoulder, thoroughly kissing me. I wondered what Blossom would say if she knew! Moments later, Dan released his hand, with the intention of turning back to concentrate on his driving. But I couldn't resist the temptation to hold his love in a lingering moment, quickly pulling him back towards me; tenderly kissing him. Dan's eyes twinkled, and I couldn't help but laugh with the wonderful joy filling my soul in his love!

Blossom looked up and propping herself against me, whispered, "I peeked," she squealed, "and he likes you, too, Maggie! A lot!"

I squeezed her hand and kept still. I think enough had been said on the subject for now even though it struck me that my heart was maybe blushing inside of me, just a little, too!

Before long, Dan turned into his drive. I didn't know why, but I kept mum, too. Ethel appeared, almost like magic, and she opened the door for his niece. Dan thanked Ethel, and put the car into gear, heading back out of his driveway. I couldn't figure out why he'd dropped Blossom off first when we drove right by my boarding house, which I thought was strangely odd. He was doing it all backwards, making a double trip when it wasn't necessary. As he pulled up to my boarding house, he took my hand in his, and kissed me.

"I love you, Maggie, and I know you have many questions, but they shall all be shortly answered, *on Saturday*," he emphasized. "All I'm asking until then is for you to trust me, please." He leaned over and passionately kissed me, long and tender, then said goodnight. I was too stunned to think of what to say, except, goodnight, as I stepped out of his car and watched it disappear around the bend, pondering his words. I'd no idea what had just transpired, and this troubling feeling held that I was being brushed aside somehow, that I thought was duly unfair. Except for the kisses, it would have been totally unbearable.

I didn't like jumping to conclusions, but I'd never liked secrets, good or bad, nor ever would. At a complete loss to understand, my joy from our happy time together quickly melted away. Without a doubt, Dan was hiding something, and I sensed as though he was using me as a pawn on a chess board; he and Ethel both, matter-of-factly. I wondered if I'd burst before I learned what was being conspired in front of me right in plain sight.

I suddenly felt betrayed in every sense; abandoned, totally beaten, and unworthy. Did I not meet his expectations anymore, I wondered? I could scarcely bear the thought, but this purest, perfect love would never falter in my soul for this amazing, extraordinary man I had fallen in love with. Well, I fretted, it would do him good if I never saw him again. I truly wondered what had happened to his courtesy and manners in that regard. Like a conspirator's scheming, plotting façade, I was more perplexed than ever, and I didn't like it any! I had no one to confide in, not even my dear Ethel now, my sister, whom I loved with all my heart.

Tomorrow was Saturday, and I truly had no clue as to how I'd ever pull through it, but I surely would, I said with gritted determination, and no one, not even Ethel or my beloved fiancé, Dan, would get the better of me. And I dearly prayed that Blossom would be nowhere near around with her giggles and questions about either of us. Surely, Dan would be wise enough to have a neighbor care for her then, where little girls had no place in meetings or boardroom like settings.

I was torn between the love in the honor that I had come to respect in my editor, Daniel Danes, and the love we'd found together. How Ethel fitted into the picture, I couldn't imagine.

I thought how much I despised puzzles, with little wonder. What was the point in cutting up a picture and then putting it back together again? Why not just leave it as it were to begin with?

Like a riddle, only God had the answers, I reflected, because He was the only One who could fit all the pieces respectively in the right places. I supposed that that surely should be enough for now. But only because He was God, I added to the postscript of my thoughts.

I reflected on the joy I'd shared with Blossom. Then, I remembered that she'd given me a paper that I'd forgotten I'd tucked away in my purse. When I opened the folded paper, tears blurred my eyes. Depicting a woman and a man holding hands standing in a garden filled with flowers, was a little girl, and but one word beneath the scene: *Hope*.

Crying softly, my heart wholly forgave her as I felt one sweeping breath of healing fill my soul with joy. I held onto that one word where love had come softly unawares, in both Dan and the gift of his sister's child, Blossom, as I longed for us to become that family in each other. I thought with amused gist as the tears tumbled down my face, that I would gladly substitute her any day for those dowdy meetings, I decided quickly! Her innocence merely wanted answers in the truth right then, as I had felt to give to her, when Dan had asked her to wait. So sweet and beautiful, I desperately hung onto that faith to bring me and Dan to the altar of our love in marriage, if for only to have the honor of this beloved, precious child as my daughter. But in truth, everything within me wanted it all . . . her and Dan together.

And it wasn't until I was cozy in bed that I suddenly sat straight up. Why, I exclaimed, Blossom had called me Maggie and not Miss Hanes! She sometimes did that, but this seemed different: almost too grown up for her. Oh, dear, I thought, I wonder what life with this spirited child would truly be like in real time every day? I supposed Dan and I would simply get used to it, I decided, smiling to myself. Furthermore, there was no doubt in my mind that she was a gift of jeweled joy and blessing in everything, just as Dan was to me, an essence of perfect love.

My head found the pillow, and I fell asleep amidst the pain in my heart that longed for peace and love within this beautiful man and the daughter of his sister, and the joy of that *Hope* I had come to find in loving them, where there, a sliver of healing adhered me to Blossom's heart, and I'd never let it go.

Perhaps, it also was a part of that trust which Dan had so lovingly asked of me to momentarily tarry and abide beneath. His request wasn't unreasonable, just obscure. Surely, I could give him that much! Even so, he should likewise trust me – in us – and not withhold anything from me. Then, I seriously considered my next thought: Could that *Hope* still truly be waiting in his heart for me and Blossom? In that moment, I saw this beautiful child with her own yearning heart. It gave me the strength to hold on . . .

Nonetheless, my emotions were frayed and near the breaking point. I never knew that love could be so hard. If only Julia was still here, my heart bemoaned, I knew that everything would be all right, and I longed for her presence, too, in this beloved sister-in-law, even though we weren't. Sometimes, I sadly reflected, we need to lose what we dearly cherish; what is most precious and beautiful in our hearts and lives, before we find it again, if it comes back to us at all. What, if anything, was God up to, working behind the scenes, that I couldn't perceive in this conflicting confusion, where love longed to find its place of peace in everyone so dear to me? With every breath of this extravagant love that lived inside my heart for Dan, I would hold on to its firm foundation in God's perfect time, should it be in His omnipotent Plan at all. But in this moment, there was no word in answer to satisfy my hurting heart.

CHAPTER 9

Something Special

I had dreaded that the end of the week had almost arrived the evening before, and everything inside of me had wished that it were over. I had supposed it would be soon enough at that, I told myself.

But when Saturday dawned, much to my relief, I awoke to a glorious sunrise, feeling refreshed and sublimely happy. Parting my lacy curtains, I was privy to seeing two robins having a bit of a tussle, the pair that nested outside my bedroom window. I couldn't help but grin, thinking that perhaps, they could have used more sleep!

Shortly before ten o'clock Dan called to tell me that he would be picking me up at my boarding house at 4:45 p.m. "I look forward to seeing you," he lovingly said.

Butterflies stole into my heart, and I replied, "Me, too, Dan. Thank you!"

The day was lovely, but I tried not to think of the grueling hours ahead when I had to play niceties. I'd never liked such secrets and I certainly didn't like playacting, especially, when it was for real. The only good part was in the anticipation of being with Dan. With a joyful song in my heart, I happily flitted about my kitchen like a bird, as I prepared my breakfast, and I could hardly wait to see him!

Dan arrived on time and pinned a gorgeous corsage of red roses with a touch of baby's breath to my dress. Kissing me, he said, "You look beautiful, Maggie! I almost want to just take you away with me, my darling, and forget the whole supper!" he complimented, his eyes shining. Then, he politely asked, "Shall we?" He opened the door on the passenger side of the car for me, and I stepped in.

When Dan was seated in his car next to me before he engaged the ignition, I turned toward him and sweetly commented, "Hmm," I teased, "it's almost as though you have an ulterior motive that holds a special secret . . ."

Smiling mysteriously, he flirted, "Perhaps, I do, my darling Maggie!"

I was at a loss for words, not having seen this side of Dan before, and gathered my thoughts to the pleasant short drive to Dan's mansion, where we arrived minutes later. He parked his car in the garage, and we walked the short distance along the avenue of trees leading to the backyard. When we came around the corner, I was astonished. The supper was to be an outdoor event in his enchanted garden. I'd expected we'd all dine in his beautiful banquet room, elegantly spacious, and charmingly tucked away across from the Drawing Room. I looked around for Ethel, but she wasn't to be seen anywhere.

"I'll just go see Ethel for a moment," I said, as Dan released his arm from mine.

"Ethel must not be troubled, my dear," he firmly said, looking into my eyes. "For the moment, you will wait outside here with the others, please." He walked swiftly to his home and disappeared inside.

"Well!" I said to myself. "What's going on here?" His turnabout mood, while not rude, was certainly questionable, especially when I had found my back to enjoying his presence. I considered turning around to go on home, but my thought ended there.

"Why, hello, Maggie!" a sweet voice said. Turning, Mrs. Durif warmly embraced me. "How wonderful to see you, Maggie!"

"Thank you, Carletta," I acknowledged.

We strode along the avenue of trees toward the garden arbor. There was no higher rung than the top, and the Durifs certainly were there, even long before I came aboard Dan's company.

Linking arms with me, she laughed and stopped abruptly. "Maggie," she said, lowering her voice almost to a whisper, "I shouldn't be telling you this, but I know how a public announcement can throw one's mind at times." I listened intently, considering her words, and finding myself having reservations about her motive, if any.

"We've long considered how well you and Daniel Danes work together. Also, I've seen your dedication to the work at hand, especially transitioning into the senior position with Daniel's temporary leave, but also, in being a personal support to him and his family, and even his household staff."

"But, Mrs. Durif," I said, not taking my eyes off hers, "it's not only my responsibility, but my pleasure. I've enjoyed being able to lend support to Mr. Danes and his family. I need no praise or recognition for that."

"That's what makes this evening's event so special," she smiled. "Maggie, Daniel, and the management of the company, want to offer you the option to buy into the company's shares, to provide you a more long-term income. You're doing an incredible job and sales have soared. As a writer yourself," she rattled on, "*Julia's Song* is the first book ever to have sold the highest number of copies in the firm. Incidentally, I believe he's just now found a company to produce the book into a film." I was totally at a loss for words as I found her disclosure unfitting at this time.

"Maggie, this night is to recognize your immense contributions and to honor you! I also understand that you're recently engaged to each other. But the company can no longer sustain your high-ranking position. That's why this is an evening to celebrate you both, but it also means the termination of your position."

Shocked, I wondered what was truly happening. This was too bizarre, even for my limited knowledge of such matters. Furthermore, it was very unlikely an employee of this standing would be dismissed in such an unorthodox manner, and I was more than certain, that it would not be Carletta Durif to undertake that task in firing me. And if Dan had found that producer, it was so precious, that I'd be the first to know, not her! To top it off, why would a company offer shares and then fire that very person who was such a tremendous asset in the company? What a muddle!

Conflicting thoughts instantly aroused suspicion and I was disappointed to be enlightened that she was less than what she appeared to be, especially when this would be Dan's place and not hers. Her personal knowledge in my affairs with Dan, was most unethical. Thinking hard as to how to properly address her raw candor, I threw the first thing that came out of my head. "What's this to you, Mrs. Durif?" I suddenly asked, pausing, facing her. "The pieces don't fit such nonsense, and you know it!"

Aghast, she seemed momentarily unnerved, then said, "But Maggie . . ."

Interrupting, I said, "I've had enough of this. Now, please excuse me, Carletta," as she stood there looking perplexed. Turning, I hastily walked away. My emotions smoldered inside of me, and I didn't care a whit what she thought! I may have gone out on a long limb, but Dan had confidentially, and explicitly told me, that he'd share updated details regarding important business in a meeting between us just as soon as was possible. And any firm with high sales applauded that writer, they most definitely did not fire them!

None of this was making any sense and I was shortly to discover that none of it was true. No possible motive came to mind, but her arrogant façade certainly wasn't fooling me one bit! In that defining moment of stark reality, I was wholly enlightened to the decaying darkness scheming within her, realizing that our friendship was finished. My feelings of respect and pleasure quickly melted away, arising with alarming suspicion, whereby I knew with certainty that this wouldn't bring any satisfaction to Dan, either.

My heart mellowed toward my beloved as I realized a solid truth: I would wholly trust Dan any day over Carletta despite what I'd been presently feeling for him, and surely, he'd have a positive answer to leaving me standing in his yard, alone, until Mrs. Durif's untimely appearance.

Looking around for Dan, I suddenly felt ill about almost being taken in by Carletta's conversation, and I needed to escape to the bathroom and splash cold water on my face if I were to endure the evening. It was more than a moment since Dan had left me standing outside, and I needed to recover from Mrs. Durif's insidious indulgence that yielded nothing good, as far as I could tell. I may not have that university degree, but I was wise enough in knowing when something wasn't sitting well. Perhaps, that's why it was properly considered intuition or better still, an inner impression from God Almighty.

Trying to understand Dan, I felt awkward and alone here, and if I wasn't even welcome in his home, then I wasn't welcome anywhere else. It was only my promise to Ethel that helped me to walk down that path to his home where I could have a bit of privacy to get my emotions back under control, that kept me from leaving, especially without even seeing Ethel or having a moment of time with her.

Ethel happened to be coming to the outside entrance of the door when I arrived. "No come in," she said, blocking the way.

"Ethel!" I said, distress filling my heart. "I don't know nor understand what is suddenly going on here, but I'm not pleased in the least, and I dare say that that somehow seems to include you. Now, Ethel, please," I begged, as tears began to fill my eyes, running down my face. "I need to use the restroom."

"No, no. Mr.'s strict orders."

Shocked, I didn't understand why everyone, including Ethel, seemed to be turning on me at the same time. "Ethel. Please," I implored. She was holding a huge plate of fruit and I suddenly heard a commotion behind her. She turned to the sound, and I quickly sidestepped past her, accidentally brushing against the plate. A cry went up and the fruit down, as the dish clattered noisily, landing on the floor in front of her feet. I briefly turned to see Ethel frantically begin to pick up the mess, calling for help.

An arm suddenly grabbed ahold of me. "Miss Hanes," he softly scolded, but a tenderness drew my eyes upwards. Daniel Danes was standing in front of me. "Come, Maggie," he gently said, pulling me with him.

"I'm so sorry, Dan," I began, but he wouldn't let me finish.

"No need for that now," he said in the kindest way. We walked speedily along the corridor and up the flight of short steps, leading to his private bedroom.

Gently escorting me into his room, he quietly closed the door, then turned to face me. "My dearest Maggie, whatever is this upset? I was on my way to fetch you just now when I nearly stumbled against Ethel and saw you at the door with her. Are you feeling alright, my darling?" he asked with concern in the sweetest, melodious tone.

119

Taken aback at his sudden change in attitude, I didn't know how to respond. I pulled the drape open where the loveseat invitingly stood, and sat down, my hands on my head. The words refused to come at first when I began to apologize again, and I felt him at my side close to me, as burning, hot tears tumbled down my face. Taking my hands lovingly in his, Dan drew me into his arms while I sobbed against his shoulder.

"Maggie, I think I know what's been troubling you tonight. Ethel confessed only yesterday that something has been bothering you since the day I asked you to fetch that file for me. Nothing more."

But I interrupted, shocked at her betrayal. "She had no right! She didn't! She didn't!" I cried; my heart broken. "That was spoken only between her and me. And, and," I burst out, as the pain seethed like fire inside my heart as a thousand burning daggers of the past collided with the present, "you told me more than once that we were as strangers, and that hurt me a lot and still does. After all we'd been through together, Dan: the journey I took with you in Julia's illness, the book I wrote in your honor; I don't understand why you ever could have thought to express that, especially when you said how much you cared for me?" I asked, as my heart felt like hot coals amidst my pain. "I wasn't much of your dearest after all, was I?"

"She didn't betray you, my darling. She cares so much about you and me that she wanted to see us happy. When I noticed you weren't wearing your engagement ring, I asked Ethel about it. That's where it began, but as I said, she didn't want to tell me, but I figured you had told her, and I needed to know the reason why. Ethel only expressed to me that you were upset with me about something and that I needed to discuss that with you.

"The only other thing I knew for sure was that it had something to do with that file. So, you see, my darling Maggie, Ethel did not betray you! I decided to take a peek for myself that night and see if I might find a clue. I did. But I don't believe it had any bearing on our relationship, so there's no need to mention it.

"As to the 'stranger' part, I did say that, didn't I, Maggie? Well, Maggie, that's when I was such a fool and I'm deeply sorry for that, and I've long since regretted it. I should have repented and asked you to forgive me, but please, Maggie . . . forgive me now, my dearest?" His lovely, blue eyes were intense and honest in his feelings, close to tears.

Then the words came so fast, I hardly knew what I was saying. "That I can do," I softly assured. "But Dan, what's it to be now when . . . when you're already married and . . . and . . . and have a son?" I stammered. "Tonight, I swear that I will be forever gone from your life. I quit it all – everything. No engagement . . . no publishing . . . and especially, no more you!" I emphatically expressed as my heart felt crushed within the agony of losing the one I'd come to love so softly unawares. Then, a realization dawned: it wasn't Dan who was the fool, it was me.

Looking unmoved, I expected Dan would spew a tirade back at me, but much to my surprise, he lovingly said, "I understand, Maggie. But I would pray with all my heart that you'd have the grace to not judge me too quickly in this and allow me to set something straight with you right now, my dearest darling." He rang for Ethel, and she appeared within moments. "You know what to do," he simply said, and nodding, she disappeared, turning to leave out the door.

I suddenly couldn't bear to stay a minute longer and gravely said, "Never mind about Ethel. Whatever you have to say, you can say it in a letter to me, Dan, but don't expect a reply back! For now, I want to go home," I said, beginning to rise. "I mean it, Dan; straight away!" I demanded, sobbing, but Dan tenderly pulled me back down, his arm firmly about me.

"Not yet, my darling," he said. "Not until you have seen my side of it." There was a pleading fervor of compassionate love that sent goosebumps down my spine. Then I couldn't figure out why he'd used the word, "*seen*," instead of, "*heard* my side of it."

Before I could protest further, the photograph in question came alive before us as a couple were escorted into the room with a little boy, and Ethel left, closing the door behind her.

"I want you to meet my brother and his wife," he said, "and their son."

My heart nearly stopped. "Dan, but, but . . ." I stumbled over my words. The resemblance between Dan and his brother was uncanny!

"I would never betray you, my dearest," he softly whispered. Then Dan introduced the people in the room. "This is my identical brother, Justin, my sister-in-law, Lil, and my nephew, George. And this," he said, smiling, "is Maggie Hanes, my fiancée, and wonderful partner at work."

Humility crept in and I wanted to hide, especially with my face streaked with tears. They acknowledged my presence, then disappeared, leaving me and Dan alone.

"Please accept my sincerest apology. I got so wrapped up in my work and the excitement of our engagement, that somehow, I neglected to mention my family. It's all my terrible fault that you've suffered so needlessly at my lack of attention to you, Maggie. And when Ethel confided what had unexpectedly occurred in a manner of speaking as a riddle, I was filled with deepest remorse, but you must believe me, my dearest, that it was totally unintentional." His eyes became serious but were filled with a love and purest tenderness, that it took my breath away. "I love you, Maggie. I hope you know just how very much I do. I know that I haven't been here for you, and you've had every reason to be angry with me. I just didn't know what to say, and I missed you far beyond any loneliness I'd ever known during my long absence. And now, work has been extremely busy, and I'm afraid it's taken center stage over you."

Taking a deep breath, he continued, "Ethel is right, Maggie. There's never been another woman in my home except you whom I have ever loved. I wondered what had happened to my brother's photograph of him and his wife and son after he'd posted it to me some time back. I guess it stuck to the file when I was working late some time ago, not realizing it. And the note, of course, it must have brought conflicting ideas into your mind. But it was Justin who scrawled those words to Lil, 'Loving you always, my sweet darling, yours ever.' I don't believe that note was meant for my eyes, and he probably wondered where it had gone to! But I must say that I'm very surprised Ethel mistook Justin for me since she is usually very astute at catching things like that when he has black eyes and mine are blue." Lovingly drawing my face to his, he tenderly said, "I ask you, please, to forgive me, Maggie, and not just this, but for what more is to come tonight that you shall shortly understand."

"I'm so sorry, Dan, and I feel so foolish about everything. I should have trusted you in every way, but some days, sometimes,..." I cried, unable to go on.

"The roses are specially so lovely tonight," he began, in that beautiful musical voice that held a lilt of beauty I'd never quite heard before, but I deeply loved as his heart measured the truth that caught me wondrously unawares. In this extraordinary moment, my heart nearly stopped as I fully understood the import of his words as his eyes lovingly looked into mine, and I knew what he was about to ask. Clasping my hands to my face, my heart was filled with so much emotion, I could hardly take it in as his voice softly continued, "I promise to love you always and I want so much to marry you – tonight."

Tears began to fill my eyes as they spilled onto my arms and Dan spoke love amidst our joy. "Don't let what gossipy Carletta Durif must have told you, tarnish my reputation against you. Ethel and I so want to make you happy, and she's worked very hard to make everything perfect for us. Maggie, remember how we planned that night to be our wedding when the roses bloomed, my darling?"

As my soul drank in his words, I nodded through my tears. "Somehow, however, it took that spill with the fruit to help me realize you were not only left out of the equation, the one who means the most to me, but that you'd never met my brothers because they weren't able to attend Julia's funeral, living in Nova Scotia. I hope that you'll forgive me for this."

"Of course, Dan! I've been so wrong and foolish and . . ." But he blew away my worry.

Holding me close, he gently said, "With everything I've put you through, Maggie, I shouldn't blame you if you didn't care to . . ." But I hushed his pain and lovingly kissed him. Sobbing, he whispered, "You still love me, after all that, and this is more precious to me than anything I've known. I've waited all my life for you, and I nearly lost you in my foolishness."

Consoling my beloved, I wept with him until I could hold back my feelings no longer. "There shall never be anyone but you for me and I've never stopped loving you, my darling Daniel Danes, and I never shall. But Dan," I quietly asked, "if you don't mind telling me, why did you only give your address to Carlie and not to me while you were in Austria to act as our go-between? And what was the clue you found in your file cabinet?"

"The clue had to have been from Ethel, am I right, my darling? There was a smudge of dough on the back of the photograph, and I was quite assured that it wasn't yours!" he divulged.

"No, it certainly wasn't, Dan!" I laughed.

"I suspect that Ethel took a peek at the photograph?"

I nodded and he laughed. "Well, while she's most respectful of me, I suppose she had to see for herself about the figures in the picture – under your influence, if I'm not mistaken, Maggie?" he suggested, teasing.

"That's right, Dan! She didn't want to believe me, so in a fit of deep distress, I challenged her to take a look, but I honestly never expected that she would! It was in that moment of deep despair that I tore the ring off my finger and threw it on your table! Ethel hid it in her jewelry box until yesterday, when I realized that I needed it for tonight's supper. She also called me up early one morning and told me she'd looked at the photograph, with the wrong assumption that it was you, only neither of us knew that at the time! I guess Ethel and I both jumped to the same conclusion, and I am immensely sorry, darling."

"Well, I suppose that clears that question up, and I think that we all learned something of great value there," he said, smiling. "Now, as to Carlie. Oh, that was nothing more than a misunderstanding as well, dear Maggie! Carlie Mills supposed I didn't want you to know my location in Austria. I tried to tell her several times, but she kept posting them on your behalf – and mine. I didn't know your boarding house address, so she left me no alternative. I'm truly sorry, and I should have long since clarified that with you. I should demote her for that!" he said.

"I understand," I said, "but I think she's much too fine for that! Perhaps, a talk might simply do?" I suggested. Nodding, he smiled. "And Dan," I hesitated, "I'd be with Blossom just to be with her," I said. "You know how much I adore her."

"I know you love her, Maggie . . . forgive me?"

"Will this do?" I teased, leaning in to kiss him long and sweet.

"Quite well, yes!" he said.

I smiled, as his eyes met mine, and joy filled my heart. Then, taking my hands in his and bending his tear-streaked face to kiss me, Dan lovingly said, "As of this moment, there's a beautiful wedding gown waiting for you in the guest room, the one we chose together. I know how cold and rude I must have seemed to you, but Ethel was so excitable about this evening, rushing about these days, that I was afraid that she'd spill my secret, and that's why I didn't want to have you talk with her in the house tonight. I didn't mean to appear so curt and . . . and Ethel has her gown waiting as your maid of honor already in that closet, too," he smiled, and the musical lilt of his voice held mine. Breathless with joy, Dan tenderly asked, "Will you marry me tonight beneath the beautiful roses, my dearest love?"

Throwing my arms about him, I cried with joyful tears, "Oh, Dan! I will! I will," I said, "but only if you'll forgive me, please! For all of it! I should have trusted you; I wanted to, but nothing made sense to me. And . . ."

But he wouldn't let me finish as he softly whispered, "Closer, my darling," and he lifted my face to his, kissing me long and tender. The passionate warmth of that love held me, and I couldn't wait to become his Mrs. Danes!

Then, crimping my brow, a few questions caught me at a crossroad. "Dan, when were you going to tell me of this tonight," I asked. "I mean, the true reason for this supper, and was asking me to marry you tonight this 'extreme confidentiality' you mentioned earlier?"

"Just as soon as the supper preparations were ready for the wedding meal, I wanted to ask you to marry me. And yes, this was the 'extreme confidentiality.' Ethel was to bring you into the house shortly, where I needed to see if that hopefully should fit into your heart tonight," he smiled. "I know it's unusual, but I couldn't wait another day to be without your lovely presence as my wife. But at the last moment, I decided that Ethel should bring out the platter of fruit and I would get you." Laughing, he said, "I guess that didn't quite work out the way I planned, did it?"

"Not at all!" I replied, laughing with him. "But on second thought, I think that God planned it more perfect than we ever could have!"

"He certainly did at that!" Dan softly laughed. "Well, I also have another surprise for you. Your parents are here, Maggie, waiting to see their beautiful daughter become my lovely bride." Stunned, I could hardly take it in. "However," he detailed, "we're going to eat first and then have that announcement that Mrs. Durif has apparently shared with you against my wishes, and that probably includes the producer whose shown interest in *Julia's Song*." My eyes grew large, and I nodded.

"I have the feeling that she also misinformed you as to who exactly owns this company, and I assure you that it isn't her!" Dan's words took me by surprise as he continued. "I own it . . . I own it all, Maggie. I should have forewarned you about her because she isn't what she always appears to be. She takes far too many liberties in the company, especially since I returned, and her husband follows her like a spoiled puppy. Well, I run and own the company. I'd have her fired right this minute, and I just may do it at that," he said, laughing, "in spite of the good work she does for the most part. But for all the trouble she's tried to put between us, I might do that just the same. What do you think?"

Overwhelmed at all my heart was learning, I relaxed, laughing with him, then said, "Perhaps, that might be wise, indeed, but right now, I'd like to marry you very much, my dearest Dan." He took me in his arms, and peace filled my heart with a joy like I'd never known as we kissed sweet and long. It was then I understood why my heart held this amazingly overwhelming joy of sublimity this morning, and somehow, I'd never forget the tussle of the robins outside my bedroom window! I hoped that they'd also made up and would keep singing their duets of wondrous joy!

"You'd better slip into your wedding dress now, my dearest," he lovingly said. "And I have this feeling that Ethel will be bubbling over with joy for you!"

As his words sunk in, my hand flew to my heart as I cried out in dismay, "Oh, no!" I spoke. "Ethel! I need to apologize to her. Excuse me, please, my darling." Dan pulled me to himself for a lingering loving moment, and kissed me, then I ran off to find my dearest Ethel.

When I tried to apologize, Ethel wouldn't hear of it. "If I fit the shoes you are wearing, I would have felt the same as you, Maggie. Besides, I should apology to you, Miss Maggie. I felt just awful terrible having the Mr. make me to keep you away from me like that," she said, her eyes loving and gentle, and her English off. "I understand your upset, and now, my dear sister, you must hurry and get into your dress. You're getting married tonight to that handsome doll of yours!"

I wasn't sure if Ethel had ever addressed me as "Miss Maggie" before, but perhaps, she had once or twice. I burst out laughing as tears filled my eyes. "Oh, that Daniel Danes is a real doll, indeed, dear Ethel!" I said softly, hugging her close in the sweetness of the moment.

I quickly went to put on my beautiful, wedding gown and reapply my makeup. Dan brought me a gorgeous bouquet of flowers from his garden that held a jeweled treasure of roses, white lilies, and the purple blossoms I loved so well, but didn't know the name of. I'd have to ask Ethel. Tom had gathered the flowers in the afternoon and kept all the bouquets, including Ethel's and the men's boutonnieres, in the fridge. Then, much to my surprise, Dan reached in his pocket, and withdrew a shimmering diamond necklace that sparkled in his hands. He gently clasped it around my neck, then lovingly kissed me. Tenderly, he whispered in my ear, "Love and kisses forever, my darling," and my heart burst with joy! Momentarily looking into my eyes, that beautiful, pure love I'd always cherished, shone brightly, and my heart felt like it would burst to the profoundness of these special moments with him. "Don't take too long," Dan lovingly said. "I want to marry you right away!" I nodded as tears threatened, and he reassured me with another kiss, then turned to exit the room.

Ethel helped me with my hair and placing my headpiece and veil just perfectly, that complemented the lacy outward layers of the material. The underlying layers were made of a polyester blend and gossamer and silk. My gown embodied full length sleeves, covered in lace, that was set off to advantage, as was the bodice. The neckline was boat-shaped, accentuating the delicate beauty of the fluency of the dress that fell just above my knees. I slipped into my pretty, white pumps and I felt like Cinderella surely did, as I took one last breathless moment to gaze at my reflection in the long mirror. Everything was beautifully exquisite!

The evening couldn't have been more enchanting, and I was so pleased that my parents were here to see me wed my beloved Daniel Danes.

Ethel had helped to prepare such a lovely meal in our honor, together with some of the church ladies, and as soon as the meal was eaten, Dan and I married beneath the gorgeous arbor of the delicately fragranced roses as their spicy perfume wafted in the air. He looked handsomer than I'd ever seen him, attired in a three-piece suit the color of the deep blue sea. My heart was so full, just like the beautiful blossoms filling my heart with song, where the gift of this special day would be mine forever!

Best of all, I was thrilled that my soon-to-be daughter in Blossom was our flower girl. She looked especially pretty in her white dress, with the exception of the bodice and sleeves trimmed in blue lace, that complemented her eyes.

Her bouquet was filled with wildflowers that Carlie had picked only an hour before our wedding. That was something that Blossom dearly desired, even though there were telltale signs of the blossoms beginning to wilt when she stepped forward to walk down the aisle. But my heart longed to please hers, and I assured Blossom that it would be an extraordinary memory to cherish through the years, and most delightful!

After we were officially married, Blossom couldn't contain herself, slipping past Ethel, where they stood near the altar with us, running happily with her arms wide open toward me and Dan. Hugging us together, we held each other close, and the joy overflowed in my heart to this treasured gift I would have the pleasure to unwrap like a rare flower as Blossom grew into womanhood in the years to come.

"I love you so," I said, "and you are mine now, my darling Blossom, and soon we shall live in this beautifully enchanted mansion!" I giggled.

"That's right, Blossom," Dan told her. "Living a fairytale life together with you and Maggie . . . truly this is a dream come true for me and you!"

Blossom giggled and said, "I love you!" then quickly let us go, and ran back to Ethel, who had tears in her eyes.

We chatted with my parents, and soon found ourselves saying goodbye to our guests. But I needed to talk with Ethel first, before we departed shortly afterwards.

Dan had asked me to leave my trousseau at his mansion that Ethel and I had shopped for when we became engaged. While I thought it an odd request at the time, it made perfect sense today on my wedding. Dan was always so kind and thoughtful, I smiled in my thoughts.

Dan had also asked Ethel to pick out a few more pieces of clothing, unbeknownst to me.

She divulged how much she had enjoyed it! "I just wish you could have been with me, dear Maggie," she said, hugging me, "but the Mr., why, he wanted to surprise you so. I hope you'll like it."

Reassuring her, I said, "I will love everything you personally and so lovingly chose for me, my dearest Ethel! I can't wait to take a peek and see them!"

A shy smile broke across her face and tears misted her beautiful eyes. "Thank you, Maggie! It was my deepest pleasure." She threw her arms about me again and softly whispered, "You please do enjoy your honeymoon, dearest sister. And me and Tom here, we'll be waiting for you, and counting every moment."

"I shall, too!" I promised. It wasn't until later that I thought back to Ethel's odd comment about her and Tom. Well, I shrugged it off, it was only fair that Ethel included Tom in our conversation, since they were both going to be caretakers of our estate, and nothing personal in it. Dan came alongside me, and I knew the time had come to leave. "I love you dearly, Ethel," I said, as I turned to go with my husband. "Now I must say goodbye, my dearest sister."

"Me, too," she said. "I love you, Maggie." And then I found myself alone with my beloved Dan.

It would be some time before I would meet Dan's parents. For now, I couldn't wait for our honeymoon and everything that would be waiting when we returned home. I knew that Dan's heart felt exactly the same as mine!

As soon as we were alone, I couldn't help but express my heart. "My dearest Dan," I began, "so you really did want to take me away tonight, didn't you, my love?" I teased.

"I really did, Maggie! I meant it with all my heart! Now, here we are and I'm so honored and proud that on this evening, you are at long last, my beloved Mrs. Danes!" Kissing me with tenderest passion, my soul couldn't have wished for anything lovelier. His

Mrs. Danes . . . I loved the sound of that and best of all, it would deepen through the years to all the joy and worth of love I would ever hold, and more, for my beloved Dan!

Dan had long since planned that Ethel would care for Blossom for the next month while we honeymooned in Europe. I was thankful for his thoughtfulness. From there, we would both take our studies together to better understand all the facets of the publishing business, and eventually acquire our certificates to teach within the field. I always loved this work, and now the opportunity to grow within the company would be a great asset.

And Dan, he blew away the discord of Carletta Durif's lying tongue. Shares, as she insinuated, were non-existent. Dan and I now owned equal partnership of one hundred per cent in everything together. She later admitted that she was jealous of me in having Dan . . . What she really meant, I learned from Carlie, was that if she could convince me of the deceitfulness within the illusion she'd created, I could more easily be pushed away, and out of Dan's life forever. She wasn't an attractive woman, nor was her husband, and if she couldn't have Dan, she'd do whatever it took within her conspiring heart of darkness. Dan would never be persuaded to such devilry, that I was certain of! And when Carlie had confronted her head-on, she determined more than ever to get rid of me. Her double expression of deviously personality-playacting was more dangerous than any straight talk I'd ever heard.

As much as I loved having my Daniel alone as we enjoyed honeymooning in Europe, as the days slipped away, my heart longed for my friends back home, especially Ethel and most certainly, Blossom. It had been hard to say goodbye, but in time, we would be together again, me and my sister, Ethel. Daniel couldn't be more understanding to my feelings, or more loving and wonderful, and now he was truly all mine, as my beloved husband.

My real sister, Amy, hadn't been able to attend our wedding, and I was delighted when she wrote of visiting us upon our return, and staying for a week.

And our dear handyman, Tom Wafer, well, he was more than capable of caring for Dan's estate, and I was assured his flowers would also hold many breathtaking moments when we returned back home!

Tom escorted Blossom to Europe where we were situated in Austria for the school term. He stayed a week, then journeyed alone back to Canada. The university kept nannies as a part of the overseas incentive package while Dan and I continued our studies. She was happy and full of expectation to this different world that was our home for a time. We loved learning and growing with her, too!

The following spring, we celebrated Easter together, growing closer as a family. I adored my husband and daughter . . . his sister's darling child. We recognized how important the cross is, where Jesus had laid His life down for the world. Our daily devotions helped to strengthen our hearts spiritually, whether we sat beneath a tree in the nearby park, or wandered over a bridge, fascinated at the river beneath its expanse.

We purchased several children's Bible storybooks so that Blossom could understand the Bible stories at her level. Dan and I loved them, too! Filled with colorful illustrations, they were amongst her favorite possessions, as well as the classic fairytale stories we still loved to read to her, as well.

Dan was thrilled when I revealed my pregnancy to him just before our return back home. "Won't Ethel be happy?" I smiled.

"My dear Maggie," Dan corrected, "she will be ecstatic!"

Laughing, I held my beloved close to me, kissing him as he kissed me back, his eyes alit with joy.

"This child," he said, "shall have an advantage. Just think, Maggie. He or she will inherit my Japanese and Mexican-Spanish, and you, my beauty," he said, his eyes misting with tears, "Your beautiful Nordic, with your gorgeous, black hair!"

"It's so wonderful, darling," I smiled, "but perhaps your ancestry's better than mine!"

"Ah, together, we," he said in softest joy. "Together, we!" he exclaimed. "God's best of everything in this!"

Kissing me with tenderest passion, my heart was so full of joy in this precious gift and the wonderful blessing of my beloved Dan, I couldn't have asked for anything more as the *Something Special*, unexpected, that had come to me. Truly, it would live out in our lives to the joys of jeweled blessing that God had wondrously given to us!

That dream of long ago before I met Dan still came to me at times, but I kept it to myself. I was happy where I was, living it out with Dan and the little girl, Blossom, who had come to us both as a beautiful blessing in disguise. I couldn't wait to share our good news of the baby with her, but Dan and I would wait until we were settled in Dan's estate back home. As for dear Ethel, I think she'd need to be seated for this special secret of ours without any doubt about it, as my husband said!

CHAPTER 10

Moving Forward!

The trip back home was uneventful, and we arrived on a rainy day. The air was fresh and exhilarating as I appreciatively breathed it in, and everywhere I looked, green was suffused in the glory of its wet beauty. Hurrying into the mansion, I settled down with a long nap. Ethel gently knocked on our bedroom door as Dan was getting up beside me an hour later.

"Supper is hot and waiting for you, Mr." Pausing, she suddenly burst out with a merry cheer, "Oh, and your Mrs.!" she exclaimed.

"We'll be down in a few minutes, Ethel," I heard Dan say. Coming back to the bed, he kissed me, pulling the blanket off of me.

"I'm cold," I said. "I just want to sleep some more."

"Not before you have a good meal," he teasingly said, looking into my eyes. "You wouldn't want to waste Ethel's delicious supper, would you, darling?"

"Oh, I suppose not," I whimpered, begrudgingly sliding my legs over the edge of the bed as my feet touched the floor a moment later.

I'm glad to hear that," Dan teased. "Our baby needs to be nourished properly, my dearest darling!"

Laughing at his humor, I challenged, "And I've never been partial to fat babies, so I think we'll just compromise somewhat on that, okay, my Dan?" He kissed me and I washed my face and hands as Dan waited and we descended the stairs together when I was ready.

Ethel served the delicious food of roast beef, mushrooms and gravy, creamed potatoes, and peas. As I began to eat the wonderful meal, my strength returned, and I looked across to Blossom, who was especially quiet. Her eyes looked sadly into mine until I kindly asked, "Is something troubling you?"

Her lip slightly quivered as she played with her food on the fork, stirring it on her plate as she kept her head down. Then, unexpectedly, she burst out, "Are you going back without me?"

Surprised at her unexpected question, I gently answered, "No, darling. Not at all. Rest your soul. Me and your uncle are here to stay, at least for some time, we trust."

"Then, you aren't going back?" she asked, her eyes questioning as she began to cry.

"No. Maybe. But not for a long time. Please don't fret and finish your food. Whatever will Ethel think? Why, she'll be hurt to find so much food, and wonder if it wasn't any good, Blossom."

"I'm not hungry anymore."

"Not hungry? Why, were you and Tom sneaking behind Ethel's back and tasting the food?" I asked, straight-faced.

"Me and Tom? No!"

"Then, what exactly?"

"I . . ."

"Come now, darling. Please eat up. Your uncle and I have a walk planned later, and you're invited! But not until your food vanishes off that plate!" I asserted with a gentle lilt.

"Okay," she said.

"And I think that Ethel can promise us quite a tempting dessert, am I right, Ethel?" I asked, as she entered the room with a tray of lovely, decorated cupcakes.

Blossom's eyes grew large. She quickly began to eat, stuffing her mouth so full that it caused Dan to laugh.

"Not so much, Blossom! Wherever will you fit the cupcakes in?" Dan asked, teasing.

Her eyes smiled as she reached for her glass of milk. Chewing and drinking, she swallowed. "All done!" she triumphantly said.

I caught Ethel's eyes, twinkling, and smiled. "See there," I noted to Blossom, "now you have made Ethel very happy tonight!" Ethel shyly turned away, gathering the dirty dishes.

"Let me help," I offered. "And later, I have something to share with you. We both do, Dan and I."

"I hurry then," she said, skipping a word.

"Well, when Blossom's gone to sleep for the night, I wonder, dear Ethel, could you join me and Dan in the garden briefly?"

"I don't see why not," she said.

"Good! Then we'll look forward to that shortly."

Dan and I wandered to the lilacs at the back of the garden with Blossom between us. "Just smell that," I said appreciatively. "Spring is such a delightful season!"

Blossom breathed in the scents as we sat her down on the bench beside us.

"We have some wonderful news to share," Dan said, "and we hope you'll be as excited as me and your new mother, Maggie," he began.

Looking to us, I held Dan close. "Yes, Blossom. We're going to have a child – a baby."

"A . . . a baby?" she stammered.

"Yes!" I murmured softly.

"And me?" she questioned, worry creasing her brow.

"Well, you will have a sister or a brother," Dan said. "Someone to love and play with and enjoy in time."

"For good?" she asked.

"Of course, Blossom! I don't understand what you're thinking," Dan said to his niece, a bit puzzled.

"I believe I do," I said. Turning to Blossom, I assured, "We love you, Blossom, and we always will. This baby will never replace you. You shall always be very special to us."

"Then, you aren't going to give me away?"

"Blossom!" Dan exclaimed, shocked as tears began to well in his eyes. "Why ever would we do that? We love you very dearly!"

Whimpering, I coaxed her to come to me, as I reached my arms out toward her. "We will always love you, Blossom, and you will need to be a big sister to your new brother or sister. I know that we'll be counting on you to give us lots of help along the way as well."

Holding her close, her tears stopped, and she hugged me tight. "I can hardly wait," she finally said.

"We can hardly wait, too!" I smiled, kissing her lovely, auburn curls.

Tom arrived moments later as requested, escorting Blossom back to the house, and in a few minutes, we saw Ethel's slim silhouette appear in the distance.

"Blossom is asleep, and Tom is with her until I get back," she said, as she joined us. "My, but isn't it a lovely night?" she said drinking it in, sitting next to me on the bench.

"Oh, it is at that!" I said.

"Well, can I do something for you?" she politely asked, turning her attention away from the peaceful view, and looking at me and Dan.

"Ethel," I said, "thank you, but we're fine. We, Dan, and I, want to share with you that we are going to have a baby in the autumn."

"A baby?" she asked. Then, her beautiful black eyes grew large, and she clasped her hand over mine. "A baby! Oh, how wonderful! I can hardly wait! A baby in our home! Just think! Oh, what joy that shall be!"

"Just as I told you!" Dan laughed. "Ethel isn't just happy about this, she's ecstatic!"

"Indeed!" I smiled.

"Did I say something funny?" she asked, perplexed.

"No, dear Ethel. Everything you said simply wonderful! It means that you are wondrously overjoyed, just as Dan and I am! Isn't this wonderful? Oh, Ethel, you'll be an aunty!"

"I've never been one of those before," she said. "I will, won't I?" Tears filled her eyes and we hugged, me and Ethel, and the handsome doll I had wed! Then, suddenly she drew back and apologized. "Oh, my Mr. I'm so sorry. I didn't mean to impose my glad heart on yours."

Laughing, Dan assured, "That's quite all right, Ethel. I think that this time, you had perfect reason to!"

"Oh, thank you!" she said, her shy way coming back. "Now, perhaps, you'd like a napcap, would you?"

I linked my arm with hers and said, "Dan and I would love a nightcap, Ethel," I gently corrected. "As for the napcap, I think we'll be having a long one shortly after when we retire for the evening."

"Oh!" she said, as the transposed meaning dawned on her. "I see. Another trick English word. Okay. I'll fix you a nightcap and then you and the Mr. can napcap all you like!"

Laughing, I assured, "I believe that you understand the difference quite perfectly."

"For now, I do. About tomorrow or the next day or the next day after that, I really can't be sure!"

Ethel arose and we said, goodnight, then Dan and I lingered a few more minutes in the beauty of the solitude of the eve. The stars seemed to dance, echoing our joy, where the hope of our baby's birth would come in its time, and we'd be delighting with the ones we loved, knowing they would echo the joy of this love in their hearts for our child, too.

It's strange how God fits everything together within the weave of His omnipotent plan. Much like that jigsaw puzzle, I mused. Somehow, I didn't mind it quite so much anymore!

The Durifs suddenly left the company after Dan and I started back to work from our honeymoon, and when I questioned my husband about the matter, he said, "Mrs. Durif and I had a terrible row regarding her treatment of you on our wedding day a few days after our return home. When I learned what ill intent was really on her mind, I knew I had to put this matter to rest and bring closure. I told her how appalling her behavior was, especially to you, and how unethical she was acting, apart from being mean-spirited; that confidential matters were only subjected to boardroom meetings, and that her privileges in the company were now terminated. Furthermore, I told her, there was no truth to any of what she had tried to make you believe. It was utterly contemptuous! She knew better . . . there was no meeting; only the supper and wedding that she had been discreetly told not to mention to you.

"Well," he sighed with a light laugh, "it's been an eye-opener for me. And I was anything but pleased when I realized her ill-intent was to drive you away so that you'd be mad enough at me to walk away on our wedding day. It almost worked, too, and had I known it then, I would never have left your side when I escorted you from your boarding house to my estate. But I know I married a wise and independent woman, and even though you were put-off, you still had the gumption to marry me that evening!"

"That's right, Dan. But I began to see what was really inside her heart, and even though I was put out with you, I also saw that you were far more trustworthy than she'd ever be, and that she was playing me. That was enough right there for me to side with you, because I knew the honor by which you lived in every day."

"Well, I reminded Mrs. Durif that we have a protocol to follow in our company. Knowing what, pardon the expression, Maggie dear, a wet hen I was sure she would continue to be, her husband, Albert, was fired as well, because the company couldn't afford him telling any tall tales back to our clients from his wife's lips. Furthermore, I had my suspicions he wasn't on the level.

"When she stomped into my office that very afternoon, while you were on an errand for Ethel, remember? she said you must have put me up to it, and that you were nothing more than a spoiled schoolgirl, and I was too blind to see that. 'She isn't worth that wedding ring you put on her finger none, either,' she had the audacity to add. Instantly, I realized jealously lurked in her heart and it made me feel sick to my stomach. Carlie had confided some questionable signings to personal bills unrelated to the firm with her husband's signature that had aroused my suspicion of him during our honeymoon in Europe upon my examination when we were back home. It had to end right then. I couldn't afford a stain on my reputation or the company, or the expenses in question I had to pay due to Albert's scheming actions.

"I immediately asked Mr. Harry Gerali, the lovely young man I'd just hired, to take over Carletta's position and escort her out of the building. She hissed like a snake in the grass, fighting against him, raising her voice in defiance, disrupting the staff, and making a spectacle of herself.

"'I know my way around here better than anyone else, especially this schoolboy you hired,' she sassed. I asserted my authority promptly, threatening to have the police called and arrest her if she didn't go out quietly.

"'You wouldn't dare!' she yelled. 'And after all the good I did here,' she said, defiantly tossing her long, red hair, her green eyes flashing like shards of lightning.

"'Indeed!' I spoke. 'That we both can agree on. But I do dare, Mrs. Durif, so don't you ever test me in this. You've lied to my wife, and I'm done with it. Shall I dare right now?" I challenged, lifting my phone. Her face flushed with anger, and she turned, as I finished, 'Furthermore, if I ever see you or your husband back here, or even as much as on the border of my property, you'll have more than me to contend with. Now, get out!' I demanded. She walked out the office door, much to everyone's relief, especially mine."

"You didn't!" I said, laughing, with an exclamation mark behind my words.

"Oh, I did, my dearest darling, and Harry will attest to it! No matter how well someone performs at their job, when they abuse their position and try to break people apart, I will never tolerate such behavior," he said, a twinkle in his eye, "and I told her that exactly!"

My hand flew to my heart as I listened, almost wishing that I'd been there in the scene from afar without Mrs. Durif knowing of my presence. "I bet she never expected such a tongue-lashing from you," I heartily laughed, "and that she surely exploded once she was off the company grounds!" I stated, giggling.

"Very likely not!" he concurred. "As for exploding, I'm quite confident that she did that exactly, too, and more than aplenty to boot!"

I was so thoroughly astounded by everything my husband had just told me, totally applauding his way of handling the matter with such dignity and grace! And I was more than certain that it took Carletta by shocked surprise, but enough was enough, and it was about time she was stood up to! Always gracious and considerate, it must have been something quite remarkably unorthodox to see Dan exert his authority without a flinch! I couldn't have been prouder of him!

I came around his desk and kissed him. "I love being your Mrs. Danes," I sweetly said. "You are my very dearest Daniel Danes," I lovingly whispered, as I threw my arms about him. "And there shall never ever be anyone as handsome or as beautifully special as you are to me."

"My feelings are mutual!" he teased. "Surely, you know, my dearest love, that there shall never, ever be anyone as lovely and beautiful and special as you are to me." We kissed long and sweet until his telephone rang. Startled, I giggled some more, then left him to his call. But my heart couldn't stop smiling through the hours of the day! And much to my pleasure, Mrs. Durif's treatment of me somehow didn't bother me a whit!

How Dan had ever put up with Carletta Durif's arrogant management all those years, I'd never know. As Dan said, her work performance was excellent, but her ethics left far too much to be desired. She showed no remorse, and we couldn't have her on our staff with such a putrid attitude. To my way of thinking, both her and her husband should have been thrown in jail for a very long time!

Like Dan, when I'd met Harry days earlier, it was a great pleasure, and I instantly felt a beautiful warmth within his presence! Young, handsome, and aspiring, he was extremely considerate of Dan's position as the boss. Immensely helpful in how to better manage the company, Harry more than proved worthy of the high praise and recommendations his former employer had given to Dan.

"You won't find a finer or more loyal man and employee," his former boss had shared with Dan, and we certainly couldn't have agreed more!

Furthermore, Harry carried a lovely disposition that was kind and passionately warm, that we both appreciated. He was respectful and pleasant to me as Dan's wife, and nothing we asked of him was ever too much. We were very thankful to God for leading him to us, and soon discovered that he personally knew the Lord, making life at the firm so transparently uplifting. It was evident that he loved people and that he loved serving with the joy of Christ Who lived inside his heart.

As had always been Dan's longing, we now came in twenty minutes early to have a time of Christian fellowship together, reading a passage of Scripture or just a few verses, and a time of prayer. Before long, other employees asked to be a part of this time with us. Together, it made all the difference in our work, setting the tone for a productive day within the honor of working under God's direction as we leaned on Him, following within the path where His goodness abundantly produced blessings overflowing to everything we did. It was the loveliest part of our workday in celebrating and worshiping our Creator with believers on staff whose hearts were to serve others with God as our Heavenly Father!

Spring's beauty was everywhere. We spent as much time as possible with Blossom, playing outdoor games, like hide-and-seek, and volleyball on the court adjacent to the flower garden. Blossom often liked to accompany us on walks, appreciating nature's glory all about us. What I cherished most of all, however, was taking walks alone with my beloved Dan after Blossom went to bed when the eve was near, and the garden filled with the lovely fragrances of the flowers. Dark and romantic, we loved to freely walk the paths of his estate as the day waned, and we grew closer in our love amidst the enchanting beauty.

Peeking out the window one morning before leaving for the office, I chuckled as Blossom followed Tom like a shadow, delighting her with his stories and sharing the new flowers he planted as they strolled amongst the beds. She could hardly wait to show us all the marvels as we labored at the office, and he good naturedly acted as a temporary nanny to her, taking it all in stride. She loved the outdoors, and as summer approached, Dan hired a nanny to give Ethel a break and allow Tom to better undertake his duties. Anna Lopez loved the outdoors, too, and I was relieved that Dan had seemed to find the perfect nanny to help Blossom be entertained during this time.

We picnicked on the grounds and took long drives to the lake, building sandcastles and enjoying the beauty all about us, like a whole, new world. Blossom didn't seem to mind any that my sandcastle building never failed to leave it slanted and crumbly with the teeniest touch! I wouldn't have made a very good architect, that was for sure! Dan was much more skilled at that than me, and we had loads of fun trying to see whose castle was the best. If there'd been a first prize for the poorest looking sandcastle, mine would undoubtedly have won the ribbon every time! As I told Blossom, however, it was in the fun and sport of trying . . . she laughed and told me that she loved mine just the same because I gave my love in it to her! It brought tears of joy I could not define to the happiness my heart was feeling!

Toward the autumn, I found it more difficult to get around. Our baby was due near the end of September, and I needed to rest more. Work took its toll, but I remained healthy.

Dan and Blossom and I were enjoying one particular day shortly after lunch, strolling leisurely along the garden paths, when she suddenly furrowed her brow, and God gave me an amazing way of sharing her childish curiosity.

"How'd the baby get inside of you?" Blossom asked inquisitively, looking at me while Dan had paused, leaving her and me alone together as we continued walking.

I was flabbergasted! How could I tell my daughter when she was still so little? But God gave me a special way to speak the truth that satisfied her little mind and understanding.

"Well, one lovely day," I began, putting my arm around her, "God decided that He wanted me and your uncle to have a baby," I said. "He thought we'd do just fine to have our own, and that He could trust us with this special miracle. He also figured that you'd enjoy having a sister or brother to eventually play with and share wonderful things together, maybe even a secret or two! So, on that lovely day, He planted a seed in me, something like how He plants the seeds in the garden with Tom's help. You remember, don't you, Blossom?"

"Uh huh," she said, listening. "I put the seeds in the ground and Tom covers them all up. And then he does a funny thing."

"What's that?" I asked.

"He thinks the seeds are thirsty and gives them a long drink of water. Isn't that strange? How come he does that, Mommy?"

"Well, like Tom, God covers the seed in me by protecting it – like it's in a dark place, but safe. Then, He breathes His life in it, and the baby slowly grows, just like Tom gives the seeds a drink of water in the ground so they will grow, too. It takes time and a lot of patience, and then one day, like the seeds in the ground, God puts His sunshine on the baby like a light, and He leads it out of the dark place, like a tunnel, where it's born. That will happen in the next few weeks and then one day soon, we'll have our beautiful baby from God."

"Ohhh," she drawled out the word. "Special, right, Mom?"

"Yes, Blossom. Very special."

Ethel called just then. It was time for Blossom's nap. "Your mother needs her rest and so do you," she said, smiling as Blossom skipped to the house.

"Ethel! Ethel!" Blossom cried, almost out of breath as she reached the house, her voice rising. "Mommy's baby has God's light and soon will be here!"

Speechless for the moment, Ethel searched for an answer in her Spanish mind. Finally, she said, "I see. God's light. Uh huh. You could be right about that, Blossom. I guess we'll just have to wait a little longer to see." Ethel glanced at me, and caught my smile, and smiled back with a quick wink. I couldn't help but laugh!

Dan and I reached the house shortly, and we beamed. "I couldn't have said it better myself than you just did," Dan whispered to me, taking my arm. "I couldn't have said it any better at all!"

Patting his hand, I teased, "Well, God wasn't caught off guard at Blossom's question in the same way as I was, and I'm sure happy for His help in this respect!" I finished.

Lingering near the roses, we paused, and Dan lovingly kissed me in this special moment. Then, with tears in his eyes, he affirmed, "I know, my darling Maggie. I know!" Then, I couldn't contain my feelings, and we cried in each other's arms in this joy together, loving each other, and loving God.

"God's light" came two weeks early on a warm, autumn morning. I'd never forget the wind blowing some of the beautiful, autumn leaves off their branches as they momentarily swirled in the current, falling gently to the ground. I couldn't wait to see the trees along the avenue and in the bower, like a garden paradise, where such a stunning portrait would fill my heart amongst its wondrous pleasure. When I did, my soul bowed to the Creator Who made the richness of this incredulously everchanging pleasure for our pure delight! The colors were brilliant and joyful! Hours after the long night was over, our precious baby was born; a son, whom we named, Carlos Daniel. He was exquisite and so, so perfect! As I lay in the hospital bed with Dan beside me, we marveled at this wonderful gift that God had blessed into our family!

"He's so tiny and so gorgeous," Dan whispered, kissing me, as I lovingly held Carlos in my arms.

It was the most delightfully wonderful feeling; I admitted. "Perfect, yes!" I answered Dan. "So amazingly perfect and beautiful!"

Strange as it might seem, sometimes, I wondered who Blossom's real father was, but when I saw Tom, as well as Dan, with her, there was no doubt in my mind that they perfectly fit that picture! Since neither Blossom's mother, Julia, or her uncle, Dan, ever talked about him, I felt it wasn't my place to ask. There wasn't even a photograph of Blossom's father, at least, not that I'd ever seen. Julia had done away with their wedding pictures, and Dan had none, either. I was only truly grateful that Blossom derived love from these wonderful examples of Christian men within Dan's and Tom's lovely characters, and in the honor and integrity they reflected. As for Carlos, I knew that Tom would come to love Carlos, but that there would be no doubt that this little child wholly belonged to his father, Dan!

Two days later, I returned home from the hospital. Life had changed for us all in the moment our baby was born, and with all my heart, I became acutely aware that we were taking a life-long journey together that we wouldn't trade for the world!

As soon as Blossom heard our car, she scurried down the few steps from the kitchen and into the garage to meet us, excitedly running toward us. We hadn't allowed Blossom to come to the hospital. We wanted the baby to be comfortable and nurse without too much outside disturbances. It would be a huge adjustment for everyone, and while we didn't want to shelter our beloved son, we wanted him to get a strong start.

Blossom didn't know what to say at first now that we were home. We had decided, that although the bloodline made our baby Blossom's cousin, he would be more like a brother to her as well.

Dan took her hand and smiled. Leading her back to the kitchen, he told her that we'd be right in. "Just give us a few moments, Blossom," he kindly said.

Dan returned to the car and helped me out, and then he took the baby out of his car seat, carefully handing him to me. "Are you ready?" he softly asked.

"I am, my darling," I said.

Blossom was patiently waiting in the living room with Ethel eagerly at her side.

"Oh, this is so exciting!" Ethel said.

Dan helped me out of my jacket and Ethel quickly stepped in to hang it up for me. I'd never quite seen her hurry so before, and it amused me, because I knew that she didn't want to miss that first glorious moment of seeing Carlos! By the time she returned, I was comfortably seated in a wing chair with Blossom at my side, peeking at the baby.

"Your cousin, your little brother, Carlos, is fragile and needs very careful attention," Dan told her. "You may hold him, but only with an adult at your side."

Nodding, she still didn't verbalize her feelings.

Dan asked her if she'd like to hold the baby. Looking deep into his eyes, she nodded. He led her to the chesterfield, and then took the baby from my arms. Placing him in her arms, I gently soothed her thoughts as Dan sat close to her. "We love him just as we love you, Blossom," I assured, "and together, we will grow as a family."

Dan hadn't noticed that the baby was gradually slipping down after he'd given Carlos to Blossom. Ethel, sitting on the other side of her, noticed with me, and tenderly advised, "Here, this is how you hold Carlos," she showed her. Carlos' legs were dangling over her lap, and it looked like he was about to slide right off! "Just a little higher will do, Blossom," she gently said. "I don't think that he's quite ready to flip over any hill just yet, so we need to be extra careful." Dan looked toward me, and his face blushed. I smiled, understanding, and giggled good naturedly, even though I could have burst into tirades of laughter! Ethel's expression of speaking would always endear me to her heart in that special way of hers!

Blossom sat very still, almost mesmerized, her eyes constantly on the wrapped bundle in her arms. "He's pretty, Mom," she finally said. "And, and so tiny," she lamely finished. After our return home from Austria, Blossom had started to call me, Mom, and I loved that! "Yes, he's pretty. Handsome. And very tiny." Ten minutes later, she began to rub her eyes. "Now, it's time for your afternoon nap," I lovingly said. "Your uncle will take the baby to our bedroom. And Blossom," I lovingly said, "You must never attempt to take him in or out of his crib, all right, my darling?"

Looking straight into my eyes, she respectfully answered, "Yes, ma'am."

Ethel accompanied her to her room, and Dan and I went to our bedroom where I nursed Carlos before putting him in his new crib. I was grateful that Dan had specially built an alcove off the curtained area where a windowed door allowed us to check on him and gave us the privacy of our room, and most importantly, where I could nurse him in the big chair Dan had especially purchased for this purpose.

"I am happy for the privacy of this alcove," I shared with him. "The curtain and lock will allow me to nurse our baby without anyone else, like Blossom, wandering into our bedroom unexpectedly. I do not want her to ever see me nursing her brother."

Dan smiled, patting my shoulder, in understanding.

"It won't be for more than three months," I continued. "But it's still very private to me, and I make no exception to it!" I smiled. Thinking, I seriously added, "That goes for Ethel, too, although she'd understand a lot better about things such as this than Blossom, and I know it would be unintentional with her."

Dan drew me into his arms, understanding, then led me to the bed. "As it is to me," he reiterated. "And I wouldn't worry about Ethel ever catching you unawares, Maggie. She's much too private for that herself. Now, I think that a nap is what we both need right now, my darling. You've had a hard ordeal with the birth, even though it went perfectly well. I want my sweet wife to rest at every opportunity."

I closed my eyes, drawn in with Dan's arm about me, falling into a peaceful sleep, where I awoke refreshed an hour later.

I tiptoed to the alcove to check on Carlos. Turning to Dan, a disconcerting thought struck me. "I think we need to keep our bedroom door locked as much as possible, darling. I have this feeling . . . Blossom may decide to take Carlos out of his crib out of curiosity, and if she dropped him . . ." But I couldn't finish the sentence.

"I will have another talk with her," he decided. "For now, it's best if we show her as much love as we can so she doesn't feel inclined to do something that will be harmful to him."

The conversation stayed with me, and I felt raw inside. As much as I loved Blossom, I didn't want anything to happen to my son. I needed comfort and Dan held me as the tears fell freely onto his bare arms.

"I could never take it if we should lose him," I softly said. "Oh, Dan . . ."

His arms lovingly held me as he comforted my heart. "We need to trust God in this," he said. "I'm sure that Blossom will understand my talk with her." Then, peace filled my heart and my tears stopped. Right there, I whispered a prayer of protection over our child whom God had brought as that light of His love into our lives. We had two children now. One born from the loss of a woman who would never see her daughter grow up, and the other from a love ever deep between us, whom we trusted God to every turning day. We were a family and the gift of all we were so blessed in would never leave our hearts, where a little girl had come as unexpected joy to us, and a baby boy, who would sustain that joy in us all.

Through the months, we never had a problem with Blossom or cause for concern. Loving her with Carlos, she was truly this beautiful child we had come to cherish in every day we lived. Then, for some reason, I suddenly recalled that wonderful afternoon when Blossom and I had spent that lovely time alone at the park. The beautiful drawing, she had tenderly created out of her love for me, would never leave my heart. Taking it out of my jewelry box, I opened the worn folds and read that one inspiring word which would take me through this initial stage of Carlos' birth. Here, the blossoms of the flowers flourished in our hearts, on to the seasons, knowing that as we trusted God to guide our lives, He'd fulfill all our days with the goodness of His love. There, His breath daily sustained us, and He is ever Lord, because of that one precious word, *Hope*, that He lovingly gave of His all to us in Jesus!

CHAPTER 11

Onward We Go!

What a day it had been! Dan and I had worked hard late into the evening the day before at the firm, and again, early this new morning. Having had nothing more than some fruit and coffee, we were ready for a substantial breakfast.

We wanted a change of scenery and had mentioned to Ethel that we thought it would be good to spend part of the day at the lake. Blossom had been invited to a birthday party down the road, an overnight, and Ethel was thrilled for us to enjoy some "space" alone together, as her Spanish mind translated "time".

After breakfast, Dan and I took a leisurely stroll outside, passing through the lovely rose arbor, enjoying the scents of the flowers and the twittering vocals of the birds flitting amongst the trees and foliage of the blossoms. We shared our morning devotions at the far end of the garden, sitting on the bench together. I appreciated the daily strength that filled my soul with song as we took turns reading verses or passages, and sharing the meaning with each other, and our hearts right alongside the joy in God's Presence.

I opened my Bible and read one of my favorite verses from Psalm 63:6-8 KJV. "'When I remember thee upon my bed and meditate on thee in the night watches. Because thou hast been my help, therefore in the shadow of thy wings will I rejoice: My soul followeth hard after thee: thy right hand upholdeth me.'

"I love the quaint expression of King David's words that are filled with thanksgiving and inspiration," I said to Dan as he lovingly sat by my side. "There's power in God's Word and His

Word is the strength within that mighty power that is Life to us – His Life. And when I think about the greatness of who He is, each day holds the encouragement we might glean in these quiet moments with Him as we give our hearts' attention and honor of worship to Him."

Dan thoughtfully replied, "Yes, Maggie. And hidden, like precious jewels within His Word, are gems of wisdom in finding hope and assurances for everything we need as that daily, spiritual bread."

"Absolutely!" I agreed. "You know, Dan, I am breathless to how beautifully poetic the Psalmist wrote these profoundly meaningful and lovely words. There's just something so extra special about them."

Nodding, Dan smiled. "There truly is and I feel the same way as you. These words are fresh and new, just like the rain, and I will never tire of reading them."

"Did you have something you'd like to share with me, too?" I tenderly asked my husband.

"Yes. Well, I've been thinking about the work we do. Almost no one considers a Christian author to be a missionary and all the work involved in preparing a manuscript that honors God, but we are just as much missionaries in our work as a person who may go overseas to witness of God's love and salvation."

"That's very true, my darling," I softly replied.

"I'm so excited about sharing this verse with you! Just listen to what St. John wrote in chapter 15, verse 16: "Ye have not chosen me, but I have chosen you, and ordained you, that ye should go and bring forth fruit, and that your fruit should remain: that whatsoever ye shall ask of the Father in my name, he may give it you.'

"Isn't this beautiful? Maggie! We were chosen to do a very special assignment for God, and I believe that this assignment has no timestamp on it according to this verse! John doesn't say that once we have done an assignment for Jesus, that's the end of it! No! He says that our fruit should remain!"

"Wow, Dan! I never quite interpreted it that way before, but that is right! That's an amazing insight of revelation in knowledge which God just gave to you!"

"It is Maggie! It is! I've always known that when God calls, when He asks us to do something for Him, He believes so much in us that He asks, then expects us to do whatever He has laid upon our hearts. Yet, in His gentleness, His immense kindness for us, He allows us the gift of freedom to choose for ourselves. But we are called nonetheless, because He chose us. Isn't that amazing?"

"It surely is!" I spoke.

"Well, every time I read this verse, I feel this stirring inside of me that God has called us to do even greater things for Him. That's why I so strongly felt that I needed to study all the departments within the publishing field, including movie making."

I couldn't help but stare into his eyes. "Dan! Movie making! Why, what a magnificently marvelous dream that would be! You haven't taken any courses on that already, have you?"

Teasing, he assured, "I actually have, Maggie, but then I changed back to the major, because I thought of how wonderful it would be to share this course with you, and I would wait until I returned, and hopefully you would marry me. Is there any point to believe that you have an interest . . .?"

I kissed him before he could continue, and breathless with joyful emotion, I exclaimed, "Oh, my dearest Dearest! I would love to take this together with you! Thank you for waiting, and now that we're married, we can share this dream together just as you wanted. Yes, my darling?"

"Absolutely, Maggie!" Dan said, kissing me. "And while I'm not quite certain what God has in mind, if but nothing more, I've been given a broader scope and greater understanding to all the staff who help bring the light out of the darkness through the quality books we put out in our work."

"Maybe no one else sees the value in everything we strive for, Dan, but long before we married, I did, and I appreciated everything in every moment that you gave to me. And after we married, to be able to be blessed by the opportunity to study with you in Austria was truly one of the most beautiful gifts I've ever known! It's also helped to make me become a better person and editor, to understand the facets of each department. I appreciate you more than I can ever say, my darling, and I want to take this moment to thank you for all the wonderful blessings you've given to me. Your beautiful, sweet way, kindness, and thoughtfulness, truly exemplifies the honor and integrity that you hold, not just to me, but also to all we serve in our positions in our work." Tears crept into my eyes, and Dan gently wiped them away as they silently streamed down my face, and his eyes began to mist. For a moment, silence hung between us as he got his emotions together.

"I'm happy to have been able to have done this for you, Maggie, and it shall always be my great pleasure," he softly whispered, kissing me. "You brought *Julia's Song* to me in a very difficult time in my life, and that is a priceless gift I shall ever be grateful for."

"To me, too," I said, "because I took the journey with you. But when you left and none of us knew what you were doing, I felt so lost and alone, and I wondered if I'd ever see you again."

"Oh, Maggie, I'm so sorry."

"Well, I felt like I'd lost a very precious jewel without your presence, like a stone was missing as Ethel once told me, of which she meant my diamond, because I really had. And my soul longed and hungered to share the Word with you – to grow and learn and be encouraged together within the truth and beauty of all it holds."

Dan listened with grave seriousness, as he lovingly drew me into his arms. "I missed you, too," he admitted, "but I just didn't know what to say anymore."

"Dan," I hesitated.

"What is it, Maggie?" he asked.

"You . . . You didn't have to take me on your journey with Julia, but you did. And I've sometimes wondered, why did you choose me? Why not anyone other than me? Why did you entrust this very personal journey with me?"

"Because I knew deep inside of me, that if I truly listened to my heart and was honest, I'd see just how very much that you already meant to me, and I found my feelings growing stronger each day for you until I realized that I loved you, Maggie. And no one else could ever fill your shoes to be the beautiful and captivating writer that you are. Nor could anyone else ever fill your shoes to the tender heart by which you create your characters, especially mine, in our beautiful story.

"I've never felt very valued as a person, and you were this beautiful gift I'd waited all my life for. Always encouraging and supportive and kind. Without you, I was lost, completely. You gave immense worth and beauty to my soul. You were always there for me, even in my long absence, and you are always here for me now."

"Even in the pain of your long absence, Dan, I've never stopped believing in you, and I've always respected and cherished what God gave to us, because what He gave to us held His very heart through our daily lives."

"I didn't deserve it, Maggie, not one little bit!" Dan said, tears welling in his eyes.

"Yes, Dan. You deserved my trust, and I'm afraid I lacked plenty of it back then! Sometimes, my mind conjured up all kinds of dire scenarios, but I always came back to the highest excellence of honor and integrity that I knew was who you are. Don't you see, my darling? It's this very heart of who you are that means this deeply honorable significance of integrity to me, and I assure you, that this shall never change, because God brought us together for a purpose – His!"

This morning held an incredible worth to take in, but as Dan and I kissed and arose, we walked hand in hand amongst the glory of the flowers, enjoying the richness of their colors and the perfume that wafted lightly in the air.

"I'm glad you're mine," Dan said, looking into my eyes as we paused before the roses. "And I will never stop loving you or thanking God for bringing you into my life that day."

"I'm glad you're mine, too, Dan," I said, "and I will never stop loving you or thanking God for bringing you into my life that day, too, even when we didn't expect to meet again that morning you helped me to locate my car!"

Laughing softly, Dan took me in his arms and passionately kissed me. "You're my Mrs. and always shall be. I treasure you more than all the lovely petals that bloom within our garden. There's no one like you, and I'm blessed beyond all measure." I rested against his shoulder, loving the closeness of his heart to mine. My heart was so full, I couldn't answer in the moment.

I admired the trees and the sensually enticing blossoms that blew their perfume to the ever-persuasive, changing moods of the wind. What a beautiful scene it was, filling my soul with rich contentment! Here, the elaborate graces of Dan's soul would keep my heart as we lifted Christ before us, and rivers of peace overflowed in abundant joy in everything we did, both within our amazing place we called home, and to the world, sharing the Good News of Truth wherever God led our paths.

My thoughts shifted, and suddenly, I paused, remembering a beautiful verse I'd read earlier in the morning. "Dan!" I softly exclaimed. He turned to face me, inquisitive. "I just recalled a wonderful verse, and I must share it with you now! Listen to this: 'I will tell of the Lord's unfailing love. I will praise the Lord for all he has done.' It's from the Book of Isaiah, chapter 63, and verse 7a from the NLT translation. Isn't that something? And so astounding? Dan! In this place, right where we are, God has given us a purpose – His Purpose, in sharing the Gospel of Jesus Christ!"

"Wow, Maggie! That is astounding! I love it! Telling of God's unfailing love and praising the Lord for everything He's done. That makes me feel very humble and very privileged."

"Me, too, Dan," I said. The tears came as we rejoiced in God's Goodness as we loved and adored and worshiped Him – our King of kings and Lord of lords. Nothing . . . nothing at all, got better than this!

When we arrived back at the house, Ethel had just put Carlos down for a nap, and we enjoyed her lovely lunch. When the meal was over, Ethel momentarily remained seated, which was quite unusual for her. I could see that something was on her mind, so I tactfully asked, "Is everything all right, Ethel? Is there something Dan and I may do for you?"

"He's such a handsome baby," she said, in that shy voice of hers, as though she didn't hear a word I'd just spoken. "He was no trouble at all, just as I told you, and I enjoyed my time with him when you took your morning walk. And yes, Mrs., there is something I'd very much like you and your Mr. to do for me. You know, I think that you both need to have that bit of a break."

So, she had been attentive to my words, I happily thought, but I wondered what this was all about. I barely caught Dan's response.

"A break?" Dan asked.

"Yes, sir. You and your sweet Mrs., for sure. I thought I'd like to surprise you."

"You did?" Dan teased, a smile shining in his eyes.

"I did! So, I went ahead and made a surprise."

"Uh huh," Dan waited, patiently.

"Well, yes, I did. Never you mind that baby of yours," she lovingly spoke. "He's all done with that nursing, and I'll take good care of him. I've already taken the liberdee," she misspoke. She hurriedly arose, returning moments later. "I packed a picnic for you," she proudly announced, "and I want you to enjoy some space just with yourselves." Handing the basket to Dan, she grinned. "Me and Carlos will be fine, so what do you say?"

I was at a loss for words, but I knew Ethel had a heart as pure as gold, and I really appreciated her thoughtfulness. But my baby . . . I missed him already.

Reading my troubled thoughts, Dan lovingly said, "We wouldn't want Ethel's hard work to go to waste, now would we, Maggie? And I for one, am very grateful!" Tactfully, I agreed because I really did, but my heart still longed for my baby boy. Then, I hurried up the stairs.

Without a word, I tiptoed down the long corridor and up the stairway. There, my baby still slept, handsome and peaceful. "Do be good," I softly whispered. "I love you so and we'll have our own special time together later; I promise, Carlos." I lightly kissed his cheek and exited the bedroom.

Heading back along the corridor seconds later, as I stepped down the stairs, Dan asked, "Are you all right, Maggie?"

"Quite all right," I said. "Ethel, this is most thoughtful and generous of you, and my Mr. and I want to heartily thank you."

Ethel smiled. "Oh, it twairn't nothing, Maggie!" she said. Why, if I wasn't mistaken, she hadn't called me by my Christian name since the Mr. and I had wed, I exclaimed in my thoughts! I couldn't help but laugh, and my heart was at rest. I knew that God had planned this special time for us, and that He was looking after Carlos and Ethel, too. All was well!

I thought of everything that Ethel so graciously did for me, and now that I was married to her Mr., she was as gracious as always, and I thought, sometimes, even more so, especially since Carlos had come into our lives. It was wonderful to have Ethel's support and trust in everything. As Dan excused himself to get our jackets, and stood in the foyer waiting for me, she said, "No dillydallying now. I want you to enjoy every moment you can!"

Joy filled my heart and I couldn't help but giggle! Hugging me, Ethel tenderly spoke, "Best you hurry now, Mrs. Your handsome Mr. is waiting for you!" Chuckling, Dan, and I said goodbye and exited the house.

It was something that Ethel hardly called me Maggie anymore. I was the Mrs. to her now, I happily said in my thoughts, and that suited me just fine!

The late morning sun streamed on the water as the shoreline came into view minutes later. The cool air was refreshing, and I inhaled of its welcome bliss. Time seemed to have no meaning as it slipped away, and we were oblivious to the beauty of this delightfully poignant portrait. With Dan at my side, it was poetically uplifting in the timeless joy within the presence of God's wondrously unsurpassed creation!

Dan and I walked along the shoreline enjoying the beautiful scene of the expanse of the lake, where we could see the distant shoreline with its towering trees. Although the view was hazy as the afternoon light waned, and a fog slowly appeared over the vastness of it, growing thicker over the water, it was just marvelous to share this special time alone with my husband. That dream had certainly taken me much further than I could ever have imagined, I smiled in my thoughts. We wandered along the cove, and much to our surprise, we came upon a small cave.

"Why, I had no idea!" I exclaimed in surprise.

"Nor I," Dan said.

Venturing into the cave, we found it to be the size of a large room, high enough to stand upright, and spacious enough to be well camouflaged from the outer world.

"I think I'd like to explore this in better light," Dan remarked. "Why don't we ask Ethel to take care of our children tomorrow and we'll have a look-see around here?"

"That sounds like a great plan!" I smiled, reaching for his hand as we exited the cave.

"I wonder if there's any more caves further on?" he said, his brow creased.

"Perhaps. Seeing that there is one here, I'd say it's a good chance that there is."

I knew that Dan held a strong interest in science, and I did as well, but I wasn't ever able to retain much of what I learned. I never had. Still, it fascinated me.

We searched for a while, but the fog was beginning to spread over the land, making it harder to see our way back to the cave. By the time we returned to the cave, I was getting quite hungry. Our basket of food was where we'd left it in a well-camouflaged corner of the cave, for which I was immensely grateful.

We exited the cave again, holding hands. "I hope the fog lets up soon," Dan said, in a concerned tone. He took out his flashlight from his pocket and clicked it on. The light glared in the swirling fog as though it was swirling with it.

"This won't be easy," he began, "but darling, I'll have a roaring fire as soon as we are able to find, and collect, some wood for it," he promised. The light was strong enough to penetrate the misting aura as it pierced the foliage growing close to shore. "Why don't we see what driftwood we can find in that brush over there?" Pointing, I turned to see a fallen tree as I followed his direction. Dan helped me up the steep incline from the shore to the land. Then, as suddenly as the fog had come, it dissipated, making our search so much easier. We found oodles of large pieces of driftwood from old and dried-up trees. It felt good to feel the warmth of the fire once Dan got it going.

We indulged in Ethel's delicious lunch. Cold pieces of chicken, potato salad, and carrot sticks, and afterward, a delicious white cake decorated with icing and coconut, topped off the meal for a perfect dessert and delightful lunch! The hot coffee warmed us on the inside, and we relaxed on a thick quilt, enjoying the lapping of the water.

When the meal was finished, Dan retrieved two lawn chairs. Sitting near the water's edge, tiny waves rhythmically lapped against the shore, quieting within the solitude of the waning evening. We enjoyed the setting sun, colors of golden hue splashing like a sunburst momentarily against the blues and wines across the wide expanse.

The fading embers of the fire softly crackled, and I drew my chair close to his. We should soon be leaving for home, I was thinking, when Dan intruded on my thoughts.

"I think we should do an overnight," he expressed. "We could sleep in the cave we discovered, and then we can search the land to see if there are any others. What do you think, my dearest Maggie?"

"Oh, Dan! I'd love that!" My heart was happy as could be.

He leaned over to kiss me, accidentally tipping his chair in the process. He caught himself before falling over me.

"Are you alright?" I asked with concern.

"Yes. But I think that you need to come in a little closer."

"Oh, so I might fall?" I teased.

Taking it into account, Dan replied, "I wouldn't want that to happen, not even for a kiss," he proposed. "Unless" he amended, "you'd consider it worth the risk?"

"I certainly wouldn't want a mishap," I carefully mulled over, "not even for a kiss! Mind you," I coyly reflected, "I suppose I could humor you this once if you'd meet me halfway!" I grinned.

"No! No!" he protested. "Not even halfway, my darling! I don't want to spoil the enjoyment of your kisses." Rising from his chair, Dan bent to meet my mouth, and kissed me passionately. Then, his footing slipped as a wave suddenly crashed on the shore, covering us with a huge spray of water.

We laughed as another boisterous wave caught us before we could move. "The wind has really whipped up," I smiled mischievously, "but we shouldn't let that unexpected distraction spoil our love any, Mr. Danes!" I couldn't resist teasing Dan as water literally poured off our clothes, dripping onto the sand in a puddle.

"I'm quite surprised at you!" he chortled good naturedly. "In that case, *Mrs. Danes*," he accentuated, "perhaps we ought to take this up in our car where I can guarantee the wind won't catch us unawares for anything or soak us to the bone!"

"As you wish, my dearest," I obliged, smiling as I looked into his eyes, and love met me momentarily in the tender grasp of his. The wind momentarily calmed as we arose shortly afterward and gathered up the picnic.

"Ethel sure went to a lot of trouble to make this so special for us today," I remarked. "Dan, we need to do something for her, too. I've been thinking . . . considering that, perhaps, we might give her a few days off as well and pay for a short vacation for her."

Putting the basket into the car and getting in moments later, Dan started the car. "That's a lovely idea, darling. But we need to plan a little. After all, we need a nanny for the children. Then, we should ask Ethel about it, because we don't want to make plans and have them fall through."

"Of course, Dan. That's my sentiment exactly," I said, leaning over to kiss him.

"I need to concentrate on my driving now," he teased. "Think those kisses can wait?"

"They might, but I've never heard of kisses being put on hold before, Dan," I scoffed. Pretending to pout, I challenged, "Maybe, I'll just close my eyes and go to sleep for a bit, and you can waken me when we arrive home. After all, you did suggest that the wind wouldn't play havoc in the car with kisses."

"I did!" he returned. "Come here, my dearest Maggie! There shall be no sleeping . . ."

The car began to fog up as I drank in Dan's kisses, long and sweet. "Mmm," Dan smiled appreciatively when I could breathe again. "No one needs a white cake for dessert when one can have your kisses!"

Blushing, I said, "But you must admit it topped the meal, Dan!" I replied, kissing him.

"Oh, it did at that, but nothing like your kisses!" he repeated, flirting. He held me close and minutes later whispered, "There shall never be anyone like you, my Maggie!"

Moments later, he released me, and put the car into drive. With the mist playfully frolicking outside the windows, the night descended in an eerie wonder of silent beauty that took my breath away. And Dan, well, I told him, there'd never be anyone like him, either! The headlights honed the road as Dan held one hand over mine and my heart couldn't stop smiling.

Ethel had kindly left a lamp on in the living room for us. She was already retired for the night, but not asleep. Dan and I quickly showered, and Ethel joined us in the kitchen afterward, appearing in her housecoat over her pajamas. Bustling about, she put a plate of finger sandwiches and dainties on the kitchen table while she waited for the water to boil on the stove.

"A hot apple drink will warm you," she said. "It must have been cool at the lake." Shivering despite the warm shower I'd just had, I burst into laughter. "What's so funny, Mrs.?" she asked, quizzically.

"Oh, nothing! But we do appreciate this evening snack. Especially the hot drink." I didn't dare glance at Dan. I hadn't even felt the evening's coolness with Dan holding me tenderly close. But I was feeling the effects of the cold a little bit now. We loved Ethel and it was amusing how she fit right in even though we weren't real family, in the true sense that is, although we were truly that to each other, and so much more!

Seating ourselves around the table, we leisurely drank the delicious, hot apple drink. Ethel's sandwiches and cookies were also delicious!

Reaching for a white cookie topped with a thin layer of butter icing, she said, "Now, I want to hear all about your afternoon, please." I couldn't feel more amused – the housekeeper and cook wanting details of her bosses' experiences! Taking it in stride, I knew that Ethel was like our own blood and we, hers. It was always so much fun to share with her!

Ethel was dumbfounded when we shared our experience of the cave. "Oh, you must go back!" she said, with a serious expression. "I think you might even find a secret there – what you call it – a treasure?"

"You know something, Ethel, that never occurred to me," Dan said thoughtfully. Excitedly, he asked, "Would you mind the children for us tomorrow and overnight, Ethel? Maggie and I are very interested in exploring that area more extensively. And we'll pay you extra well for this extended favor."

"Oh, sure. Anything for you and the Mrs.!" she gaily chortled. Then, her brow furrowed, and she voiced her thoughts, "But extra pay . . . No, no! That be my pleasure to have the joy with your lovely children!"

We thanked her for her kind consideration for the snack and the offer of which we knew she was loving every moment with our children! God truly blessed us more than we could have ever asked of Him in this!

Dan excused himself and called up Harry Gerali, although the hour was getting late. "I'd appreciate you filling in for me and Maggie tomorrow," he began. "We have important work to do elsewhere. Should anything of importance arise, please get in touch with our housekeeper, Ethel Rodriguez, and she'll let you know where to find us. Otherwise, Harry, enjoy tomorrow and we'll look forward to seeing you on Monday."

"Certainly, Mr. Danes," he politely said. "I appreciate your call. Have a great weekend and then I'll see you and Maggie on Monday."

"Thank you, Harry. Goodbye for now and enjoy your weekend, too."

Harry, we knew, could always be trusted to perform the duties with gracious care which were unexpectedly required of him, and like Ethel, we were very grateful for his presence!

We bid goodnight to Ethel and tumbled into bed, happy for all the blessings that had come to us, where sweet dreams awaited upon the waning eve. As we laid our heads down upon the wonderful comfort of our pillows, I was explicably drawn to the peace of the night before us. It was then that I recalled an incredible verse that I'd meant to share with Dan earlier in the day. Somehow, I felt it couldn't wait until the morning. Gently nudging him, I said, "May I tell you something before we sleep, my darling?"

Dan sat up and said, "Sure, Maggie."

"Well, I read a special Bible verse this morning I'd wanted to share with you, and I didn't remember about it until now. It's another verse from the Book of Isaiah, Chapter 42, verse 4, but the funny part is, I don't recall where I read it, but I think it was from one of my devotional books. I don't even recall what version it is, but I suspect that it's from the King James Version. Anyway, it says, 'I the Lord . . . will hold thine hand, and will keep you.' Isn't that beautiful, darling? What an amazing promise to know that we have the God of the universe caring, providing, and protecting us! And He is our Good Shepherd and Healer through it all."

Dan was stunned. "It's a remarkable verse, Maggie. It almost feels prophetic . . . I wonder . . ." But he kissed me and laid back down again. Before I could express my sentiment to his words, he was fast asleep, but it almost felt prophetic to me, too.

161

I lovingly kissed Dan and he stirred, but didn't awaken. In this profound moment, my heart held the gift of love close to his as I looked to God each day, and the joy of Dan's heart in same. Turning over, the stars in the darkening sky twinkled like they had their own secret. Contented, I closed my eyes as I felt my beloved's arm about me in the warmth of his love. I knew that he would always be my precious stay, guarding and protecting me and our household through the hours within the gift of the night's welcome solitude and blessing. Of course, I smiled to myself, God would watch over us all, like no One better than He ever would!

Chapter 12

Unexpected Adventures

Peering out the large picture window in our bedroom the following morning, I slowly perused the lovely arena on the other side of the pane. A misty fog was swirling in play, but the hint of dawn was simultaneously slowly overcoming the darkness of the night. I felt Dan at my side, and turning, he softly kissed me.

When we entered the kitchen, a note was propped on the table. Ethel had scrawled a message affirming that our picnic basket was prepared and in the refrigerator. I couldn't resist drawing a heart underneath, and penning the words, *"Thank you!"* to her!

We had a quick bite to eat, and shortly afterwards put on our jackets, about ready to leave. But first, I needed to slip into my children's bedrooms, where they were both still asleep, as was Ethel, and so I kissed my baby and daughter in my love. Little wonder Ethel was sleeping late this morning! I'd momentarily aroused in my sleep and heard her arise just after 5:00 a.m. in the quiet of the hour, knowing that she was preparing our meals for us. "Such a marvelous person," I whispered in my heart before contentedly falling asleep again until Dan awakened me at six-thirty. I wanted to throw the covers back over me, but he gently pulled them out of my reach, and leaned in to kiss me.

"Rise and shine, my Maggie," he softly whispered.

As we set out, quietly closing the door, the sun was just beginning to peek over the horizon, tinting the sky in lovely tones of pinks and mauves and blues. The warmth of the sun's welcoming touch grew in strength as it touched my face in the chill.

The robins began to sing in clear notes of richest beauty, and I drew in a deep breath. I could understand a little why they awakened so early upon the dawn. But I doubted that they appreciated the sunrise like us, although I was certain that they did appreciate their own gifts in God's blessings to them. Their melodies stretched far and wide within the glory of the morning that never failed to fill my soul with a song in my heart to endless praise!

I kept in step with my beloved Dan at my side as we walked along the avenue of trees, where this new day held a bounty of blessings just waiting to be discovered. The wind gently rocked the branches like a cradle, creating open spaces as sunbeams splashed in merriment, dancing to its rhythm as the first rays of light burst upon the new day. It almost seemed as though the sun had a secret, too, streaming in between the apple blossoms, filling the air with their enticing fragrance; a good kind of secret I didn't mind!

Dan had parked our motorcycle on the road, and the walk along the avenue of trees was exhilarating. We didn't want to leave our car on the road at the edge of the shore when we arrived at the lake, so Dan opted for the motorbike. I wasn't thrilled about the idea, but it certainly made sense. I didn't mind riding with my husband, as he was a very responsible driver. Even at this early hour, I was assured that he'd obey all the laws of the road!

"Just listen to that song!" I exclaimed, pausing. He abruptly stopped beside me. "What a beautiful morning this is!"

"It truly is," he smiled. "But let's continue, shall we, darling? This basket of food is heavy."

Chortling, I grinned. "Best you not drop it, my love," I gleefully replied. "We wouldn't want the birds to swoop down and start the picnic without us!" I teased. "For if you do," I couldn't help pointing out, "just perhaps, it's a way for them not to have to work for their breakfast this morning!" I couldn't resist saying.

"Goodness me!" he said, furrowing his brow. "I think I can make it just fine to the bike. Let the birds work for their daily bread," he complained with a lilt in his voice. We walked a few steps further along when he suddenly cried out. "Oops!" he exclaimed as the basket shifted. Quickly righting the basket, we hurried down the avenue, where presently, he placed it carefully in the back container of the motorcycle. I didn't say a word, but I couldn't help myself from laughing gaily, either!

The view along the shore road was lovely and minutes later, we arrived at the lake. Waves billowed as if in fanciful frolic, splashing plumes of water droplets high into the air as the wind's strength hailed the new day. We caught the full sunrise over the water; exhilarating and awe-inspiring, as its hues dappled the water in golds, blues, and plum mauves.

Arm in arm, we found a sheltered spot and celebrated this moment as Dan took out his King James Version New Testament and read a few verses from the Psalms.

"This is a wonderful verse, Maggie. From Psalm 104:24. 'O Lord, how manifold are thy works! In wisdom hast thou made them all: the earth is full of thy riches.'"

Looking across at the vastness of the lake, I couldn't have agreed more. "This is lovely, indeed, Dan. Who but God could have created all this diverse wonder: the water in the basin of this immense lake, the sand on the shore, the trees, and shrubs on the land in close proximity, and the sky and clouds above, especially the air that we breathe?"

"That's very true," Dan replied. "Here's a lovely verse we can hold on to. This verse is from Psalm 71:3: 'Be thou my strong habitation, whereunto I may continually resort: thou hast given commandment to save me; for thou art my rock and my fortress.'"

"That's truly beautiful," I said. "God is our strong habitation, our rock, and our fortress. And He's given life to us through the cross because of all Jesus accomplished for us."

Dan and I shortly linked arms, wandering along the seashore. "What an inspiring scene!" he appreciated. "This reminds me of this verse from Habakkuk 3:2a in the NIV. It exults, 'Lord, I have heard of your fame; I stand in awe of your deeds, Lord. Repeat them in our day, in our time make them known; . . .'

"You know, Maggie," he acknowledged, "hearing the gentle lapping of the waves and all the raw beauty here, I can't help but praise our Creator, knowing how powerful and strong He is. It just thrills my heart, and like King David shared his thoughts, I want to always stand in awe of everything God does. Yet, in all the wonder of His creations, He's still small enough to fit inside our hearts when we surrender our lives to Him. Isn't that truly amazing? To me, it's almost incomprehensible just knowing that God loves us this much in everything."

"To me, too, Dan," I softly replied. "God's world is astounding, but what's most amazing is that He invites us to have Him come and live inside of us."

"I just want to say a prayer in gratitude to Him. Shall we kneel before Him in worship, my darling?"

"Absolutely!"

Dan and I knelt on the sand and his prayer deeply touched my heart. "Dear God," he prayed, "we are so privileged to be here with You in this beautiful oasis of solitude. Thank You for giving us life! Thank You for giving us Jesus! And thank You for being with us here as we share this time in Your loving Presence. In Jesus' Name, Amen."

As we arose, my soul was refreshed. I looked to the sky, where the blue met the water so precisely, that the division of colors were almost indistinguishable.

"God can do a lot out of little," I softly remarked. "After all, He created the whole world, and He did that out of nothing . . . Just imagine that, and He had to think up all His ideas, too! And you know something, Dan? God, being the Word, spoke Who He Is as that very Word, and in that, He created the breathless beauty of the sunrises, as well as the gorgeous sunsets. He flung the stars into the sky, each in perfect place. He set the sun in perfect mark, too, just as He did the moon. Besides this, He holds the universe in precise sync! That alone should bring us awe and wonder to humbly bow our hearts in praise, and worship Him as Lord over all!"

Dan completed my thoughts by adding, "That's right, Maggie! His majesty and beauty of nature exclaims His greatness; undeniably and fully visually, and it shows and tells us Who He Is. Here's an incomprehensible thought: When I think of the power that it took for God to create our world, and when I see this wide expanse of water, the water is subject to Him in every way. It cannot escape the basin it's contained in. While there's terrible tsunamis around the world at different times, even there, eventually, the water must obey its Maker, to return and stay within its basin. The shoreline holds it back. Just as He spoke worlds into existence, His words still rule today. How can anyone doubt the handiwork of His creation, and how can anyone refuse Him as the Creator, and His Son, Jesus, as the Way, the Truth, and the Life?"

"I don't have the answer," I said, "but I do know that the greatest gift to living is found in Him Alone. Staying on the high road, we will always find His footsteps leading us on the right path toward Him when our hearts are found in the right place to Who He Is.

"And I don't honestly know what I'd ever do or where I'd ever be if not for God. He has given us everything abundantly from His hands. We just need to reach out and take hold of it; to claim the blessings, because He is our Father, and He wants to give everything to us to live our lives in Him for others. As the Bible tells us, His Goodness is unsearchable."

Appreciating the wondrous solace and beauty all around us, I leaned my head on my husband's shoulder as we watched the water lap against the shore. "It sure is pretty," I said. "Pretty and joyful."

We began to walk again along the shoreline when Dan interrupted. "I want to tell you something confidential," he shortly said. "Come, my love, the cave we discovered isn't too far away from here. I want to share that with you once I get a fire going." Carrying the basket in his free hand and holding mine in the other, minutes later, we entered the cave. Pulling a flashlight from his pocket, Dan played it around the interior. "Hmm," he said, taking it in. "Someone's been here, if I'm not mistaken. There are remnants of a fire. See, over there," he said pointing. Squinting, I could just make out a neatly stacked pile of wood. "That wasn't there before. I'm sure of it!" Dan firmly said.

"Well, what if the person or persons return? Dan, I don't feel comfortable sleeping in this cave or any other if there's someone prowling around this area."

"We do have protection," Dan quietly said. "I always carry my gun with me, as you know. For now, I think it's safe enough."

Dan started a fire, and it took the morning chill away. It was really cozy being sheltered in the cave. I felt happy and sleepy.

Dan opened a thermos of hot coffee that we enjoyed with Ethel's delicious biscuits, and my sleepiness abated. Then, Dan took my hand in his and startled me with something that was furthest from my mind. "Darling, I've been thinking very seriously about something. Now that we are both qualified in all the fields of the publishing industry, what would you think about it if we went back to Austria and taught?"

"Taught? I'm not certain I'm that qualified," I said, furrowing my brow, "and there's still plenty to learn," I admitted. "But that's never been far from my heart, and I've always had a longing to teach and fill eager minds with knowledge! In what way are you thinking, Dan?"

"Well, a few days ago, I received a telephone call at the office, and the Director asked if we'd be interested in teaching positions."

"But what about our life here? And our children? How long would we be gone for?"

Laughing, Dan said, "Slow it down, please, my dearest! We'd teach during the regular school term and return here in the summer, maybe even for Christmas and Easter holidays."

"But what about our children?" I persisted, my heart instantly becoming lonely at the thought of possibly having to leave them behind.

"We would take them with us. And before you can ask, I propose that we take Ethel with us to be their nanny. The school has generously offered to pay her wages, including our flight and travel expenses."

Throwing my arms about my husband, I kissed him tenderly. "Oh, Dan! That sounds just wonderful to me, and I say, yes, to that! I couldn't bear not to have my children, and Ethel, why, she's priceless, and a part of our family! Just think how happy that will make her, too!"

"Wouldn't you miss Tom?" Dan teased.

"*He is handsome,*" I began, playing on my words as Dan's shocked expression finally settled. "But then again, I've already married my handsome doll, and I really believe that one is plenty enough for me!" I smiled. Dan didn't seem to have his voice yet, so I sweetly continued, "Oh, and I'm quite certain that in the winter, Tom could manage our big house by himself. He's a smart fellow and there's not so much to tend to that he couldn't do it on his own completely. I mean, he does, anyway. Just that he'd have no cook."

"Oh, dear! I wonder how he'll take that?"

"Maybe he won't mind too much," I said.

"But about Ethel. I thought we were going to do something special and pay for a vacation for her?" he queried.

"Well, why don't we propose your plan and take it from there? Going to Austria will be special for her, but if she doesn't have any break and cares for the children here as she would there, only the location will change. Dan, she needs that vacation!" I suddenly declared.

"Yes! I agree. Well, then. Let's see if we might find some treasure here to help pay these expenses. Not that I really need it, but wouldn't it be simply grand if we did?" he asked, delight teasingly shining in his eyes.

"It would, Dan! And" I teasingly added, "it might not hurt to keep the pauper away!"

"Well, I think we needn't worry about becoming paupers," Dan laughed. "But" he seriously changed the subject, "You didn't answer my question. Wouldn't you miss Tom, too?" His eyes were teasing yet wondering.

"I believe I clarified that quite nicely," I said. "But if you want a straighter answer, of course, I'd miss Tom! But when I have you, I think that it fairly answers your question, darling!"

"Put that way," Dan conceded, "it surely does!"

If anyone had told me that there was real treasure here, I would scarcely have believed it. But I recalled the story of Jesus telling one of His disciples to go look in a fish and he'd find money enough to pay the taxes. Sure enough, he did! I tried to imagine if that were me Jesus had asked, I'd have been scared half to death to peek into a fish's mouth! I wonder, too, if the disciple had a hard time catching the slippery mammal? And that's something like how this unexpected adventure happened - a treasure discovered that held its own mystical aura, but of course, not in the mouth of a fish! It was a good thing, too, because, honestly, I didn't have any desire to open any fish's mouth! Not even for a treasure! But strangely enough, I couldn't take the full credit for uncovering the mystery behind it!

Dan and I enjoyed our day. We walked along the shore in search of more caves, breaking for lunch at noon. We'd just turned around to go back, when I tripped over a hidden piece of driftwood covered in inches of sand, except for a broken branch protruding out that I hadn't noticed. Stumbling, I nearly fell. Right on the shore, we were walking close to the occasional shrubs and trees, that grew in thick groupings of groves, their roots, notably well-established underground, beneath the fine, white sand. Clutching at some overhanging branches cascading to the ground to break my fall, the branches suddenly parted, revealing an opening. Much to my surprise, the overhang was like a densely camouflaged canopy, concealing the entrance of a hidden cave.

"Wow!" Dan exclaimed. Cautiously peering in, he was totally taken with it. "I think it's safe for us to spend the night here, Maggie. No one's been here and I doubt anyone has discovered this cavern. I'll go back and get our gear."

It was about twenty minutes later when I heard our motorbike approaching. Dan pulled right up, and he led it into the cave, parking it against the east side of the wall.

"I didn't see anyone," he said, "and nothing suspicious. Let's take a look and see how wide and deep this cave is, Maggie. You didn't explore it, did you?"

"Only a bit. I wanted to stay near the entrance and keep a sharp lookout for anything unusual, but everything was fine."

"Good!" Dan took two flashlights from his pocket and handed one to me. "I'm going to keep my gun at the ready, too," he said, and I didn't argue with that.

The cave was quite deep and unusually wide.

"I think we should set up about halfway into the cave, Maggie. I want to keep a fire going throughout the night and it's getting late into the afternoon already. I managed to get some of that wood from the first cave on the motorbike, but it won't be enough. I'd like us to quickly peruse the area and see what we can find. Then we'll have supper and rest before retiring. I'm really thirsty, though. Please check and see what Ethel has in that other thermos, would you, my darling?"

"Sure, Dan." I rummaged in the basket, drawing out a huge thermos and a package of Styrofoam cups. Unscrewing the lid, I was happy that it contained water. "Oh, Dan. She also put in a few bottles of different juices, too."

"I'd really love a taste of that water right now," he said.

I poured a cup of water for Dan and handed it to him. He gratefully drank it down, handing me the empty cup when he was finished.

"That really hit the spot. Why don't you gather the napkins and dirty plates while I take a peek outside to ensure that we're still alone?"

By the time that Dan returned minutes later, I was eager to move on.

"I believe it's safe to say that there's still only the two of us here. Are we ready to go then, Maggie?" he asked.

"Yes, Dan."

The air felt warm, yet a coolness was beginning to pervade the region. He guardedly scrutinized the surrounding area through the cascading, leafy branches and nodded.

"It's all right," he said.

Taking my hand, we exited the cave. We walked past the cave and found an abundance of driftwood, which seemed to be everywhere. The sand was beautiful and pristine, as though no soul had ever walked upon its smooth surface. It appeared that this far away from the road into the lake area, was desolate, and untrodden. Carrying different sized pieces of driftwood until my arms were full, we made several trips.

"Perfect! That will do just swell!" Dan said at last, sitting on the blanket after emptying his armload. I joined him. "That should get us through the night, but I think it's warm enough in here that I won't need to light the fire for a couple of hours," he commented. "How about some lunch now?" he asked.

"You read my thoughts, Dan," I agreed. "I sure am getting hungry, too." Rising, I went to the basket, and opened containers of chicken, macaroni salad, and a bean salad. We satisfied our ravenous appetites and rested, falling asleep for a good hour.

When I awakened, Dan's arm was lovingly straddled over me, and I couldn't move. Nudging him, he awakened.

"My arm is sore, Dan," I complained. "You had your arm so tightly over mine that it feels almost numb."

"Oh, Maggie, that can't be. It must be from carrying that wood. Here, let me see," Dan gently said.

In just moments, my arm was hurting so bad, I couldn't keep from crying. "What did you do to me?" I whimpered.

Dan shone his flashlight on my bare arm and instantly pulled it back. "Maggie, I need to get you to the hospital right away," he quietly said. "I don't mean to alarm you, my darling, but you've been bitten. Your arm is red and swelling badly. I'm so sorry, darling." Helping me up, he said, "Sit as still as you can." He tore a piece of his shirttail and made a tourniquet. He sucked as much poison out of my wound as he could, spitting it onto the cave floor. Then, moments afterward, Dan helped me to the motorcycle, then started it up. Looking down at the ground, a spider scurried away, so ugly, that it made me shudder.

"Hurry, Dan," I begged.

Within fifteen minutes, we reached the hospital. Dan explained the situation and I was immediately ushered into an examination room.

The doctor questioned Dan, and the moment he examined the site in question, I couldn't help but cry out.

"Mrs. Danes," he kindly spoke, looking directly into my eyes, "I know this hurts a lot, but you'll need to be very still. I'm going to inject you with an antidote first, and then a strong antibiotic that will work over five days." The nurse prepared the two injections after swabbing the intended area with alcohol and handed Dr. Morris the first needle. "Ready, now, and steady," he quietly said. The needle hurt terribly as it was thrust into my arm. Then, came the second injection. When he was finished, Dr. Morris advised, "You must be kept very quiet during this time. No unnecessary activity." Helping me down from the examination table, he said, "You may go home now, but I want you to see your family doctor immediately if there's any change. Otherwise, everything should be just fine." Smiling, he said, "I do trust that your adventures will lead to safer ground from now on with your husband."

I slept fitfully, but in a few hours, my arm was feeling somewhat better, and the swelling, slightly improved. Dan insisted on taking his work home to keep an eye on me. I loved his nearness and the loving dearness of his heart by which he constantly hovered over me. When Ethel learned of what had happened, she doted on me when Dan was busy elsewhere, or working with the daily duties and demands with the firm, and I was ever grateful.

It was hard for me to be quiet and hardly see my children. They brought boundless joy and strength to my heart in the small amounts of time that Dan allowed them to be with me. It was then that I was reminded of that verse I'd felt so strongly compelled to share with Dan just before we slept that night not too long before we enjoyed our adventure, but for my misfortune. Sitting straight up, I realized that it could have been much worse, but God's hand of grace was with me through it all. Now, I understood why. It said, "For I the Lord thy God will hold thine right hand saying unto thee, Fear not; I will help thee." Isaiah 41:13 KJV. It wasn't just a wayward feeling that Dan, and then I, had had, it was God's impression that He was with us through the storms that unexpectedly buffeted our lives when we least expected them; had no idea they were coming. Sharing my heart with Dan that night, he could hardly speak, he was so moved.

"Yes! I remember that now," he softly said as the tears rolled down his face. "Maggie, that was confirmation given prophetically for this very incident! Something really touched my heart that I wholly took in and believed when you said that God was caring, providing, and protecting us. And without a single doubt, He certainly is!"

"Yes, Dan. The Holy Spirit led me to that verse, and it emphatically spoke to me. It wasn't until I shared it with you that I felt at ease, little knowing the significance it would hold not long afterwards."

The unexpected also came in wondrously lovely ways as well. It was hard for me to be laid up, and when the doorbell chimed the day after the incident, the unexpectedly thoughtful gift of Harry Gerali's heart helped to soothe the longing for my children, where it left my soul breathless to all the goodness I held in God's love, and the caring people He surrounded my life with. I still missed my children, but it somehow made it easier to bear, seeing the flowers, and the love that went behind such care.

Stopping by the following day after my recent encounter, Harry held out a gorgeously enchanting bouquet of beautiful flowers. My heart soared with inner emotion, that I could scarcely speak. Tears began to fill my eyes as I softly brought the bouquet close to inhale their fragrance. The scents were heavenly! I could only imagine what Ethel would say when she came home from the market with Tom!

"Oh, Harry!" I exclaimed. "Thank you so much!" I joyfully cried in glee.

He bent his face to mine, tenderly kissing me on my cheek. "I did say I'd see you and your husband on Monday!" he teased. "I hope you'll forgive me for being a day late?" he chuckled.

"I don't honestly think that I'd have any reason to be upset with you!" I playfully joshed back. Smiling, I exclaimed, "The flowers are lovely, Harry!" I exhorted. "What a bountiful posy of carnations, baby's breath, tulips, and daisies; every one, so special and beautiful!"

Blushing, he answered, "Well, I'm glad to hear that, Mrs. Danes, because I thought that I might just bring you a fresh arrangement again in a few days or so!"

"Ohhh!" I gasped. "That would delightful, but you needn't do that, Harry!"

"I'll have to see to that," he remarked, "and it shall be my pleasure, because I have something rather unique in mind that can't be found in any florists' shops!" he mysteriously said. His eyes twinkled, and cheerily hinting at his surprise, he continued, "Maybe, I'll bring you a buttonhole or two of wildflowers from the nearby meadow where I live!" he proposed with an air of intrigue. "The flowers are a scream with color as far as the eye can see, dotting the woodland in its own serenity of joy, and I'm sure you'll love them!"

"I'm sure I will, and I'd like that just fine, Harry!" I graciously admitted, my heart aflutter.

The colors engaging our presence for the moment, were exquisite against the greenery, and I didn't know how much fuller my heart could be. And I supposed I'd have to wait for the next bounty of such abiding blessing until Harry filled my soul with the blossoms across the wild span. With the joy before me, I could wait quite well!

Dan entered the room, pausing where I was sitting on the divan in the living room, admiring the blossoms. "Wow!" he exclaimed.

"What a treasure! I can assure you, Harry, that I'll adore the flowers as much as Maggie! They're magnificent!"

"I'm pleased to hear that," Harry said. "I couldn't wait to bring some merriment to your Mrs.' heart and I hope you'll both enjoy them!"

Excusing himself after a few minutes, the delight I felt left me breathless to every lovely petal on the stems. Dan went back to his work in our writing room. I fell asleep, awakening half an hour later. Peering out the window, I slowly scanned the backyard, absently drawing my attention to the bower. My back suddenly stiffened, and I sat up straight, not daring to move. My first impression was that I was still dreaming. I rubbed my eyes and looked again. Then, I found my voice, softly crying out with excitement, where Dan was instantly at my side. I pointed toward the arbor. A doe had paused just inside the trellis, standing motionless in its stance, so immense; its eyes shining, and entrancingly beautiful!

"I've never seen anything like this before!" I said with a catch in my voice. Mesmerized in its beauty, emotion swept over me.

"Nor I, Maggie," he gently answered. "I wonder . . ." The doe remained perfectly still, alert to every sound. "Maggie," he softly whispered, "just supposing this is God's way of reminding us of His Care over us? Especially you . . ." he considered, his voice suddenly trailing in the moment. "It's so surreal," he finished, "that I can scarcely fathom the depth of what I'm feeling, knowing how good God is to us."

I cried in his arms as his words took hold and he comforted me. "My darling, I'm so sorry for the trouble that came to you. May God forgive me for this misadventure." Holding me close, Dan wept in my arms as my own tears continued to fall unbidden.

The doe unexpectedly turned its head, and in a flash, gracefully disappeared across the yard as though it had feet light as an angel's wings. "Wasn't she enchantingly stunning?" I praised, as tears welled in my eyes, spilling onto Dan's arm. "There's no doubt in my mind that this was a divine encounter; a miracle!" I expounded. Nestling my head against Dan's shoulder, I added, "My beloved darling," I said, holding him close, "I love you dearer than dear, but I'm assured that this truly is a blessing from God even though, sometimes, it's hard to wait in time through one's healing."

Nodding, he kissed me in my tears, where I could no longer contain all the goodness of the greatness of our God, fully assured of His love that would carry us, and continue to see us through.

We found encouragement in our devotions, and I loved Dan's beautifully musical voice as he quieted my pain in his wondrous presence in song, sitting by my side, or working near as I slept through the days.

Knowing how much I loved roses, as many bouquets that filled our home, remarkably, not one of them contained a single rose. I think God saved that gift just between Dan and me. The diverseness they all encompassed, however, was rich in color with gentle, spicy fragrances that I loved!

The staff shared Harry's sentiment, bringing me wonderfully lush posies that filled our home with their entrancing glory. And true to his word, Harry's extravagant indulgence afforded every pleasure in this joy toward my healing. Wild delphinium blues and forget me-nots were a stark contrast against the baby's breath and pink and orange tiger lilies that I was especially smitten with that Harry had given, amongst his numerous sprays.

Amongst his many, wild buttonholes, much to my astonishment, I was left speechless when he presented me with a delicate flower that literally grew in cow pastures, and I'd long since cherished. They'd always been a childhood treasure that I loved to this day, appropriately named, cowslip. Placing the arrangement on a table, the pure, orange petals seemed to dance in the light streaming through the open window as my soul was mesmerized in the joy of their exquisite beauty. Here, my heart flourished in these manifold blessings and love as my pain gradually lessened and I found that full healing when my medicine was completed.

By the fifth day, I felt perfectly recovered and healthy again. "I'm well now," I told Dan one morning, "and I'd love to sing a song with you!" We often sang together, just as he and his sister, Julia, had enjoyed with each other, too. Like a garment of praise enjoyed, here our love drew us close, as we worshiped God upon the evening's cool in our beautiful garden within the arbor of the sensually trailing roses, or simply took pleasure in the walks along the avenue between the stalwart, tall trees.

Before he could reply, I heard a gentle knock on our door, then Ethel rushed into the room, out of breath, which was totally unlike her. Leaning against a chair, she finally caught her breath and stood up straight. "I'm sorry to bother you," she began, "but for some time, I've been meaning to give you this. It just kept slipping my mind with the Mrs. and all," she apologized. She held out a coin and I wondered where'd she gotten it.

"I don't understand," I said, as I turned it over. It looked to be a rare coin with an Indian Head on it that was U.S. minted. "Where did you get this?" I asked, perplexed more than ever.

"Remember, when you and the Mr. went to the lake – to that cave you accidentally found. You must have picked this up along with the lunch." Still not getting the gist of her talk, she continued. "Well, what I mean to say is, I almost threw it out with the soiled napkins that were in the bottom of the basket. See, when I picked up the napkins and the bottles all together like, I heard a clink, so I carefully checked through every napkin."

"My goodness!" I exclaimed. "That's right! It was just before Dan, and I were about to rest after supper. A sudden strong gust of wind had blown the branches upward, causing a draft, and the napkins scattered everywhere just as I was about to gather them up."

"I don't recall that at all," Dan remarked.

"You wouldn't, because you quietly stole cautiously outside to ensure that we were still alone. I remember it well, because you took your gun with you as an extra measure. By the time you returned, I'd just collected the napkins and food wrappings and put them in the basket. I didn't want them to fly out, so I weighed them down with both the full and empty juice drink bottles Ethel had packed for us."

"Well," Dan said, as I handed him the coin and he carefully examined it, "I can tell you right now, ladies, that this is worth a pretty penny."

Ethel looked downcast. "Just a penny?" she bemoaned. "And after all the trouble I went to, to give it to you!"

"Oh, no, Ethel! It's a strange way to say it perhaps, but it means that it's worth an enormous amount of money. If I'm not mistaken, I believe that's what the 'pretty' stands for," Dan patiently explained to her. "The fact that it has an Indian Head on it makes it extremely valuable."

"Really? Oh, Mr.! Well, pretty or not," she said, "then, I'm so glad that I found it for you!" she exhorted.

"I'll have this appraised immediately, but I wonder how it came to be there?" he asked, a quizzical expression on his brow.

"I haven't the answer," Ethel said, and I couldn't help but smile!

"Nor do I, Ethel," Dan thoughtfully replied, "but perhaps, it was a visiting American or Canadian," my husband mused, "and somehow, the wind or waves carried it into the cave, unless the coin was dropped unawares within the cavern, but there's no way to ever know for sure. Anyhow, thank you, Ethel! We do appreciate you bringing this to our attention," he said most appreciatively.

We said goodnight and Ethel left. I truly was dumbfounded by it. "Imagine that!" I said, scarcely daring to believe it. "But Dan, don't you think that Ethel should receive part of the reward for rescuing it? She's so sweet and honest and I think that she should be rewarded somehow!"

Kissing me, he smiled and replied, "Certainly, my dearest! When we have the exact amount that the coin is worth, I want to give Ethel the surprise of her life!"

CHAPTER 13

Riding High!

W hen the coin was appraised, we were aghast at its value. The Indian Head cent, also known as an Indian Head penny, which had been produced by the *United States Mint*, was indeed, rare. We learned that this coin had been designed by the Chief Engraver at the *Philadelphia Mint*, a man named, *James Barton Longacre*. This penny had been produced from 1859 – 1909. We were enthralled with such an incredible find and Dan and I decided to give half of the money to Ethel. After all, without her, we'd never have known. Yet, without me, there'd have been no coin for her to find.

"This is most generous of you both," she shyly thanked us when we gave her a substantial cheque. "But I didn't find this treasure without you, ma'am, and it rightfully is yours."

"Oh, not at all!" I smiled. "You earned it, and we want to be this blessing to you that you've always so graciously been to us."

"Well, I do thank you most kindly." Her black eyes were shining with gratitude.

"Ethel," Dan said, as she turned to leave, "I think this belongs to you, too." Handing her a sizable amount of cash, he said, "Maggie and I want to give you all of the money from the coin, and with this, we hope that you'll use part of it to take a well-deserved vacation wherever your heart desires before we head for Austria."

"Ohhh!" she gasped, tears welling in her eyes as Dan pressed the bills into her hand. "This is too much," she began to protest. Then she threw her arms about him and danced a happy dance as Dan twirled her about. When she let go of him, she threw her arms about me, too. "Oh, Mrs.! You are both so kind, and I will think hard where I want to take my trip."

"Well, as it happens, Ethel, we stopped by the *Traveller's Paradise* office, and picked out a few brochures for you."

"Oh, thank you!" she gratefully said, as I handed them to her. "I will gladly look through these, every one!"

Ethel chose a lovely place to visit on her vacation and we were so delighted for her! I wanted to buy her a few clothes, and several days later, I took her shopping with me. "I want to purchase a few items for you, Ethel, so please, drop your shyness and look to your heart's content! Whatever you feel you'd like to have, Dan and I want to give this to you as a special gift for everything you do for us and our children."

"But I love to do for you all!" she said, almost in a hurt tone.

Laughing, I took her arm and led her into a ladies' dress shop. "I know you do, dear Ethel, but this is just a special way to thank you in showing our appreciation to you for everything. Okay?"

"Okay," she shyly smiled, looking into my eyes, and I knew her heart was smiling, too!

Ethel decided on an emerald-colored dress with blue, shimmering highlights, that, with every movement, drew out her eyes in sparkling contrast as she turned to peer into the mirror. It was gorgeous and reminded me of the lovely colors of a peacock.

"It's perfect on you," I praised. "And it's cotton with just a little polyester, so it'll be cool when you walk along the beach in the heat. I love it on you!"

"I kind of like it on me, too!" she laughed.

"Well then, what else would you like in here?"

"Umm. Really, Mrs. This is already quite enough."

"Not for me, it isn't!" I exclaimed. "Let's see now. What about that lovely coral blouse over there," I pointed, "and the matching capris? It's adorable! Would you like to try that on?"

"Maybe. But . . ."

Her eyes roved to the next aisle, where an unusual portrait was depicted on an attractively stunning sundress, which gracefully hung on a hanger. I couldn't help but fall in love with it with her.

"It's delightful!" I joyfully exclaimed, when I saw it up close with Ethel.

The background of the sundress was a lovely blue, and beautiful orchids in coral-wines, pink, and shades of varying mauve, intermixed with white, orange, and pink lilies, were elegantly drawn across the wonderful simplicity of the skirt on the right hand-side going upward to the bodice. What I loved best of all, however, were the blue roses tucked in-between, lending an aura of rich tranquility in pleasured bliss.

On the left-hand side, seaweed likewise, similarly sketched, portrayed a large seahorse amidst playful bubbles. Shimmering sparkles, dancing in the light, enhanced the whole beauteous effect, where the picturesque loveliness came alive in an entrancing and wondrous feeling of explicit joy. It was breathtaking!

"Oh!" I said, admiring the sundress. "You must have it, Ethel!" Gently taking the sundress from off the hanger, I handed it to her, and Ethel's eyes sparkled, but she didn't say a word! "Please try the dress on right away!" I insisted, encouragingly.

Moments later, she captured my sentiment, like a picture out of a book. The colorful, vibrant hues wanted for nothing, perfectly accentuating Ethel's delicately refined, and natural beauty. It was most becoming; both sophisticated and endearing, against her Hispanic ancestry as her face beamed with expressive animation.

"It's so pretty on you!" I declared. She smiled and slipped back into the dressing room to change into her street clothes. But when she came back out and handed the dress to me with misty eyes, I knew her heart loved it, as did mine!

Hugging me close, she softly whispered, "I'd like to take it, please, my Maggie dear, if but you don't mind that any."

"For you, my dear Ethel," I lovingly replied, "it shall be my honor in every way!"

The blouse, capris, and sundress fit her attractive, thin frame perfectly and Ethel looked like a model in the clothes.

"I think you should take them all," I encouraged, "but I also would love to buy something with lace, and something white and blue. Let's pay for these items and then shop at another store, shall we?"

The clerk wrapped the packages and I paid for them. We exited the store, and on our way to the next shop, I noticed a shoe store. "I want to buy you a pair of sandals, Ethel." Pausing, I gently took her arm and guided her into the store. "Aren't they pretty?" I asked, admiring several as we made our way to the back of the shop.

"Oh my, yes!" she agreed.

Ethel couldn't decide between two pair, and so I decided that she should have them both. "Variety is good for any apparel one desires," I said, "so I think we might just purchase them both. What do you think?"

Ethel had the sandals in her hands and started to put them back. "Too much," she said, matter-of-factly.

I laughed and retrieved them. "*Not* too much for you, Ethel!" I emphasized. She tried them on, and they were a perfect fit, and so adorable, the first pair especially reminding me of a little princess' elegantly delicate and dainty pair of slippers. The sandals were wrapped and paid for and we headed to the next shop.

As we walked along the sidewalk, Ethel asked, "Excuse me, please, Mrs., but is, what you say, apparel?"

"Oh, that means, clothing – clothes."

Giggling, Ethel looked into my eyes and remarked, "Such funny English words, aren't they?"

"Yes!" I answered. "But you do so well, dear Ethel. I dare say, I'd hardly make a dent half as good as you in knowing two languages!" I cheerily laughed. "But never be afraid to ask me anything, Ethel, because that's the way to learn, and it shall always be my pleasure! As a matter-of-fact," I added, "I don't get all the English words right myself at times because they're mixed with several languages. No wonder you keep telling me it's 'crazy English,' again and again!"

We laughed, and she smiled in appreciation and said, "You and the Mr., always most kind to me." Then, much to my surprise she comforted, "Don't worry any, Mrs. You do quite well with English, I say!"

"Thank you, Ethel! And me and your Mr. are more than happy to help you anytime," I graciously acceded.

"No worry, ma'am," she said looking into my eyes as her mind tried to put it into perspective. "I wanted to come to Canada – your

America – and live my life in your beautiful country. So, I just kept on learning."

Patting her shoulder, I continued. "Now, about that shop over on Lilac Street," I said, to change the subject. "It's just a bit further over that way," I pointed out, pausing on the street. I suddenly felt Ethel gently looking over my shoulder, totally absorbed in my words. "I've only been in there a couple of times myself, but their clothes are beautifully fashioned and so feminine. I'd like to see what they might have for you." Noticing that Ethel seemed to be tiring, I suggested kindly, "After that, we can lunch at one of the restaurants."

"Oh, I'd like that!" she commented as I opened the door of *Ladies Apparel*, and we entered the shop a couple of minutes later.

The clothes were exquisite, and it wasn't hard for us to find what Ethel would look adorable in. A lovely, blue dress, unique from the one just purchased, with a lace bodice and delicate, lace-capped sleeves, drew my attention and immediately captured my heart as I gently rifled through the dresses on a rack near the serving counter. I loved the touch of lace at the bottom of the dress, too! It was absolutely stunning!

"Blue is so pretty," I said. "It's always been my favorite color. It's going to be charming on you, Ethel! That is, if you're interested?" I proposed, hoping she'd agree. Her hands tenderly touched the material and she nodded with pleasure shining in her eyes. She slipped into the dress, and I drew in my breath when Ethel came to stand outside the fitting room. The clerk, looking on, smiled. "Oh, Ethel! This is you!" I celebrated. "It's just gorgeous with your lovely, black eyes and beautiful, black hair!"

"It sure is at that!" the clerk enthusiastically agreed. "I think that you shouldn't wait a moment to take it!"

"Thank you!" Ethel shyly smiled, her face aflush.

"Is there anything else I may help you ladies with?" the clerk asked when Ethel had changed back into her blouse and pants.

"Yes!" I said, smiling. "Something in white with a touch of lace, preferably."

Pausing, the clerk's eyes suddenly brightened, and she said, "I know just the item! Follow me, please, ladies!"

183

When I saw the dress, I could hardly take my eyes off it. "Ethel, could you use another dress on your trip?" I asked.

The white dress was exquisitely tailored with a blue sash over the waistline and white lace that impeccably detailed the shoulders. It had a boat neckline, accentuating its beauty. The dress was accented with tiny, blue stones that sparkled in the light along the slight swirls of the full skirt, which fell just above the knees. And much to my surprise, a pair of white shoes, adorned with shimmering blue stones, beautifully completed the apparel. When Ethel slipped the dress carefully over her head, its lovely, flawless beauty filled my heart with joy!

"But it's too big in the waist," Ethel said, disappointment showing in her eyes. "I cannot wear it."

"Not to worry," the clerk assured. "We have an excellent dressmaker who will readjust that for you at no extra charge. That is, if you wish to purchase it."

Looking at herself in the full-length mirror, Ethel's reflection stared back at her. Twirling softly, a smile slowly widened on her face.

"Oh, I do!" she suddenly exclaimed.

"Then, it's settled. If you have time to wait now, I'll summon Abby and she'll make the adjustment. It won't take long, and if you have something else to do, it'll be ready within the hour."

"That's very kind," I said. "That'll be fine. And now I'll pay for it."

Ethel and I enjoyed a leisurely lunch, but I could tell that she was anxious to get back to the store.

The dress was ready and waiting for her. She tried it on again, and the fit was definitely improved. "I made an extra adjustment," Abby said. "I slightly shortened the length and fitted, or tightened in, I should say, the loose waistline, by cutting out a long piece on either side of the full skirt. Do you like it?"

"Oh, it's perfect!" Ethel exclaimed. "Thank you!"

Abby's eyes expressed her gratitude as she smiled and praised, "It's absolutely stunning on you, ma'am, and I'm most happy to help!" Glancing at her watch, she gently said, "If you'll please excuse me ladies, it was delightful serving you, but I have another customer waiting on my services."

I drew in my breath to the exquisite beauty that added this special pleasure of joy in Ethel's heart. The clerk seemed especially pleased as well. "Abby, she's a very kind soul and loves to satisfy our customers," she said. "Now, is there anything else I may help you with?"

"Yes!" I exclaimed. "Ethel, I want you to have a new purse for your trip."

"No! No! No!" she shook her head. "Much too much, dear Maggie. What will the Mr. think of me with you spending all his money on me?"

Laughing, I said, "Well, this is *my* money, at least mostly, and gifts don't count as 'spending!'" I chortled. "As for Dan, he more than generously told me to buy whatever, and how much, my heart fancied for you! So, there's nothing further to talk about it!" I assured her, smiling. Turning to the clerk I asked, "Would you have just what we're looking for?" I inquired.

Understanding, the clerk led us to the opposite end of the store. "I believe this would be quite pleasing, especially in your travels, am I correct?" she asked.

"Yes!" I answered. "But not for me. Just Ethel."

When we reached the purses, Ethel's eyes grew large.

"Oh, my! Look, Maggie! There's so many to choose from."

"Well, how about something like that black one – on the top shelf next to you?" I suggested. "It's not too big, yet not too small. It will be easy to carry, and I think it should have enough compartments. Except for your white attire, it will suit the colors of all your other clothing today, and we can also choose a white purse for that purpose."

The clerk, standing beside Ethel, offered to reach it. Handing it to Ethel, she was delighted as she opened the two zippered compartments on the top and checked out the front and back zippered smaller compartments. The top compartments also had two extra, inner zippered, sections that were ideal for small items. Ethel tried the purse over her shoulder and the length was a good fit. Looking at the price tag, however, she groaned, handing it back to the clerk.

"Thank you, but I no take," she said.

"Yes, you take!" I insisted.

"No. Too much."

"Ethel, this is our gift to you, and Dan and I will decide what's too much and what isn't, and I assure you that this isn't!" I turned to the clerk, handing her the purse, who had an amused smile on her face. "The tables got turned some time back," I said. "I was the housekeeper and Ethel, the cook. Then I married the Mr., as she calls him, and now I'm the boss! And sometimes," I giggled, "the boss needs to be bossy!"

Looking almost directly above me on the shelf, I caught sight of the prettiest white purse, and asked the clerk to take it down. "Just look, Ethel," I praised. "Isn't it darling? Here," I said handing it to her, "try it out." Holding my breath, tears misted in Ethel's eyes.

"Oh, my! Maggie, it's so, so beautiful! I don't even need to look inside; I dearly love it already." Her hands trembled, and she passed it back to me. "You look inside," she said.

I opened the purse and gasped. It had a lovely blue lining and two good-sized zippered compartments. "It's just marvelous, Ethel!" I exclaimed. "Very exquisite! Oh, you must have it!" I tilted the purse for her to look, and her hand flew to her heart.

"Oh, it is!" she breathlessly exclaimed, impetuously expressing her sentiment. "If you truly don't mind, Maggie, I would like it very much."

"Of course, Ethel!" Turning to the clerk, I said, "I think she found her 'Cinderella' purse. Please kindly wrap this for me."

As I was about to hand the clerk the purse, I didn't realize that I'd inadvertently stepped too close to the shelf, and I bumped hard against the sharp corner of it as pain shot through my shoulder, nearly causing me to lose my footing. Gripping the purse hard, its price tag was clearly visible.

Ethel's eyes were fixed on the mishap, and then the price as I gave it to the clerk. "I changed my mind, Mrs. This is too expensive."

"Well," the clerk interposed before I could say a word, "because you've purchased quite a lot, the store has a huge discount, and this will totally cover the price of the purse, so it won't cost her a penny. In fact, you have another twenty dollars due, so I will just deduct that from the total bill."

Ethel put her head down. "Really?"

The clerk laughed. "I'm more than sure, madame."

"Can't win," Ethel softly said, but there was a hint of pleasure in her words as she looked up to me and then at the clerk, smiling.

"Do enjoy your day, ladies, and thank you for your purchases today. And ma'am," she gently said, "I hope you'll love the trip your Mrs. and Mr. are giving to you!" Blushing, Ethel nodded and quickly followed at my side. She kept quiet on the drive home, and my heart was inwardly smiling.

When we arrived back at the house, I helped Ethel take her packages to her room. "Thank you, Mrs.," she said. "But everything you and the Mr. gave to me is too much, I still say."

"Not for you it isn't, Ethel. And we couldn't be happier to do this for you! If it makes you feel any better, I'll let you in on a little secret. But you mustn't ever tell another soul, especially Dan, alright?"

"Alright!" she said.

"Dan and I just received notice that at the end of this month, we're both getting a raise. Let me tell you, Ethel, Dan's is really big, so it will please him much for you to accept everything he asked of me to give to you, because we have an opportunity today to be this blessing to you, okay?"

"Okay," she said, but I knew she still felt uncomfortable with all the spending we were giving her.

"And even if Dan and I weren't getting these raises, Ethel, we would still want to do this for you, so I want you to try to think about how much we love and appreciate you, especially with our children now. You care for them so beautifully and with such love in your heart, and that means so much to us."

"I'll try, Maggie, but it's a lot for me to take in."

"Well, you've been super generous to us, and now that we can give you something extra, we really want to from both the bottom of our hearts! Please take a rest, and we'll see you later in the evening, okay? Then tomorrow, we will browse another store that should have a colorful purse that's more casual that you might wish to use with any of your apparel. And I have something especially in mind for you that you'll just simply adore!"

"Okay, ma'am." Then, hugging me, she whispered, "I love you, Maggie Danes, and I sure do thank you for this pleasure!" Joy effused from her soul, and I think that I finally got through to my beloved Ethel! I couldn't wait for the morrow to come!

The following day, Ethel and I went to a store I'd always loved, which was in a pleasant area across town. The purses were beautiful and their prices, most reasonable; almost a 'steal,' I'd have to admit! Looking over the selection, Ethel found an absolutely charming purse that would perfectly fit her dresses and casual attire. It even had a matching change purse.

She oohed and aahed over it with joy, clasping her hands to her face. "It's . . . it's so grand!" she delighted. "Oh, Maggie, I love it!" We purchased the item and had an early lunch topped off with an ice cream cone.

"It's a joy to give you this pleasure," I said, looking across the table at her. "It's grand for sure, and I admire the vivid hues that contrast so well to your Hispanic coloring and hair." Pausing, I added, "And there's something else . . ."

When we'd finished our food, we walked over to another store adjacent to the one we'd just been in. "You'll need some casual T-shirts, and this is the best place to find them. You need to also have a couple more pairs of capris and perhaps, long pants, Ethel," I commented.

"Mrs.!" she said. "No! No! No!"

"But you need them, Ethel, and I want to help."

"But I can use the money from you and the Mr.," she insisted. "You'd think I was a mere pauper," she mused, laughing.

"No!" I emphatically said. "Not this time! Remember, that I told you that Dan and I are getting a lot of extra money by the month's end next week. You keep that for a rainy day and let me have this one last pleasure. In fact, I insist on it, and my 'insist' is stronger and bigger than yours!" I cheerily laughed.

Her eyes grew large as she thought it over and looked at me, first with a shrug and then an innocent query. "I suppose I'd forgotten already about that, Maggie. What does a 'rainy day' mean?" she asked, puzzled.

Laughing, I said, "It means, when and if you should ever get into a tight spot, like your money isn't enough for everything, then, if you've already put aside some of it, saved it, that is, you'll have enough to use for that very time."

"But I don't lose money on rainy days, Maggie." Looking perplexed, she suddenly blurted, "Oh, you're fooling me," she said, unsure.

"I'm not, Ethel. Ask Dan or Tom if you don't believe me."

"Okay, I believe you," she said, but there was an almost amused, and hidden perception behind her words that didn't quite seem to fit, and her eyes were mysteriously smiling, almost in a wistful reflection.

Turning back to my thought, I said, "Let's take a peek and see what's available."

When the purchases were made, Ethel was both happy and a bit upset with me, but I couldn't keep from smiling, knowing that Dan and I were able to bless her for everything she always so graciously did to care for our family.

In the days leading up to her departure for her trip to Hawaii, Ethel asked to talk with me near the avenue of trees one night after supper. "I'm sorry for being a bit of trouble, Maggie, for seeming ungrateful," she meekly began, "but it was so, so much, that I am not used to being given. Your loving heart truly means everything to me, and I want you to know how very much I appreciate and love every gift jeweled from your and the Mr.'s heart to mine."

I hugged her close and whispered, "I know, dearest Ethel, and don't you worry about it any. I understand your heart completely and it is such a heart of purest gold."

"Gold, yes, Maggie. Just like yours and my Mr.'s."

We sat in silence on the bench for a time, and then walked together back to the house.

"I'll miss you," we said, almost in unison, as we both turned to face each other just as we reached the porch. Hugging, we held each other for a long moment, drying the tears that misted in our eyes.

"Dan and I," I commented quietly, "want you to enjoy every breathless second in Hawaii," I assured. "Just hurry back as soon as you can when your plane lands on Canadian soil, my friend, because I don't want to miss you a moment longer than I have to without your loving presence."

Looking lovingly into my eyes, Ethel smiled as she answered, "I promise, Maggie. With all my heart, I promise."

Minutes before her departure, I handed Ethel the package I'd recently purchased, and her eyes inquisitively looked into mine. "I didn't forget that something extra special for you," I quietly began. "Time had slipped away on us that day we shopped, and, and . . . Ethel, I can't wait one more moment; please open it!" I excitedly burst out. Ethel stared into my eyes and nodded.

Slowly unwrapping the box, as she opened it, total surprise showed on Ethel's face. "Oh, Maggie, dear!" she exclaimed in astonishment. "How lovely!" Tenderly, she withdrew an exquisite, gold-plated, heart-shaped locket, lovingly fingering it before pressing the tiny button that would unlock it. I had inserted a photograph of her on the left side and me on the right.

"What do you think?" I curiously asked.

"Why, Maggie, it's beautiful!" Impulsively, she hugged me as tears filled her eyes. "I will treasure this always!" she softly whispered. "Thank you so very, very much! I see it's time to go, but I shall always remember these sweetest moments with you, Maggie dearest! I love you!"

"I love you, too, Ethel!"

I watched until Ethel disappeared, and turned my attention to Dan. "I love you, too!" I softly teased.

Dan couldn't resist chuckling, and said, "That was really special, thinking of such a wonderfully unique gift for our Ethel," he said. "I'm sure going to miss her."

Tears filled my eyes. "Me, too," I said. Dan held me close, and we left the airport. Like him, my heart was already missing our dearest, most beloved, Ethel, but I still had my beloved, I consoled myself. He was enough, but still, I'd miss her glowing presence with us every day.

I knew that, when Ethel left, she was *Riding High*, and both Dan and I were thrilled for her! But that ache I'd known when Dan invited me to be his assistant at the publishing firm after I'd first come to work in his home, unsuspectingly crept back into my heart now, and I couldn't help but feel sad. I knew how much her loving presence would be missed in the days to follow, and I could barely stand to be without her love as my precious sister.

Crying softly into my pillow, Dan comforted me that night as tears fell unbidden from my red and swollen eyes, and the heart that fervently broke along with it. A whole fortnight away from my dearest Ethel whom I deeply loved. I didn't know how I ever was going to stand it as my beloved Dan tried his best to comfort and assure me, holding me close and loving me, through these very dark moments I was missing her so. And interestingly enough, I said in my thoughts, if that *Indian Head cent* had never come to our attention, I'd not be missing my dearest Ethel at present. If I had to blame my broken heart on something, I concluded, it was all because of that *Unexpected Adventure*!

CHAPTER 14

Tall in the Saddle

In the excitement before Ethel's vacation, Dan and I had completely forgotten about finding a suitable replacement temporarily during her leave. The following morning, Dan called the agency where I'd gotten my job with him before I came to work at his publishing firm, and because it was a diversified agency, he was able to hire a nanny for the duration that Ethel was away. It was a busy time of year for us at the publishing firm, and we were relieved to have a caregiver for our children.

Anne Fletcher was delightful and patient, and we liked her immediately. The children took to her, and that gave us peace of mind.

I coaxed Dan to create that story with me that we'd planned on long before we married.

"I didn't realize how much work creating a book is," he remarked. "I've only seen the effort from this end." Creasing his brow, he said, "Maggie, will you come and leave your editing and help me with this scene, please?" he asked.

I read through the material we had started and frowned. "See here," I said. "That doesn't sound quite right. I think this scene suggests more flamboyance on the part of the character relating to the flowerbed around the setting. Let me see now," I paused, thinking. Leaning over him, it suddenly came to me. "How about we say it this way?" I suggested. Dan moved his laptop toward me so I could more easily type my thoughts as I began to compose on his laptop, and the words began to come so fast, I could hardly keep up with them. When I was done, I moved over so Dan could peruse the content. "It's likely not perfect yet, my darling," I said, skimming over the material, "but it does lend that celebration that's anticipated in this scene."

Reading it through, Dan hesitated before responding. I began to feel uncomfortable. Perhaps, it wasn't what he was looking for after all. Then, he slowly drew his arm about me and smiled. "Maggie, my dearest, I don't know where you get your ideas from, but this is truly wonderful! The fluency is beautiful; it's graceful, and just what I was looking for, complementing the enchanting backdrop of the setting. Its simplicity brings that feeling of breathless joy forward, heightening the aura surrounding the main subject, as well as lending an airy, welcoming, and grateful voice that I'd missed. In fact, I'd have to say that it's downright exquisite!" he praised. "You have a unique way of seeing things than me that complements exactly what the scene now portrays. As you say, this scene depicts a celebration of what the character is feeling, and that flamboyant gist is perfect, without a doubt! Thank you very much!" Kissing me, I smiled.

"I'm glad to be of help in this!" I said. "Well, darling, do you need me for anything else?"

"Not at the moment. But Maggie, I believe we really complement each other in our creativity, and even though I'm encountering stubborn knots, I am really enjoying this collaboration with you!"

Kissing him, I couldn't resist adding, "Me, too, my darling! I am loving every moment of it with you! And don't forget," I reminded him, "you created the character, so my hat is off to you! I merely worked around the setting as to how the character imagined, and saw, the scene!"

Near the end of the day, I happened to glance at Dan through the glass window of his office, and he seemed to be deep in thought. I wondered what was troubling him now, if anything. I didn't wish to intrude, but unexpectedly, he peered through the window straight at me, and beckoned me to come.

"Are you alright?" I asked, concerned. He looked tired and weary from the day's work.

"Oh, I'm fine, my darling. Right now, all I want is you at my side. You know, I stumbled on another knotty scene, and I was thinking that, perhaps you might help me out again?"

Laughing, I said, "I'd be happy to! But why don't you leave it for now? If you post it to our email at home, I promise to take a look at it this evening, and we can work on it together."

Dan seemed a little upset over the whole thing. Maybe, he expected me to do it now. "Or is that too late?" I asked.

"Oh, no. Not at all. I appreciate this, Maggie. For now, I believe that a break will be good to clear my mind. Well, time to head for home," he commented. "I hope that Anne made us a good meal. I sure feel hungry."

We were the last to leave the office and arrived home just after four o'clock. A wonderful aroma wafted in the air as I opened the door and entered the kitchen.

"Something smells so tempting," I smiled, taking off my jacket. Stepping up to the counter, I peeked into the oven. "Whatever you made, I can hardly wait to eat, and my husband is starving!" I commented.

"I hope you like it," Anne shyly said. "I made a lazy cabbage roll casserole. Also, a mandarin salad and sweet potatoes."

"Oh!" I exclaimed. "No wonder the house is filled with such a wonderful aroma!"

Blossom entered the room, running toward me. "I missed you, Mom," she said, giving me a big hug.

"I missed you, too, my darling," I said.

"Is the baby sleeping, Anne?" I asked when Blossom left my side to hug her uncle.

"He is. I can go check on him right away if you'd like me to?"

"No. That's fine. I'll go. Why don't you just sit and relax for a few minutes before serving the meal?"

"Thank you, ma'am," Anne politely said. "I just put the casserole and potatoes in the oven half an hour ago, so it'll be ready at five o'clock. If you need a snack, there's a bowl of fruit and those crackers you like so well. I'll be happy to quickly fix that up for you if you like," she asked.

"I think I would, please," I replied.

As I climbed the stairs to my bedroom, I suddenly felt almost ill with hunger. I was very grateful for Anne's consideration of the snack and enjoyed it with Dan after I'd checked on our baby. Leaning over the crib, I lightly kissed Carlos' forehead, and tenderly stroked his face. Dan affectionately patted his tummy and smiled lovingly up at me, taking my hand in his. His eyes seemed to convey a hidden message – a secret yearning – and it almost felt like he was already thinking of having another child with me! I shall love that, I smiled in my heart, but not for some time! He kissed me most tenderly, and my heart merely smiled in the warmth of that glow, as I turned my attention to Carlos again. He was peacefully sleeping and looked like a prince, the sweetest ever to be born, I thought to myself! I was tempted to awaken him and hold him in my aching arms, but I left the alcove where he peacefully was sleeping, and quietly left. We rested until 5 p.m. when Anne called us to the table for supper.

We found Anne to be as equally capable as Ethel. But it still took some adjusting and there were those days that I found myself missing Ethel terribly. I tried to hide my tears, but one night, as I walked alone through the avenue of trees and onto the beautiful flower garden, I couldn't help but cry my heart out. I finally reached the bench where the lilacs were silhouetted in the moon's warm glow as its light splashed across the path. The birch trees behind the lilacs swayed in a musical lilt with the wind, their branches providing a beautiful canopy overhead. Thoughts of perhaps never seeing Ethel again flooded my imagination. Or maybe she'd find a man to marry and leave us forever. What if something happened on her trip? Then suddenly, a lone figure sat beside me, wrapping me in his love.

"Dearest Maggie," he lovingly, gently spoke, "what is troubling your heart so?"

"Ethel!" I cried, in one word. "What if she's gone forever? Oh, why did we ever give her this trip, Dan? Why?"

"Because she was deserving of it. You know how happy you made her shopping that day. And she'll return. I promise."

"Promises can't be made in the unknown," I said.

"But they can, my darling. I mean, this isn't a thoughtless promise." Reaching in his pocket, he pulled out a wrinkled letter and handed it to me. "I truly apologize for forgetting to give you this letter today," he said. "It's from Ethel. Why don't you open it and read what she says?"

I eagerly tore open the envelope and began to read the soothing words that gathered like a fragrant bouquet of flowers in my sadness. My heart began to quiet as tears flooded my eyes.

Dear Mrs. Maggie,

How are you? I'm having a wonderful time, and everything is so beautiful! I think of you and Dan and the children every day and pray that you got a nice person to help you out in my absence.

Walking on the beach at night is like being, what you say, in a fairytale book, but I know that this is real! The sunsets and sunrises are extraordinary and breathtaking. I think that I could live here all my life and still not believe that I was in this exquisite setting and in this perfect paradise.

I have something to tell you, but it will need to wait until I am back with you. Just a secret between you and me. No Dan. Not until later, anyway!

Just a few more days in this gorgeous paradise, then home to you, dear sister, as we had planned! I miss you and I can't wait to see you, Maggie!

Please, could you ask Tom to pick me up at the airport if your Mr. be too busy?

My love,
Ethel Rodriguez

Beneath her name, Ethel had drawn a heart.

"Is everything all right with her?" he asked.

"Oh, Dan! Yes! Perfectly all right. She's having a wonderful time and says that she'll be back home on Friday. That's only three days from now. Just think! Our Ethel is coming home!"

"She would go nowhere else," Dan lovingly said, as he embraced me in his arms, and softly kissed me. We lingered in the beauty all about us and I could hardly wait until Friday arrived.

I was so happy that my heart felt free and light to all the joy just waiting in the days ahead. Only three more days until Ethel would be with us again! We needed to celebrate, I told Dan. I hoped he would agree to Anne putting out a spread for us to welcome her homecoming. And with everything that needed to soon be readied for our travels to Austria, I wondered, too, if just perhaps, Dan would accede to keeping Anne on until the day we departed.

Anne worried that Ethel might think she was overstepping the boundary. I assured her that Ethel was so, so sweet, it would be a joy for her to have someone to help her with the duties and preparations for our plans ahead.

When Ethel arrived back home, she was both excited and tired. Her plane had been delayed a few hours, but she called to let us know, and it wasn't until that evening when she placed her feet on our estate again.

"Oh, I'm so happy to be back on this splendid Canadian soil with you again, even though I just loved my trip in Paradise!" she exclaimed, hugging me as if there were no tomorrows. When she'd greeted everyone, she sank into a comfortable chair in the living room, and Anne, who was busy rocking Carlos to sleep, slowed her pace until the rocker settled, and she carried Carlos to his crib upstairs. She appeared shortly with a steaming cup of lemonade and freshly baked biscuits.

"Mmm . . . this just hits the spot," Ethel appreciatively praised. "I'm going to plop into bed right after I've eaten every crumb." Anne beamed, and together, we shared the evening snack with Ethel.

I suddenly remembered something. "Ethel, would you mind taking the second guest room next to ours tonight? Anne is staying on until we leave for Austria, and . . ."

"Oh, no, ma'am," Anne interrupted. "I will move out tonight so Ethel may have her room back."

"But you have everything of yours hanging in the closet and the dressers. You don't mind, do you, Ethel? Just for tonight? We had a painter come and so this is why we put Anne in your room," I explained.

Ethel looked so tired, and I hoped we hadn't upset her. "Not at all," she pleasantly said. "Just as long as I may now put my head to the pillow."

Anne looked uncomfortable, but Ethel waved her hand, saying goodnight.

"I had Tom bring in your bags and place them in the guest room already," Dan gently said. "He was good enough to oblige and help me."

"Oh, Tom! How is he? I'd like to thank him before I sleep," Ethel said.

"Tom's already departed, but he said to tell you that he has a surprise and will show you it tomorrow."

Tears filled Ethel's eyes and I wondered why. "Tom, he is so good to me, like you," she said, and I thought that rather an odd statement. But she seemed to be especially content in the moment and my thoughts were immediately drawn back to Tom again, and I'd no idea why. We said goodnight as she arose and hugged us. "So good to be back. So good!" she said, disappearing down the long corridor moments later. The curiosity part in me yearned to know what significance lay behind those words concerning Tom, if any, but I had to curb that curiosity for now, and I hoped it wouldn't be forever! As patient as I usually was, there were times when it seemed like the sand had run out of that imaginary hourglass of mine, and it nearly drove me crazy!

Anne gathered the dirty dishes and took them to the kitchen.

"Just leave them, Anne," I said. "It's late and the morning's soon enough. Go have yourself a good sleep tonight."

"It's no trouble and I don't mind, but if you wish . . ." she said.

"Whatever takes your fancy, but the morning is truly soon enough," I smiled, hugging her goodnight.

When I entered the kitchen the next morning, the sinks were empty, and a lovely aroma permeated the room. "Why," I said in surprise to myself, "Anne must have changed her mind and washed the dishes after all last night." But when I stepped into the dining room, Anne was nowhere to be seen, but Ethel was already up and about, humming softly.

When she saw me, Ethel greeted me with a big, warm hug. "Breakfast is almost ready," she said, placing the silverware at the respective plates. "You and the Mr. must hurry to enjoy it hot. And where is Anne?" she considered.

"Anne? I wondered that myself, Ethel. She must be tired from tidying the kitchen last night and doing up those dishes, and the excitement of meeting you, I assumed," speaking a bit run-on.

"She no done it," Ethel said, still slightly bent over, putting the last place setting of silverware down, then standing straight up.

"She no done it?" I asked, using Ethel's poor English. "Then, who?"

A voice behind me softly chuckled. Turning, I was shocked to see Tom quietly come up and stand next to Ethel as he took her hand in his. For now, that went over my head, not thinking much about it, except that Tom was glad to see her, and I temporarily dismissed the unlikely significance of him taking her hand. After all, I considered, he had the right to miss her, too!

"Why, Tom! Did you smell the wonderful breakfast cooking, also?" I asked.

"Me?" Still holding Ethel's hand, my thoughts began to trail in different directions. While it was unusual for Tom to do so, I felt confused, but said nothing. Ethel took walks all the time in the garden. It wasn't hard to see that she was drawn to the flowers every day, so it was only reasonable to understand that they had missed each other. Furthermore, I'd often seen them conversing together, deep in thought at times, bending over the flowers together. Tom rarely entered the house, and . . . Then, the realization hit me.

"You, Tom. Did you do the dirty dishes from last night this morning?" I voiced my thoughts out loud.

"Yes, Mrs. Danes. Ethel and I did them together. We made the breakfast together, too!"

"But . . ."

Voices suddenly drifted down the corridor, but Ethel and Tom remained, still holding hands. I heard Anne's cry of surprise as she entered the kitchen to find everything in order, and breakfast's pleasant aroma wafting in the air. Blossom appeared moments later, coming to stand at my side.

"How did this happen?" Anne asked, dismayed, looking about. "Oh, I'm sorry, Mrs. Danes. Please forgive me! I slept fitfully and I see the clock is half past eight now. My apologies. But what's that wonderfully delightful aroma?"

"I know!" a voice behind me piped up. "And what a lovely surprise it is! Lefse keeping warm in the oven, and fresh strawberries in the fridge as well as a casserole dish of potatoes, and freshly baked cabbage buns." Dan came quietly behind me, holding me close with his arms about me.

"That is a lovely surprise!" I agreed. Turning to my husband, I suddenly said, "How would you know what's for breakfast in the fridge, my darling?"

"Well," he laughed, "I admit that I was up earlier and caught these two at it. Ethel was just placing the strawberries in the fridge."

Pausing in thought momentarily, I said, "I see." I drew my attention back to Ethel and Tom. "Oh, but Ethel and Tom, that's too much work, but we thank you ever kindly."

Ethel began to reply but was interrupted by Tom. "Well, I best be off," he said, releasing Ethel's hand. Her eyes looked into his like liquid love for a brief moment, and I wondered what was up. Tom did have a surprise for her, Ethel had told me, and I was more than eager to learn about it than ever! It really seemed like he had missed her a lot! I supposed it could get lonely in the garden as he went about his work, even though he loved it, and perhaps, he had a lot to share with Ethel in that regard.

"Tom," I said, as he started to walk to the door. "You surely haven't had your breakfast, so please stay, especially with all the work you did to help our Ethel. You and Ethel be our guests today. Making this lovely meal is more than enough work for today, and I want you both to relax and enjoy yourselves."

Tom seated himself next to Ethel, a little too close, perhaps, I thought, especially when there was ample room, and I was beginning to have my suspicions, farfetched though they might be. But Ethel could hardly stop from smiling, and she barely touched her breakfast.

"You eat like a butterfly," Blossom said, noticing. "Maybe you will fly like one, too!" she innocently said. Blossom adored butterflies, so she misunderstood the "bird" part of the true saying, which went, ". . . eat like a bird," meaning, just a little. Somehow, I thought her perspective was a lot quainter and so very exquisitely lovely!

Ethel choked on her coffee, tipping the mug as she overcompensated in an attempt to place it back on the table as it poured out all over the table, and onto her. "I spilt some on my dress," she said. "Beg your pardon."

I began to ask her if she was hurt from the hot liquid, but Tom immediately pushed back his chair, and taking Ethel's arm, escorted her up the stairs as they excused themselves from the table. I wasn't sure what to make of it.

Tom was waiting for Ethel at the door while she changed her dress, and stepping out of the room, she was now wearing the cool, coral blouse and capris I'd purchased for her trip. Something just had to be up. I was curious as to what Tom might be to her, and I would have loved to have tagged along, at least at a distance!

An hour later, Ethel gently knocked on my bedroom door. "Mrs.," she looked into my eyes imploringly, "would you mind if Tom and I spend the day together? He said you gave him the day off and I want to accept his surprise to me. He said it's in the city."

I put my arm about her shoulder and lovingly said, "Of course, my dear Ethel. You certainly deserve to take the day off to have your pleasure, as I said earlier. Enjoy it with Tom," I chuckled, and said in passing, without pausing, "but I shall be anxious to know something about it whenever you feel you wish to share it with me!"

"Oh, thank you, Mrs.! Thank you!" She kissed me lightly on my cheek, something Ethel had never done, and her face blushing in the morning glory within the warmth of the day, hurried out of the entranceway of my room, running down the corridor as though she was as light-footed as a deer.

"I know that feeling," I said, joy arising in my heart. "I know it all too well. But could it really be? I think that Ethel's riding *Tall in the Saddle*, I smiled to myself, and it made my heart so happy, I didn't know if I should laugh or cry, but I figured that eventually, they'd come together! I was rather surprised that Tom had something special in the city for her. I was quite sure that it would have led them to the flower garden they both adored so and took such pleasure in.

With all my heart, I longed to talk with her before they left, but in their excitement to start out, time didn't seem to hold their horses down at the "hitching post" a moment longer than was necessary, I chuckled to myself. That left me no alternative but to curb my curiosity a while longer. In that waiting, I prayed with all my heart that love had found its way to my dear Ethel!

CHAPTER 15

A Secret Revealed

Anne appeared rested and seemed to enjoy her duties as she went about her day. By early evening, I heard Tom's car pull into the drive. He stepped out, walked to Ethel's side, and opened the door for her, helping her out. Her hands were laden with packages, and Tom then opened his trunk, and pulled out a few more bags.

Tom helped Ethel by carrying the purchases to her room. Anne had cleared out her stuff, and Ethel appreciated her room back, although she hadn't minded the night in the second guest room.

I innocently hurried up the stairs a few steps behind them, hoping to have a little chat with Ethel in case she remained in her room for the night. I expected she was tired from her long day out, but I wanted to hear a bit about her trip. Knowing what a gentleman he was, I didn't expect that Tom would be keeping her any, except to help with the packages, then bidding her goodnight.

Tom was relieving Ethel of her handful of packages after setting the ones he was carrying down on the nearby table. I happened to be walking toward her room at that precise second, hoping he'd be soon out the door, but to my astonishment, the door stood slightly ajar, and I could see that from the short distance I was away from her room.

Tom turned to face Ethel, and lovingly smiled. To my utter amazement, he gently bent his head towards her and passionately kissed her. In that moment, I knew my heart was right in this. I didn't want to be seen, and quietly hurried to my room and closed the door, pausing to get my thoughts in proper perspective. I felt all in a dither, when a voice suddenly questioned, "Whatever are you doing facing the door, my dearest?" I nearly jumped out of my skin, my heart right along with it!

"Oh my, Dan," I said. "Please don't ever sneak up on me like that again!"

"What's the matter with you today, Maggie? You seem to be bothered by something. Is there anything I might be of help to you?"

I nearly fainted! Right then, I knew that I needed to get my emotions under control. Dan mustn't know . . . not yet. Not until Ethel and Tom decided it was privileged information to share with us.

But what explanation could I honestly give my husband? Then, it hit me. "Dan, I'm just very glad that Ethel is home safe and that she's feeling so happy. I can't wait to have her tell us all about her trip."

"Oh, well, that makes sense. Are you sure that's all?"

"For the moment, that's all," I replied. Before he could respond, I went to the bathroom and splashed cold water on my face. I heard Carlos awaken from his nap and Dan lovingly take him out of the crib. When I came out of the bathroom, I suddenly felt extremely tired. Dan was about to hand Carlos to me, but I managed a smile and asked, "Would you take him, darling? I'd like to rest a little, if you don't mind, and I'd most appreciate it."

Understanding, Dan merely shrugged and lovingly replied, "Sure, Maggie." Lifting Carlos in the air in a playful gesture, Dan exited the room with him, softly closing the door behind them. I knew that everyone would more than be happy to give our son attention while I got my thoughts together and my emotions under control. Closing my eyes, I was soon asleep.

Dan called me for supper just after I'd awakened. I glanced at the clock. It was six, and I was feeling more like myself again as my thoughts drifted back to Ethel and Tom.

Tom stayed for supper, which wasn't unusual, then afterwards, he and Ethel took a walk to the garden when it was finished.

"It's such a lovely night," Ethel said. "The stars – so pretty."

About an hour later, Ethel knocked on my writing room door, and asked if we might take a walk through the avenue of trees. "Tom has left, and I need to share something with you."

"The secret you mentioned in your letter, Ethel?"

"Yes, Mrs. But there's a chill come up, so best you put something warm over your blouse."

I threw my cloak over my shoulders and waited for Ethel to get her shawl. Closing the door quietly behind us seconds afterward, we soon enjoyed the night air, walking along the avenue. The sky was breathtaking as the moon arose high in the sky and the stars above twinkled, where the world was perfect, and at total peace all around us. We were enthralled by the wonder before us!

With eyes shining bright, the joy of Ethel's words filled my soul, and I wondered how I'd never seen it between her and Tom before. "Tom asked me to marry him while I was in Hawaii," she said. "We've been spending months together, especially when you and the Mr. retired for the evening. We'd sit by the far garden, walk the avenue of trees, and wander amongst the flowerbeds. Such joy I've never known before."

"I see," I said, not knowing what to say.

"Well, I fancied him the first day I came to work for the Mr. – before you and the Mr. met. But he didn't seem to notice me at first. Then, one day, he, what you say, snuck into my kitchen and said he'd like to take a stroll with me. I didn't know what that meant. He laughed and said, I'd see! I trusted him, so I told him that I would be happy to take that stroll with him, and he was always the great gentleman.

"Every now and then, when I'd wander the garden, I'd unexpectedly find him at my side. 'Your eyes are like shining stars, glinting in the darkness of the light like the moon,' he'd tease, 'and so, so very pretty.' At first, I felt funny about that. But then I asked a friend of mine, and she told me he was complimenting me.

"Another time," she continued, "he tiptoed so quietly into my kitchen just after you and the Mr. went to bed, that I didn't know he was there. Then you turned around and called out to me, and he hid behind the shadows of the kitchen door."

Laughing, I asked, "What did I want?" I inquired.

"Oh, that!" she smiled. "It was when you couldn't sleep, and you asked me to make you a hot lemon drink! Well, Tom stayed behind the door all the time I was fixing it, because he didn't dare want to have you catch him! After that, I always made sure that you and the Mr. stayed put in your room – no wanting hot lemon!"

"That's why you asked me every night if we wanted anything else before retiring?"

"Yes! But Tom tried to stay out of my kitchen after that. I met him at the back door, where we visited each other in the garden. Some nights he just waited in the garden by the fountain."

"And tonight?" I curiously asked.

"Tonight . . . oh, Mrs. Maggie, tonight he asked me to be his wife for sure and look what he put on my finger! Stones! Beautiful, glittering stones! Isn't it pretty?"

"Oh, Ethel! I'm so happy for you and Tom! You're engaged! And yes, the stones are pretty. But we call them diamonds. How exquisite your ring is! I can't wait to see Tom and you together and share my joy with both of you, just as I'm sharing it alone with you right now! So, this was your secret?"

"Uh huh. Isn't it grand? Just grand?"

"Just grand, Ethel! Just grand!" We hugged and cried and laughed it seemed, all at once. "I'd like to tell Dan about your special news this evening," I said. "Is that okay with you?" I asked.

"Oh, goodness, yes!" she happily cried. "You must!"

I was about to say how happy this news would make Dan, too, when a startling realization hit me. "But Ethel," I said, "what about Austria? And working for me and the Mr.?"

"I . . . I want to go, but my heart wants to stay here, *with Tom,*" she emphasized. "We want to marry right away. But, Maggie, I have something especially important to tell you, a special secret to share with you, and we'd like to know right away. Tom, he wants to build a special greenhouse for you and the Mr. To grow rare flowers and win ribbons and lots of money for you. He asked me . . . he asked me if I'd still care for your home and if I do, then he hopes to build the greenhouse on your land?"

"What a wonderful project!" I exclaimed. Considering, I continued, "I'm sure that you and Tom have thought about this for some time," I slowly said, scarcely taking it in, carefully choosing my words. Ethel's eyes lit up, nodding, and I quickly encouraged, "That's such a lovely gesture, but I need to talk with Dan. So, Ethel, I don't want you to worry about it any. My imagination is already picturing so much beauty and joy that I can hardly wait! I know Dan's heart, and I'm sure that he'll understand, and agree wholeheartedly. You've really taken me by surprise, and I'm just thrilled for this unexpected venture, and it's most worthy of our attention! Not to mention your engagement to Tom tonight! Would you like me to talk to Dan this evening, or as soon as I can?"

"Would you? Oh, Mrs., that would be most grateful of you," Ethel said, hugging me as tears ran down her cheeks. "I can't wait to tell Tom!" Then, she turned around and was gone before I even had the chance to hug her and bid her goodnight. My goodness, I said to myself, this was the first time this ever has happened! Chuckling, I understood, reminding myself of what a man can do to a woman she's in love with, and him with her!

I also knew that Ethel got the grateful part wrong, but I didn't have the heart to correct her. Especially, when I knew only a couple of words in her Spanish, I told myself. I long understood her meanings, and this was no exception. But thinking on that as I walked back to the house, perhaps it wasn't misplaced after all. Dan and I would indeed be grateful . . . grateful to have their dedicated loyalty and friendship. I knew deep inside my heart that Dan would understand as I, and there'd be no need for persuasion. I believe that in itself was enough to hold *A Secret Revealed*, and everything that had so wonderfully come to us, which more than said it all! Then, much to my surprise and delight, as I was leisurely walking back to the mansion, a shadow was suddenly coming toward me, until the light of the moon fell on a beautiful face, illuminating her presence.

"Oh, Mrs. Maggie," the voice breathlessly said, as I lingered on the garden path. "I was so happy to tell you my good news that I couldn't help but skip along to meet my Tom for a while as we'd planned. But now he's gone home, so I want to give you a hug and say goodnight to you as we always do, if you don't mind too much. Maybe, you'll forgive me a little in this, too?" she asked, her eyes questioning, but hopeful.

Linking arms with her, I heartily laughed. "Well, dear Ethel, I surely forgive you! I perfectly understand, too. That's exactly how I felt when I knew that Dan loved me, and I wanted to run as free as the deer in the forest!"

"You did?" she exclaimed, her lovely eyes growing large, fully comprehending everything her heart similarly desired as mine had.

"I did!"

"Wow! Do you think all women feel that way?"

"I don't know the answer to that, but I'd expect that most of them do," I replied.

"I see. Well, Maggie, Tom asked me to ask you if you would be my matron of honor and Dan his best man? Do you think you could? We'd love to give you that pleasure on our wedding day!"

"Oh, Ethel! We would! We would!" I happily exclaimed, tears filling my eyes. "We couldn't ask for a higher pleasure! Thank you so much for this!"

"Well, now, Maggie, I suppose the night is calling me to lay my head on my pillow. But I won't run ahead of you this time. I'd like to walk, side by side, with you back to the mansion."

"Of course, dear Ethel! Nothing would give me more joy!"

A Secret Revealed. Mmm hmm . . . I think I was walking there right alongside my Ethel like a light-footed doe, and I could hardly wait to see what else this wondrous future would bring to us all!

The lights of the lanterns along the backyard bathed the mansion in welcoming fortitude. And I don't suppose that I ever did mention that the garden was beautifully lit through the night as well – a lovely artistic design of Victorian lanterns amongst the paths within the walkways of the flowers which Tom had designed with Dan shortly after we'd married.

The frogs were singing in the creek, bathing my soul in the ritual of their musical accord. As ugly as most frogs are, (aren't they all? I paused, considering my thoughts), I smiled to think that God had imparted such a gift to us, if we but had the ears to hear, and the time to listen to the blessing of their chorus! And we'd even find His humor more than there within the joy of their songs!

I knew that I wouldn't sleep for a while, but Ethel immediately retired for the night once we entered the house. I didn't feel like being alone, longing for some companionship. When I asked Dan to sit with me, he willingly agreed. We fixed a bowl of fruit: grapes, kiwi, cantaloupe, and melon. Dan poured two tall, frosty glasses of cold lemonade to enjoy, along with a medium-sized platter of Ritz crackers, my very favorite, and thinly sliced marble cheese.

"I have a surprise for you, darling," I began, as we sipped our lemonade. "Tom and Ethel became engaged tonight, and they have asked us to be in their wedding party. Isn't this wonderful? I knew you'd agree, don't you, my love? So, I said yes on your behalf as well as mine."

Dan set his drink down and thoughtfully considered. I didn't know what he was thinking, and I was becoming rather concerned. He had to be equally happy as me about Ethel's engagement to Tom, but perhaps, I should have privately asked him first before speaking on his behalf about the wedding party. But I was so sure he'd agree, after all, why wouldn't he?

Then joy flooded my soul as he lovingly said, "My beloved darling, this is a precious gift so lovely, I hardly know what to say about Ethel and Tom's engagement. And you are also truly wise in knowing what my heart feels and desires, sometimes more than I do. But in this instance, there's no other wonderful answer than in the privilege this gives me such total and great joy to say yes with all my heart for the honor of being a part of their wedding party!"

Deep joy filled my heart as I set aside my lemonade, and I threw my arms wholeheartedly around my husband's neck. Holding him tight, I kissed him in deepest love as he tenderly held me, kissing me back.

"Thank you, my darling Dan!" I blissfully said. "I know that this will be a day of wondrous rejoicing together, and I am looking forward to it, soon, just as Ethel's heart desires it to be!"

"As I am, too," he said. "Well, my Maggie, I believe I've had enough food, darling," Dan flirtishly hinted, his eyes mischievous and twinkling. "Are you soon ready for bed?"

"Yes, Dan. I'm just as ready as you!" I think the greenhouse would have to wait a little bit longer, I told myself. Ethel's engagement was news far more than we could hardly take in at the moment, I smiled to myself, let alone thinking about such exciting adventures!

We put away the food we hadn't eaten in the fridge after we'd satisfied our hunger and headed for the bedroom. The quiet of the night was lovely . . . stars glittering like jewels against the sky. The frogs had finished their symphony and the birds had stilled their song.

Slipping into my nightgown, I soon joined Dan. He held me close, kissing me in tenderest passion. He always managed to be the first in bed, it seemed. Maybe, because he simply threw his clothes on the chair next to his nightstand, whereas I didn't want my clothes to crease, and carefully hung them in the closet. For whatever reason, there was no better gift than to have his love at my side. I loved saying goodnight with kisses and tenderness in the nearness of his loving presence. The dawn would come soon enough, I told myself as I clicked off my lamp on my nightstand. I closed my eyes, dreaming of flowers blossoming against a forest of trees as I walked through a meadow. Beyond a hill, where I appeared to suddenly stand moments later, several swings suddenly appeared where the forest ended, and two little girls and a boy were having the time of their lives enjoying this pleasure! Then, the scene faded, and the colors of a rainbow appeared as rain softly began to fall upon the earth. The children got off the swings and twirled themselves with glee, merrily laughing, then holding hands, enjoying the rain. A woman appeared from afar with a man at her side, but everyone's features in this scene were indistinct from where I was seeing this beautiful joy played out. When the children saw the couple from afar, they ran with delight toward them, but their faces were hazed in that distance, so I could not identify them from the hill where I stood. It was here that my dream ended.

Upon my awakening the joy I felt within this nighttime dream would come to linger throughout my busy morning, and I pondered whether it held any meaning. I put it aside, concentrating on my work at the office. I forgot about it in the weeks following until, in time, I would reflect on this dream through the heart of my daughter, Blossom, and it became more real within its hidden meaning, and neither I nor Dan would be disappointed in it at all!

CHAPTER 16

Meadow's Bliss

Harry Gerali wanted to see me one morning as he stepped into my office and lightly knocked on the partially open door. "I know how busy you and Mr. Danes have been lately, and I thought a change might do you both good. I'm wondering if you'd like to see the meadow where I picked those posies for you – at my place," he emphasized. "The blossoms are constantly changing and I'm sure you'll love the view!"

"Oh, yes, Harry!" I exclaimed. "We'd love to!"

"Well, it's my housekeeper's day off, but I already asked her if she'd whip up a nice supper for us, that is, if it suits you. I know this is short notice, but sometimes, that seems to work better than any engagement we plan!"

"Thank you, Harry! This is so thoughtful of you! It will suit us perfectly, and I'll give Ethel a call not to expect us for supper tonight. Perhaps, if you don't mind, you'd tell Dan for me?" I asked.

"Sure! I'll be happy to, Mrs. Danes!" he cheerily said.

As he turned to walk out of my office, I said, "Just one more thing, please, Harry."

"Yes?" he politely asked.

"From now on, I'd very much like for you to address me as Maggie!" I giggled.

He stood there thinking, then smiling, answered, "As you wish, Maggie! It shall be my pleasure!"

I was so excited about seeing Harry's meadow! I tried to imagine the blossoms dressed in varying hues, their petals softly tossing in the wind. But when we arrived, I couldn't have been more pleasantly surprised or inspired. The meadow was truly an amazing and iridescently picturesque panorama of breathtaking beauty stretching farther than the eyes could see, and incredibly more than my heart had envisioned!

We joyfully walked a narrow, stone path that Harry had laid down shortly after he'd purchased his homestead and the meadow that went with it, wandering carefree along the lavish beauty of its immense glory.

Brown-eyed Susans, multi-varied colored cosmos, bluebells, delphiniums, lupines, bachelor buttons, cone flowers, and several other blossoms none of us knew the names to, were a medley of ecstatically prolific joy.

Wild roses, with their enticing fragrance, bordered the east side of the parcel, where they blended with a showcase of purple lilacs flanking the meadow on the west. Their perfumes wafted in wondrous scent over the land!

There were even those wondrous cowslips that Harry had brought to me, brightening the meadow with their cheery, orange hues tucked amongst the white daisies and baby's breath, stealing almost unnoticed, upon the gentle breeze. I'm just perplexed how the "slip" ever fits into "cowslips," I thoughtfully considered. Why simply not have said, "cow flower?" Oh, well! That's life, I chuckled. But could it be, I pondered, because a cow had slipped amongst these gorgeous, orange blossoms, and was so named?

I hadn't seen bluegrass since I was a teenager, with their tiny, blue flowers. Here, they flourished amongst the meadow floor, plump against their short, dark-green stalk, always one of my favorites! They resembled grass so much, that they were well camouflaged between the greenery, although their stems are darker in hue. In perfect measured days, their dainty, violet-blue flowers unfurled their petals, exclaiming their praises to the world! I think that this bluegrass blossom may take the name, *Blue Note Blue-eyed Grass* or perhaps, *Blue Grass Lily*, but because it's been so long since I've had the privilege to see it again until now, I can't be quite sure which it might be. It was always aptly named *Blue Grass Weed* in my childhood years, and sometimes without the *Weed* attached!

Bluebells, perfect, and divinely unique, always held me fascinated within the heritage of their spellbound joy, as these danced this day to the rhythm provoked upon the wind!

Poppies of various colors accented the richness denoted, and much to my surprise, Harry showed us a place where wild violets had found their own special niche at the end of the meadow, thriving in a lovely sonnet to the contrast of the prolific setting before us.

But my soul especially adored the lady's slippers that were sweetly nestled beyond the violets, and I loved them best of all! There, situated at the edge of the nearby brook, and breaking the thick woods extending from Mr. West's mansion next door to ours, it was a picturesque portrait. The brook followed around the land from our place, all along the backside of our street to behind Harry's property, until it met the river two miles upstream. Not only did the more commonly yellow colored lady's slipper thrive here, but a gorgeous specimen in pink also captured my soul's delight in every corner of my heart! Aptly, there was no disputing the charm of the lady's slippers' prolifically profound uniqueness. Such intricate details exclaimed praises of celebration within this amazing beauty that only God could paint upon His magnificent handiwork. To the speckled exquisiteness that dotted the "inner sole," and the carefully crafted blossom, no wonder God declared that all of His creations were "good" after He'd finished His work, then rested on the seventh day!

Delicate, extravagant beauty . . . the meadow flourished here, where only the God of the universe, Creator and Lord of it all, could bring such imagination to life as the fingerprint of His love to earth for the glory of His Name and the delight of our hearts. The power of His spoken words, through the life of His very Breath, richly blessed and nurtured this perfect meadowland in words my soul could not adequately express or contain to the depth of gratitude I was feeling. I pondered the question as to whether, any writer could?

Mesmerized to the enchanting dragonflies and butterflies fluttering amongst the blossoms or resting on petals of every color of the rainbow, I could have watched all day! Drinking to their full content upon the nectar of the flowers, they freely ruled this expanse of land to the breadth and width of its stunning beauty! This vastness was intriguingly lovely, and I'd never before been privy to such numerous numbers as dwelt within this safe, unspoiled oasis.

Bumblebees were aplenty, too, and their buzzing wings were a blur as they serenaded the blossoms. Like a painter's palette, they had whatever nectar they desired. Since a little girl, however, after I'd been bitten just under my eye as my cousins and I made our way with our grandfather to the field where he "smoked" the bees to extract the honey, I was extremely cautious of this wondrous little insect. Instantly, my eye had swelled, closing shut almost completely from the sting. And it hurt a lot! I never wanted a repeat of that!

After our souls were satisfied, Harry led us along the path back to his modest home, where a delicious meal of lemon chicken, creamed potatoes, and a salad tossed with walnuts, mandarin orange pieces, and dried cranberries, was spread before us. His cook, Suzanne Wilcox, beamed at our compliments!

Harry wanted us to see the meadow when the sunset came upon the eve. As the colors were drawn upon the canvas of the sky, we stood in breathless praise to the blessings of this precious abode, where God's hand was seen upon the meadow fair. Fragrances drifted over the land, rich and spicy. The panorama took on a different perspective, lovely in its own choosing to the exotic wonder portrayed upon the scene. I worshipped in my soul as my heart took it all in.

As I looked to the sky, and the deepening mauves and blues upon the scene, and smelled the scents of the flowers, and saw their little heads nod off to sleep, I found my soul refreshed to the lush array before us. My heart was so full and appreciative, it was almost too much for me to take it all in at once. I had no idea that such beauteous wonder thrived so close to our home!

The moon arose, full and bright like a sheath of translucent beauty awash in its iridescent glory, leaving my heart breathless to the magnificence within its transcendent celebration of joy, and the awesomeness of its priceless worth.

Within the pervading darkness against the clouds that momentarily blocked out the moon's light, fireflies emerged on the scene in myriad numbers. Rising across the meadow like dazzling lanterns flitting amid the blossoms, they swooped and rose upon the wind like aerialists on a highwire. The profound loveliness of their presence gracefully performed, as if on stage, to the wonder all around us within an alluring exquisiteness. Like lights carrying bobbing lanterns darting between each flower, it was as though the fireflies were tucking them in and bidding them goodnight! Beautifully entrancing, against the deepening darkness of the night in the shadow of the nearby woods, they appeared as prisms caught unaware, and as shimmering as diamonds in their marvelous display! I'd never seen anything like this before! Truly, it was a colossal extravaganza of awesome wonder!

Here, the aesthetic solace of this enchanting masterpiece within the meadow, like an endless garden, surpassed my deepest yearning to stay within its abiding canopy forever. I aspired to run through it to my heart's content with the sun on my face, and dance in wild, joyful laughter amongst the glory of the flowers at my feet; twirling and swirling, then being lifted like a ballerina in my beloved's arms! Holding hands with Dan, skipping through the meadow . . . oh, how my soul yearned for this glorious honor of pleasure!

I also yearned to lightly walk, as though as angel's wings, when the night became aglow to the dance of the fireflies, through its tranquil stillness, or within the winds that played upon it, and the moon that kissed the flowers in the light enshrouded like a protected shield all about it!

Effused upon my heart, the meadow imprinted a song of sacred joy that I couldn't find the words hidden within my soul to even share with Dan; only the God I loved and served. Even there, I discovered that there are some things that words cannot describe.

Gathering my thoughts, I took one last look at the expanse that Harry owned, and I knew his heart well to what he cared for with respective regard within this wild gift of blessing that he wholly cherished. I also knew his heart better, appreciating the person I was privileged to work with every day. Such gentle nature was borne from total surrender and as the guardian to everything which God had entrusted into His care, because He knew how much Harry's heart would always respect and appreciate the work of His hands. I couldn't have imagined a more profound gift that God had given to this wonderful heart in Harry. Captivated within this sphere so near, it was evident to see that Harry certainly was an excellent caretaker for our Lord in every way!

The time had all too soon disappeared, and before long, we found ourselves bidding Harry goodnight at his doorstep, profusely thanking him for the joy of the evening!

"Anytime you find your hearts yearning for the flowers, please come and visit my meadow, whether I'm at home or not," he graciously invited. "It shall be a pleasure to share the blossoms with you!

"Do you know something? I was ecstatic when I stumbled on this gorgeous field of flowers that the owner I purchased the property from, later admitted that he'd completely forgotten about! Imagine that! But since it was a private sale, there was no one to remind the old gentleman, I suppose, and he was quite the character! And such a lovely man!" Harry chuckled, pausing. "I'm truly grateful for this home and meadow," Harry said.

My gaze fell on the far-reaching meadow; admiring every blossom extolling its joy. Mesmerized in the richness inspired on the land, I almost missed Harry's next words.

"Well, I found it; this adoring meadow!" Harry enthusiastically exclaimed. "Amidst a wall of tall grass, no less!" he chortled. "But hidden inside it, cheery colors flashed in the sunlight, calling for a closer inspection. That's when I realized this beautiful treasure was here, and it's been a special place to me ever since.

"There isn't a moment that it is lost from my heart. Regardless how my day has gone, it's like a solid rock; immovable; firm, where it blesses my soul every time I come to abide within its appreciative solace, even to the changing seasons.

"When I caught my first glimpse of these gorgeous blooms," he said, "I stopped in my tracks, totally dumbfounded! I could feel God's Presence all around me, and my soul just burst with praise to the magnificence of its astounding wonder.

"From that moment, this profoundly entrancing, and ravishing beauty, has left its sacred imprint on my heart. And I sensed that it is more like a 'prayer garden,' calling my heart here every day within its quaint and lovely peacefulness," Harry wistfully finished.

"That's amazing!" Dan said. "It truly holds this wonderfully captivating aura, as you say, in a very uniquely special, and sacred abode."

At the moment, I was as overwhelmed as he; enraptured in its perfect glory. But I found my voice and warmly said, "We really enjoyed this evening, Harry, and we thank you for this kind consideration! I'd love to come again and see the changing seasons of the flowers!" I said, giving him a hug.

"We both will!" Dan graciously agreed, shaking his hand.

"We've been wanting to have you for a meal and visit as well, Harry," I invited. "We'll have to make it soon! Ethel will love to prepare a spread for you!"

"Oh!" he shyly said, "that will be lovely, but really, I don't need a spread! I'm just a simple man!"

"Well, that may be so," I returned, with a smile, "but Ethel will see it quite differently! I don't believe she grasps this English word of 'simple,' yet! But that's fine by us! She loves to cook, and she loves to please. I'll let you know when, Harry. Now, we'd better say goodbye to you!"

To my surprise, Suzanne appeared at the doorway, asking us to wait, reappearing almost as quickly as she'd disappeared. "Harry has a little gift I'm sure will please you," she said, handing me a huge bouquet of wildflowers from his meadow.

I was speechless but found my voice to thank her and then Harry.

"It's my pleasure, Maggie!" he said, smiling. "I'd almost forgotten, so it's good that Suzanne reminded me just now!"

Life was so good, I said to Dan as we drove home and soon retired for the night. So, so good! I couldn't wait to see what the morrow would bring as I kissed my beloved goodnight and dreamed sweet dreams upon the warmth of the night.

When I awoke, I wondered what special gift we could give to Harry. Nothing came to mind, but I prayed it surely would. He was one of the kindest men I'd ever met! I didn't have a meadow, but between us and God, we truly would be able to surprise him in a pleasure most befitting his friendship, of that, I was sure!

CHAPTER 17

Diamond of Love

It wasn't hard to see that Dan loved Ethel, not just as an employee, but as a good friend, and that Tom was a special friend from years back when he and Dan had met at a garden event. Ethel Rodriguez had arrived in Canada when she was twenty-six years old, and Tom Wafer, of Scottish and English ancestry, who had been born and raised in this area, were both loyal and caring people.

When we retired the following night, Dan and I talked a bit about Ethel and Tom's engagement, and then I shared of their dream to build a greenhouse. Dan was absolutely elated.

"To think that this romance was going on right under my own roof," he said laughing. "What an incredible blessing!"

"It truly is," I said, kissing my darling. "And the greenhouse?"

"That's something I've been considering myself for some time, Maggie. When I took biology in school, I also took a horticulture class. Flowers have fascinated me ever since I can remember. I think this is something we need to give our blessing to in the dream that they wonderfully share together. It's a wonderfully magical and marvelous dream! Just imagine, Maggie! Deciding what flowers, they have in mind. I've always loved orchids; there's so many varieties. Well, let's leave this for another day, my dearest, and get some sleep, shall we?"

Dan lovingly kissed me and before I knew it, it was morning. Where had the night gone to, I wondered? If just one kiss could give such blessed rest, I pondered, as my thoughts turned to the new day, I wonder . . .

We wanted this adventure to be something extraordinarily special. We asked Anne to prepare an outdoor barbecue tray of foods, and Tom would attend to the barbecue. We decided to leave for the office early, so that we could still accomplish a full day's work but be back about three.

We were delighted with the lovely supper Anne had prepared. Ethel helped, but Carlos was fussy most of the day, teething, and so much of the day's attention was spent with him. Tom already had the barbecue fired up when we returned. Blossom was to stay with a friend, Rachael, down the street, a sweet girl about her own age. They got along very well. Ethel had just put Carlos down for a nap and explained that he hadn't slept any throughout the earlier part of the day. I wanted so to hold my baby, but I didn't want to disturb his sleep knowing how tired he was, especially with the meal that was prepared for Ethel and Tom to celebrate the proposed greenhouse.

"Ethel, why don't you rest a spell while Anne gets everything out on the picnic table?" I asked.

"Oh, okay," she said, none protesting.

Twenty minutes later, Tom offered to check on both Carlos and Ethel. She'd fallen asleep and moaned when he lightly knocked on her door. "Ethel. Ethel. Time for supper," he said. Waiting outside the door for her, when she didn't respond, he slowly opened it.

"I don't feel so good," Ethel said, trying to sit up.

Tom stepped to her side as she lay propped on her pillow. Feeling her flushed face, he instantly knew that something was wrong. "You need to see a doctor, darling," he said.

"What for?" she asked.

"You're burning up. Have you a thermometer?"

"In the bathroom cupboard."

Tom hurried to the bathroom but couldn't find it. Calling 9-1-1, he asked Ethel if she could walk.

"Of course, I can walk, Tom! Why ask me such a foolish question?" Trying to get out bed, Ethel would have fallen if Tom hadn't caught her. "What's wrong, Tom? Who are you calling?"

In answer, he immediately put down the telephone receiver, and throwing back the blankets, scooped her up in his arms. Yelling for help, Dan rushed in.

"My goodness! What's happened?" he asked Tom.

"Don't know. She's burning up something awful. Help me get her to the porch." A siren strengthened as it pulled into the driveway. An ambulance attendant instantly aided Tom and Dan. Explaining the situation, the attendant's driver came to assist, pulling out a stretcher.

"She's my fiancée," Tom said. "I'm coming with you."

"Okay. Let's go!"

We stood in silence, hardly daring to speak. "We need to get to the hospital right away," I said. "Anne, would you look after things here, please? And grab my purse and coat and Mr. Danes' wallet off his dresser." Anne was back in a jiffy, and I ran through the door, telling her we'd call if we needed to. Dan already had the car driven out of the garage, waiting for me.

I stiffened my backbone, gritting my teeth, as I stepped into the car and Dan, and I drove to the hospital. Silence was between us, but it seemed perfectly normal and understandable at the moment. Ethel had seemed quite fine throughout the day, but then the recollection came to me how she'd suddenly felt so tired caring for Carlos and needed a rest before supper. That wasn't like her at all. Fidgeting, I felt exhausted.

We arrived at our destination in a few minutes at the visitor's parking area. When we entered the hospital, the nurse said that Ethel was already in a room, and we needed to hurry if we wanted to see her before she was prepped for surgery. My heart nearly fell out. The nurse led us to her room. The doctor was just leaving, saying that Ethel was resting comfortably and asking for me. "You may see her only very briefly. We're going to be operating as soon as the room's prepared."

I didn't want to voice the question, but we needed to know what it was all about. "Why do you need to operate?" I asked, pointedly.

"Miss Rodriguez needs her appendix removed immediately or it may burst. Has she been complaining about pain?"

"No. Not that we know of. She just arrived back from a Hawaiian trip last evening, and in fact, has been especially happy. She just became engaged to Tom here." Tom was sitting at Ethel's side, and Dan was standing next to him.

"But that's strange. It can sometimes happen like this, but it's rare. She came in with a very high temperature, and we've given her medication to lower it. It should work quickly. She did express pain during my examination, but apart from the high fever, did you notice any other symptoms?"

"She seemed tired this afternoon, but my baby is teething, and he didn't sleep all day. With the return trip and excitement of her engagement, she appeared in good health otherwise. She was very tired, come to think of it, the evening she arrived back and went to bed unusually early."

"Alright. Thank you. The best thing you can do is to go home, and we'll call when she's out of surgery."

"How long may we expect that?" Dan asked.

"It's hard to say. Once she's in recovery, we'll know better. At least two to four hours."

Before we left, I slipped by Ethel's side and Tom went to be with Dan. She lay there looking pale but managed a smile.

"Maggie," she reached for my hand, "if something happens to me, there's a paper in my jewelry box for you."

Tears misted my eyes, but I bravely said, "Ethel dear, we won't have need of that paper. You'll be coming home with us in a few days, so you must not think such thoughts."

"But, in case . . . promise to take care of things for me?" Her eyes were pleading, and I didn't know what to say.

"Just get all the rest you can and let the doctor do his job. We'll be praying every moment for you."

"I love you," she said, looking lovingly up into my face.

"I love you, too, Ethel."

The attendant entered the room, and I exited her room. My last image was of Ethel being wheeled down the hallway, where she soon disappeared from view. I turned, and joined Dan and Tom, and we left together.

Dan called the minister when we arrived home. Anne had a worried expression when we told her the news, then a smile lit her eyes. "God is looking after her. Rest assured; He will see her through."

I suddenly felt weak with hunger. An hour had passed since Ethel had been taken to the hospital.

Tom offered to barbecue the food, but none of us felt much like eating. Tonight, was supposed to be so extra special.

Pastor George Hokan, and his lovely wife, Coral, came to join us for the meal and then have a time of prayer. It helped my appetite to have them here with us. Judith Madison, Coral's younger sister, who lived close by, sat next to me at the table, detailing her work week. She was as sweet as she was pretty.

"We were quite busy with the quilting. But it's coming along, and you'll have to see it, Maggie. The ladies are enjoying the work, although it's something I'm in need of getting used to!" she softly laughed.

I laughed with her, knowing that quilting wasn't my forte, either.

Anne, sitting on the other side of Coral, seemed exceptionally interested. "Oh, quilting is such a pleasure!" she shyly said. "I used to do a whole lot of that and sell to the locals, even in the big city."

Totally taken by surprise, I said, "You did?"

"Yes, ma'am. I've made several."

That got me thinking. "Coral, perhaps it's not my place to say so just at the moment, but I know a beautiful, young lady, our housekeeper, who recently became engaged, and she's lying in that hospital right now, as you know. This would be a lovely gesture if the ladies' group would create a special quilt for her wedding."

"Oh! I'd love to help, too," Anne quickly pleaded.

"That's a very lovely idea," Coral remarked, her eyes smiling, "and I'm sure we can have it ready with many hands and hearts working together on this project."

Everyone seemed to have finished their meal, and Anne began to gather the dirty dishes. Tom came to help her. Coral and I brought in the leftover food to the house.

Then, we gathered in the living room for a time of special prayer for Ethel. Just when we finished praying, the telephone rang. Dan picked it up, and his concern turned to relief. Hanging up moments later, he related the conversation. "The doctor says that everything went well, and Ethel is progressing favorably in recovery. He'll give us an update in the morning."

Tears filled my eyes. I looked across the room at Tom, and his eyes were also wet with tears. I could only imagine the emotion his heart was feeling. He arose and said goodnight, and quickly left, letting himself out. Coral and George Hokan left almost immediately after Tom, thanking us for our hospitality. "We'll keep praying for Ethel," he said as they exited our home. "Please keep us posted." I stepped outside with Coral, and we hugged and lingered on the porch. Judith had arrived in her own car and followed. We hugged, too, and as their vehicles disappeared, we found ourselves alone. The night air was so perfect. Dan came to my side, and we decided to walk along the paths amongst the flowerbeds.

"This has certainly been a hard day," he commented.

"Yes, but God is with us and He's watching over Ethel, too." Dan took my hand in his, and it made me feel better. A slight breeze began to stir and in the darkened eve, fireflies danced in acrobatic pleasure.

"You know, Dan, ever since I was a little girl, I can remember the joy I always felt in seeing the fireflies at night when I stayed at my grandparents. My cousin, who was several years older than me, so the story goes, swooped a few in his hands and imprisoned them in a jar one evening. Then, he snuck into my sister's bedroom and tucked them between the sheets. You should have heard the howling when Amy flipped the sheet over and these tiny beings, with their glowing lights, arose from their entrapped prison! Once she realized what they were, her perspective changed."

Dan couldn't help but laugh at that. "It must have really made her mad!"

"Yes, it sure did! Recognizing these glowing lights, Amy immediately got over her fright, marched to her cousin's room, flung open the door, and proceeded to give a tongue lashing the likes, I'm sure, of which he'd never had! Waving her arms in the air, she had a flair for the dramatic, she vowed in no uncertain terms, to get back at him for it, but as far as I know, that's still on the table, so to speak!"

"Well, I suppose that's long forgotten by now," Dan said.

"Not with my sister, it isn't! Oh, I don't think she'll ever play a prank on him as she vowed, but Amy does threaten it from time to time whenever she travels that way down to southern Manitoba to visit Lawrence's sister, Delora. 'If I didn't care so much for her,' Amy says, 'I'd never set foot near the border!' I honestly believe, however, that, while she unobtrusively meets Lawrence, she doesn't mind as much as she puts on! We were always close cousins growing up, and a few fireflies haven't deterred her any from making the trip each summer," I finished, taking a breath.

Dan couldn't resist as he said, "I wonder if she ever considered a truce by making him a firefly pie?"

Horrified at such a thought, I began to reply when Dan took me in his arms and kissed me. "I hope, my dearest," he lovingly said, "that you will never repay me for my wrongs in any way."

"Oh, no, Dan. Of course not!" I assured. "I would bless you because that would hold so much more sweetness for both of us, don't you agree?"

"Mmm hmm," he said, kissing me, his words lost but for the sweetness of his tender, Mmm hmm. "But sometimes, darling, I dare say that it might not happen until after you've had your words with me!"

Blushing, I merely replied, "That's sometimes true, Dan, but I will promise to improve over time in our marriage." Before he could respond, I leaned in close where passion burst, and that "Mmm hmm" was hushed upon the kisses of our hearts.

Ethel made a full recovery and Tom was beside himself with joy. "Now, we can soon be married," he happily said.

It was wonderful having Ethel back home again, and we kept Anne on, knowing that Ethel needed to gain her strength.

"But I feel fine and well able to continue my duties," she said, protesting a little.

"Fine, yes! And we want to keep you that way!" I firmly said, smiling before we headed out the door to work. "As to the 'well able,' Ethel, we've long since known and never doubted your immense capabilities! But the doctor also made it very plain that you need to rest and regain your strength. That shouldn't be too much to ask, I don't think, considering you and me and Dan can count on Anne. Now, never you mind any. Anne is more than capable and she's happy to stay and help us out."

Ethel frowned then shyly looked into my eyes, grinning. "I no win this one either, Maggie, will I?"

I couldn't help myself from laughing, remembering how hard it was for her to accept the gifts of clothing that Dan and I wanted to purchase for her trip. Taking her hands, I smiled and replied, "No, my dear Ethel, you won't win this one, either! And just so you know," I teasingly said, "you needn't try to persuade your Mr. any about it, because he and I stand on firm ground together on this, okay?"

"Okay!" she laughed.

Dan overheard the conversation as he was coming along the corridor and seeing if I was ready. Just then the doorbell rang. It was Harry Gerali.

"I hoped you wouldn't mind me stopping by, but I wanted to pick some flowers for Ethel. Oh, there she is! Hello, Ethel! I brought you some cheer to speed your recovery! As a matter-of-fact, I decided to pick two bouquets, so that Anne could enjoy her own, as well."

Handing Ethel the large vase of flowers, tears began to fill her eyes and she looked into his eyes and softly exclaimed, "Oh, how so very beautiful they are! Yes, thank you, Mr. Gerali, so, so much! I will enjoy them, every petal on the blossoms!"

Dan called for Anne and she relieved Ethel of the flowers by placing them on the corner table where she could see them. When Harry handed Anne a slightly different bouquet, equally lovely, telling Anne they were for her pleasure, she became rather emotional, but held her composure, thanking him profusely. I glanced at Dan and tears were misted in his eyes. He didn't have to say a single word. His smile said it all.

Harry said goodbye, saying that he'd be in to work an hour later. "I made it up last evening, just as I promised," he told us, "unless my appointment should be delayed."

"Take as long as you like, Harry," Dan reassured. "We won't worry if you're later and you won't need to make up the difference for that if you should be delayed. We hope your appointment with your sister goes well."

"Thank you, now I must hurry, or I'll be late picking her up," he said.

"I think such a nice man needs to find a good woman to be his wife," I said offhandedly when the door closed behind him, and I saw Harry leave down the street. I'd no idea where that thought came from, but it was innocent, and easily dismissed in the room with my husband and Ethel, and even Anne. For some unknown reason, however, in that very moment, I happened to look across the room at Anne, and I saw her blush. She hurried out of the room as though she needed to attend to something important that she'd almost forgotten about. That came as a light of realization more than I dared hope; why, she would be perfect for Harry, I told myself! Could it be the same with her and Harry finding love, so unsuspecting as it had been with Ethel and Tom, and me and Dan were too blind to notice? I dared not tell anyone, not even Dan. I wondered what he'd ever think of that.

My thoughts returned to the tasks at hand, and I said, "I suppose we should be leaving, too, my darling."

"Uh huh," he answered. "In just a moment." Patting Ethel softly on her shoulder, he said, "I am sure that you and Anne will fill your day with the joyful wonder of these flowers."

He assisted me with my jacket, and I waved, adding, "Just be sure to leave a piece of that wonderfully delicious apple strudel for me and my 'doll' that Anne promised to bake this afternoon, Ethel! We'll see you just after four this afternoon."

For a moment, a puzzled look crossed her face, then slightly blushing, she remembered the meaning and happily said, "For your doll and you!" she smiled. "Trust me, ma'am, I shan't forget!"

I was so glad that Dan loved the idea of a rare flower greenhouse. I'd completely forgotten all about it, and it had apparently slipped his mind, too, until one evening, I happened to be out strolling along the paths of the flowerbeds when I practically bumped into Tom around the bend in the walkway.

"Oh, my goodness, Tom! I'm sorry! I'm afraid I had my head elsewhere admiring these beautiful flowers." His eyes were smiling, and it suddenly hit me. But before I could say a word, I heard soft footsteps, and Ethel came around the turn.

"Hello, Tom and Mrs. Isn't this a beautiful evening?" Ethel said with immense appreciation etched in her tone.

Looking upward to the sky, I had to agree. The sun was still shining, dappling the leaves in joyful play as the gentle wind bent the branches ever so slightly, like a child contentedly rocked in a rocker.

Eleanor Lee Gustaw

"Just beautiful!" I exclaimed. "I wonder, Tom," I suddenly asked, "I don't mean to interrupt your time with Ethel, but would you mind getting Dan for me and asking him to join us at the water fountain near the back of the garden?"

A quizzical expression crossed his face, but he politely assured that it was no trouble, and went off to fetch my husband.

"Let's enjoy a leisurely walk to the fountain, Ethel," I said, linking my arm with hers. "I just recollected something quite important, and I want Dan to join us."

Ethel nodded, understanding, and we slowly made our way, where we sat on the welcoming bench beneath the shade of the lilac branches and the maples, that towered high into the sky amongst the birch trees.

Tom soon appeared with Dan, and the men sat respectively with me and Ethel.

"Dan," I began, "the night that Ethel fell ill, we were going to announce that special secret, remember?"

"Oh, yes!" he said.

"Well, why don't you tell Tom and Ethel our plans?"

"Sure."

Anticipation and eagerness shone in their eyes, and Ethel leaned forward.

"Maggie and I both agree that we would like you to set up the greenhouse of your dreams, right *here*, on our estate, Tom. Just as you'd mentioned," he emphasized. "As you know, there's that area of land that has had nothing done with it on the other side of the avenue of trees, and I believe that would be a perfect spot."

Tom's eyes grew large, and he seemed almost mesmerized at the prospect. Ethel's eyes were captivated, as she suddenly grabbed ahold of Tom's arm, and joyfully exclaimed, "How wonderful! Tom! Your own greenhouse! Oh, thank you, Mr., and Mrs.!"

I was so happy, I felt like crying. Instead, I controlled my feelings momentarily as I said, "And that's not all! We thought that because there's so much available land, we'd like to build you a cottage where you may live so that you'll be close to your beloved greenhouse and work. Then after you're married, you and Tom won't have to travel every day. And Ethel, we'd still love to have

228

you as our employee, but perhaps, you may wish to work alongside Tom, and Anne can run the house. What do you say?"

"I think that's very generous and kind of both of you," Tom said. "But Ethel," he turned toward her, "would you prefer to work fulltime with me and leave the housekeeping to Anne?"

"I would only if I may visit the children and my Mrs. anytime."

Unaware of anything in his tone that prompted this question, Dan and I were soon thrilled with her unexpected revelation. But in this moment, I was almost sorry that I'd tentatively given away Ethel's position, but I really didn't think that she'd give it up so easily. A part of me felt like crying. I couldn't imagine no Ethel to be in my kitchen or available on the slightest whim for me to see and share my heart. But she was soon to marry, and I needed to let her live her life the way she chose, and with Tom. Trying to sound calm, I assured Ethel that this was quite acceptable with me.

"We already spoke with Anne, and she's agreed to stay on. And Ethel, we want you to know that Dan will renegotiate your salary to reflect your efforts working in the flowers I know you love so with Tom. I mean to say, that he wants to give you a raise, my dear friend!"

Then, Ethel was at my side, holding me as unbidden tears streamed down her face. "You know," she confessed, "I've always loved flowers and I studied them where I lived in Mexico across the U.S. border, long before I came to work for you. I have studied extensively and specialized in the field of rare flowers, such as orchids, that I so love," she said. "In fact, I've always had a special heart for your great and beautiful country, which eventually brought me here. And now it's my homeland, too, and I'm a citizen of this country, Canada. I even have my degree," she revealed, pausing.

Shocked and astounded, we looked at Ethel almost in disbelief. And it was then, in that moment of truth that I realized that we all have dreams, but sometimes, our paths unexpectedly change, and they are lost for a while, like love, until God shines His heart to that hope again, and our dreams find their place within the destiny our lives were meant to hold. I finally found my voice and expressed my question. "But then why wouldn't you have worked in this field all these years?" I asked.

"Because, as a young professor, it was too far away from where I lived to find another place to work. See, one day I decided I'd had enough where I was presently employed at a university not very far from where I lived. And" she continued before I could interrupt, "one of the professors, a colleague, he, what you say, make google-eyes, at me all the time. So creepy like," she said, shivering at the memory. "He wanted to take me out on a date, but I told him I didn't have a clue what he was talking about! I asked him how he could think of something like that when dates are consumed, and it made no sense. He didn't find it very funny. I did know what he meant, and I think, to my shame, that it is the only lie I've ever told!

"Well, he got rough with me one day while I was leaving the campus, grabbing my arm real tight that I couldn't help but cry out. Hoping no one had heard my cry, he forcibly slammed me against the door and told me that I'd better do what he wanted, or it would be too bad for me.

"To throw him off, I meekly nodded, and he released his hold on me. I saw my opportunity, and without a second thought, I kicked him so hard in his shin, that he bellowed, grabbing his leg with both hands, but trying to still grab ahold of me as I broke free. But I flung open the door, slamming it in his face, and ran as fast as I could until I safely reached my car. I put the car into gear and stepped on the gas just as he stood outside the building, his fists immediately flailing in the air and his face red in a fit of rage.

"I telephoned the next morning and told my top superior that I quit. When he politely asked why, I merely said, 'Some people are gentlemen, while others are goats, and goats don't belong in such fine institutions like this one unless they wish to get butted good for it in time.' My top boss was shocked, I could tell by his tone, as he asked, 'Whatever are you talking about, Miss Rodriguez?' I wasn't about to spend my morning stirring in the mud, so I simple-like stated, 'you might ask that old snake, Professor Milling, about that,' I proposed, hanging up the phone. It dawned on me that such likes of evil men have no fences to the borders. And that's when I came to work for Mr. Danes – a real gentleman!" she shyly smiled, her eyes alit with sparkling gratitude.

We couldn't help but laugh, but I totally understood, trying to picture the shock on the professor's face when sweet, innocent Ethel stood her ground with him! "Fences seem to only apply to those of honor," I agreed, understanding her language of wording. "That must have taken some courage," I commented.

"Not at all! That day I made sure it was the end of it!" she said. "I just had had enough of his stupidity, and I didn't think twice about it, either! He kept coming to my classroom as I finished up to leave for the day after his lectures at the university were completed. While I was sorry to give up my status as a professor, I was totally done with trying to get away from him most days. So, I really didn't have time to consider this courage!" Pausing, she added as an afterthought, "I also realized that he couldn't do anything about the situation because he'd implicate himself. He couldn't be sure, either, whether I'd told anyone, or divulged it to the higher up. As those thoughts crossed my mind, I took everything inside of me I could, and gave him a piece of my mind in that kick with my high heel!" I was about to speak when she added, "And I hope he hurt good for a long time afterwards, too!" she giggled, thinking of the recollection.

"That's not very sympathetic, Ethel, or ethical conduct as a professor," I said, with as much of a straight face as I could muster. "But am I ever proud of you!" I burst out laughing, as everyone joined in. Then, turning to Dan, I said, "I'm glad I married a prince and not a goat!"

Tom could scarcely contain himself, trying to picture the scene, and Dan's shocked expression followed sheepishly as he hugged me.

Tom reached for Ethel's hand and lovingly said, "Ethel, I'm sorry you lost such a wonderful position and opportunity, but I assure you that that old goat of a professor did me a huge favor. I'd never have met you and I love you so! I'm hoping you'll say it's our greenhouse together, my darling!" Tom lovingly said, adoringly looking into Ethel's shining eyes.

Ethel nodded, as tears streamed down her face. "All ours!" she softly whispered.

Tom was beside himself with joy. "Just think," he tenderly said, "what we'll be able to do together with our flowers here!"

Laughing and crying happy tears, I knew what a wonderful husband Tom would be to Ethel and a wonderful wife she'd be to him. I'd thought highly of Tom the first time we'd met, and my respect for him has never wavered. He was a gentleman of rare and lovely breeding, like Dan, I thought; well, most days! And I surmised that Dan could say the same of me!

"God sure has His surprises," I remarked in teasing gesture, smiling.

"Oh, that He does!" Tom assured.

Ethel looked into his eyes that held such love for her and then into mine. "Mrs. Maggie, do you think that it would be too much trouble if Tom and I married amongst these beautiful flowers – our beloved garden?"

Tears misted in my eyes, and I could scarcely whisper, the joy was so full in my heart. Tenderly, I took her hand and said, "Not at all, my dearest Ethel. Not at all, for you shall always be our wonderfully special and beautiful *Diamond of Love*, and there shall never be anything too small nor too big for you to ask that Dan and I won't do for you – and Tom," I lovingly answered. "Nothing at all, dear Ethel!"

Then, Dan and I arose and left Ethel to her beloved fiancé. Such a beautiful evening, I said in my thoughts as Dan held me close. A beautiful evening, indeed!

CHAPTER 18

Holding the Future Dreams

Where a lost love may be found, only the heart truly knows. There may be times of no return in some, or sometimes, it may be a long time before love finds its full circle of breath again. When Dan had left us and seldom responded through those long, uncertain months, I sometimes lost hope that he loved me, or that he'd ever return to me again.

As I saw the beauty of love blossom and grow in Ethel and Tom's lives, and how they respected and cherished each other, my heart embraced each perfect gift to my soul. And I prayed that their love would never face that agonizing pain of separation as mine had known. Seeing such wondrous joy alit within their eyes was a precious, sacred gift, and I knew it came from within every corner of their hearts.

To whatever our dreams, I always knew that they held the thread within the weave of which the tapestry was drawn upon. When I looked back at my own life, writing had always been a part of it. I never lost faith in my work, but I had lost faith at times that anyone would appreciate the same stories that God had placed within my heart. Sometimes, I wondered why He ever chose me to be a writer. It had to one of the hardest jobs there is! Yet, as I poured myself into my work to life's realism in various aspects, I always knew inside of my soul that this would be a part of my life's calling from Him. Because I was ultimately working for the Lord, I was challenged to strive in giving my very best in highest excellence, but there also would be the challenge within that talent to refine my skill until a word, sentence, or scene, couldn't be expressed any better.

To each of us, the dreams of our hearts needed to be nurtured. Some dreams needed extreme skill. Other dreams simply needed to be revived! Wishing for the dream to happen, won't. But even a small step would begin to unfold its value, where some dreams held priceless worth just waiting to be writ upon a scroll, painted upon a canvas, studied through years of learning to be a scholar, doctor, teacher, or perhaps a simpler, yet vital life in being a dedicated housekeeper, among many, but no less valued.

I should have seen the dream that Ethel held, where we had taken almost daily walks through the paths within our garden. She seemed to know all the names of the flowers, but I thought she'd simply learned them bit by bit through the years gone by. The tenderness by which she'd tend the plants had always intrigued me until the revelation spoken that evening that she was well studied, with a degree at that, brought it into perfect focus and complete understanding!

I suddenly thought back to something as Dan and I leisurely walked together, hand in hand, to our mansion. Back then, through the years gone by, I hoped my words would both keep Dan encouraged and focused, and bring him back to himself when he was so betwixt and between after his sister, Julia, had died. Wandering off for months at a time and coming back to his home in the spring, I'd lovingly said, "Dan, the wild roses shall bloom again soon. Remember them with me, my dearest." It was my way of asking him to stay.

He wept in my arms and I held him close. "God's love shall always be in my heart for you, to every moment of our lives, my dearest Dan," I gently whispered. Although it took some time, it was a firm foundation for which he could reflect on in the days ahead.

As God had impressed Jude 1:21 KJV upon my heart that afternoon, I shared it with Dan, adding my own sentiment. It says, "Keep yourselves in the love of God, looking for the mercy of our Lord Jesus Christ unto eternal life." And that which I had prayed so much for Dan to know my purest heart and love for him, eventually came in time to every step along his journey.

Seeing the joy of Ethel and Tom's love tonight, made me feel so loved by our great and awesome God Who had blessed me with my heart's desire in my husband. "I love you, Dan," I softly said. For an answer, he swept me in his arms and passionately kissed me. It was enough for me, just knowing that God's Plan is always wiser and more beautiful than my own could ever be! For Ethel and Tom, this night was only the beginning of a wonderful relationship that would soon lead them into their own marriage. I think the flowers will know how much, too, I smiled to myself! There was just no mistaking it - love and flowers. What a marvelous combination it surely was!

The evening before the wedding, Ethel shyly came to my door where I was working on our book with Dan. "I'm sorry to disturb you. Please, Maggie? Could we take a little walk right now?"

I was quite surprised, since Ethel had never made such a request before, especially knowing that Dan and I were busy creating the material for our story. Pushing back my chair, I said, "Yes, Ethel. Of course! Dan and I could use a break right now." I glanced at Dan and a knowing look in thought crossed our minds together. He smiled and gently squeezed my hand, and I arose. I fetched my shawl and gathered it about my shoulders, closing the door quietly behind me as I turned to walk with Ethel.

When we stepped outside, she asked, "Would you mind if we walked down the avenue of trees instead of the rose garden?"

"Sure, Ethel. Whatever you like; I don't mind." Ethel's heart was with the garden, but she did love the avenue, too. I knew she had a special reason for choosing the latter path.

When we had walked halfway down the avenue, we paused and sat on the bench that Dan had the original architect create within a quaint alcove, and she queried, "Thank you, Maggie. I didn't want to accidently run into Tom at the garden so I thought the avenue would be safer. Remember, my dear Mrs., when you mentioned to me about the 'rainy day' and what it meant?"

"Certainly, Ethel."

"Well, I hoped you wouldn't mind so much because I asked Tom what it meant, just as you said," she confided, "because you did tell me you wouldn't mind if I asked Dan or Tom. I wasn't sure in that moment if I could trust the Mr. because you may have told him, but

I did trust Tom, and I didn't suppose there was much of a chance you had revealed it to him," she emphasized.

I could hardly keep myself from laughing, wondering what Ethel's point was! "Oh, Ethel!" I teased. "Now, I understand, but I was rather wondering about your expression then when I had no idea, except a few suspicions, about you and Tom courting! What did he say?"

"Oh," she thought back, "I said to Tom, 'I came across something rather peculiar and I hope that you can tell me what you think. What does it mean when a person uses the words: 'a rainy day,' Tom?' We get lots aplenty of those!

"He laughed and replied, 'Well, sometimes, my Ethel, it rains. A lot. But 'a rainy day' is meant figuratively. That means, it doesn't really rain, but because it isn't pleasant always when it rains, or convenient, a person infers it's not pleasant when they've fallen on hard times, meaning that they don't have enough money. When such 'a rainy day' comes, however, it means that in this financial difficulty that has occurred, if not for putting aside some money for it, there wouldn't be enough money to go around to pay the bills, or whatever it might be needed for.'

"I didn't know what 'go around' meant, so I said, 'Go around,' where, Tom?'

"He smiled and said, 'It means there's not enough to pay the bills, so if a person has saved money, then it will help to have extra for that 'rainy or unexpected day,' such as if a person needs to buy shoes because the old shoes aren't good to wear anymore, or if a person suddenly needs to travel and needs to buy gasoline, but it can be anything. Simply said, money put aside will help in hard or difficult situations, referred to as 'a rainy day.' So, it means there's now enough to 'go around' and pay the bills.'

"So, I finally had my answer confirmed, and Tom was a bit taken that I understood it, too!" she happily exclaimed. "But" she continued with a frown, "I wonder then, Maggie, if a person *does* have enough money, might it be called a 'sunny or unrainy day?'"

Tears welled in my eyes. "That is a very good question, Ethel, but no, we only refer to it the other way – when we *haven't* saved. We don't call enough money for that a 'sunny or unrainy day,' but I think that's a very clever way to see it, because that is also very true.

"And dearest sister, I'd never fool you, Ethel, not like this, and I have to laugh. Tom did a swell job of explaining it to you," I gleefully smiled, "even though he did rather beat around the bush to do that! Why, if I didn't know what it meant myself, I think I would have been quite confused!" I chortled.

Looking a bit flustered, Ethel asked, "I suppose I should still study this crazy English of yours because, Mrs. Maggie, what does 'swell' mean?"

Hugging her, I whispered, "It has more than one definition, depending on how the word is used," I explained, "but in this context, it means, very good. Apart from the many words he used, Tom did a very good job to explain it to you. When you come to the lake with us when there's a storm, Ethel, you'll see that for yourself," I explained.

"Oh!" she said. "I see. Well, I'm so sorry, Mrs.," Ethel cried. "I won't no more doubt you – ever, and I hope you please, will forgive me?" she asked with concern.

Amused, I said, "Oh, Ethel, I wasn't offended in the least; quite the contrary!" I assured her. "So, I want to see my dearest sister happy again and tomorrow," I encouraged, "you shall wed that doll of yours! So, you must have the best sleep of your life tonight!"

Giggling through her tears, her eyes sparkled in the evening's fading light as we continued walking to the end of the avenue and back home again as the lamps lit our path, burning brightly, illuminating the way in the darkening night.

"I love you so and you are more precious to me than you could ever know," I said, "and I shall always treasure the gifts and the joy we shared before I married Dan and the gift of Tom, who you shall wed tomorrow!"

"Dear Maggie," Ethel whispered so softly I could scarcely hear her, "I love you this dearly, too. A treasure. Yes, you too, are this special treasure I shall love and cherish always!"

When I returned to Dan, he asked no questions. Taking me in his arms he lovingly said, "Tomorrow shall change all our lives, but I have this feeling, darling, that the change shall be a turning point for us in the best God has yet to come!"

"Yes," I said. He released me, and I slipped into my pajamas and was soon held within Dan's arms again. "Thank you so much for understanding tonight," I whispered. "I am very grateful for you, and I love you dearly." Tenderly kissing me, I smiled as Dan, and I said goodnight moments later. I closed my eyes, and before I knew it, it was morning; a beautiful, glorious day that we would celebrate to honor the love that came and was very shortly to be in covenant as husband and wife between our dearest friends.

On this day of Ethel Rodriguez's and Tom Wafer's wedding, she rushed to my study, gently knocking on the French door of my writing room. "Mrs. Maggie," she breathlessly exclaimed, "Tom and I have something special to share with you! Come quickly, please!"

She gently pulled me by the hand and rushed me out the door. The mid-morning sun was warm and cheerful against our faces, splashing the leaves in dappled beauty as I wondered what the excitement was all about. We hurried along the avenue of trees, went behind them, and there was Tom with a huge, wrapped box in his hands.

"Open it!" Ethel said, enthusiasm etched in her voice.

I removed the lovely, blue wrapping and gasped in pure delight. "Oh, Ethel! Tom! How beautiful! What exquisite orchids!" Admiring the gorgeous lavender-mauve blush color, I didn't know what else to say.

"I'm glad you like them, Maggie," Tom softly said. "Ethel could hardly wait, and I was beginning to be concerned they had missed the train. This is merely a little something for everything you and Dan are doing for us. It's one of the rarest varieties of orchids. While this, of many hues, seems plain, it's not very suited to successful grafting, and this is what makes it so rare. Many horticulturists give up too soon, but Ethel and I will work closely together, determined to create a beautiful hybrid. I ordered one for the greenhouse, too, and Ethel and I are inspired with some ideas that should help us in trying to grow a new crossbreed from it. We already chose the perfect color of orchid to experiment with, a plum-cherry."

"Oh, that will be breathless," I exclaimed, "and this is already so beautiful, I know you'll succeed! But I think that you'd better take care of my orchid for me."

"Not at all! You and Dan just enjoy it. We'll keep our eyes on it, but we want you to keep it in your home. Ethel and I plan to have lady's slippers, too. And many more," Tom smiled, his eyes a twinkling. Just hearing Tom talk, my soul was filled with the many possibilities of the beauty they would surely create for our pleasure and to God's glory!

Ethel's eyes were dancing with joy, and she couldn't resist the challenge. "Just perhaps, now, Maggie, you might be surprised at what we can teach you about the beautiful flowers that grow in your garden, and the beautiful flowers that shall grow in the greenhouse!" Ethel fairly glowed in admiration at the thought, and her face was aflush with anticipation.

Laughing with her, Tom put his arm about her and smiled. "Now, that's a fascinating inspiration, Ethel. Getting your Mr. and Mrs. to share in our greenhouse!"

The construction had already slowly begun on the greenhouse, but it would be a few weeks before Tom and Ethel could begin their dream. We walked back to the mansion and Tom carried the box into the house, momentarily placing it on the table in the dining room. Ethel gently and carefully, lifted the lovely, huge vase out of the box, filled with specialized earth, careful not to injure the pretty blossoms, and Tom asked where it should go.

"Right here," I said, indicating the buffet. "There should be plenty of room, and we can enjoy it throughout the day."

"That does seem the place," Tom agreed, placing the vase carefully on the buffet. "Will you look at that!" he said with an exclamation of pleasure. "It's just perfect! Now, we will soon get married," he said, gently hugging me, then clasping his hand with Ethel's moments later, she looked up into his eyes, where her love met his in fondest joy.

And come to think of it, I said in my thoughts, Tom had never expressed any personal sentiment to me as he had right now, but I smiled, loving the gift of his heart to mine! I realized his gratitude was beyond measure, and his expression, joy in that gift of the greenhouse. It filled my soul with explicit blessing, and I could scarcely wait to walk into the completed greenhouse, and step along the aisles, marveling at the joy in each flower that would come in time to Ethel and Tom in their love of creation's flowers from our wonderful, great, and awesome, Father, God!

Anne busied herself in the kitchen, preparing a light lunch for us. Then we'd have the wedding amongst the lush array of the beautifully fragranced, trailing rose arbor that I so loved. Ethel and Tom would be spending their wedding night in the city and fly with us the following morning to Austria.

Blossom was so excited to be their flower girl! Dan was Tom's best man, and I was Ethel's matron of honor. When the ceremony would be over, the sitter would take Blossom back to the house, and she'd eat with Blossom and Carlos. Carlos was still too little, of course, to be dining regular style at the table, but I made sure that Blossom, especially, would be happy to be with the sitter for the duration of the day.

We hired a caterer to prepare the supper meal so that Anne would have time to enjoy the day with us. Well, I smiled to myself, I think that needed a little rephrasing! I was secretly pleased that Harry Gerali had asked Anne Fletcher to be his escort for the wedding when he learned of this, and she had quickly accepted his pleasure!

"Isn't this a grand, grand day?" Anne asked me, smiling into my eyes.

"Grand, it is!" I answered, smiling back.

When the lunch was over, I coaxed Ethel to take a brief nap. "You want to be fresh for your ceremony," I said, "and then I'll help you dress in the beautiful gown in which you shall be wed."

"Oh, Maggie! It's really happening, isn't it? A man loves me for me. And most importantly, he loves God. Do you know that we used to meet real early in the mornings and have devotions together just inside the arbor where the roses are so lovely?"

I hadn't known, but my heart was filled with joy in it! "That's wonderful!" I said, hugging her.

"Well, Tom said that no one would ever figure out how God puts all that lovely perfume in the flowers, because that's God's special secret. You know, I think he's right on that!" she smiled, with a happy lilt in her words. "And we still also love to wander in this beautiful garden, and to sit beneath the tall maples and birches within its enclosure, and share our hearts with each other and with God, as well as admiring all the shrubs, adding to its immense beauty."

Feeling emotion rise in my soul, I softly said, "That's such an exquisite niche, and yes, Ethel. I know just what you're meaning! No one but God could think of such beautiful gifts for us!"

"And no matter how hard we try, we won't know God's secret until we get to Heaven," Ethel affirmed.

"Yes, Ethel, that's true. Some things belong to God alone, and what's most important, is that we love Him and appreciate these incredibly amazing gifts that warm our hearts so. Now, if there's nothing more, please have a bit of a nap, my dearest friend."

Ethel laid down on her bed and closed her eyes. "Oh, Maggie," she said, before I reached the door, "I'm so glad that one of God's special secrets – His gifts – came to me in you."

I couldn't restrain my feelings any longer, and I rushed to her side falling on my knees. "Oh, Ethel! You are one of the greatest gifts that God has given to me, too!" I buried my head on her bed and cried my heart out, and it wasn't long before tears filled Ethel's eyes, and we cried for the joy of all the riches that were ours because of this one man, Daniel Danes, that had brought us together. Then, I arose, and Ethel turned on her side, and was soon fast asleep.

Just before three o'clock, Pastor George and his wife, Coral, arrived at the garden. While I was finishing the last touches with Ethel, I had the neighbor girl, Louise Walsh, watch Carlos during the ceremony that would soon take place. She was capable and eager, and loved watching him whenever I needed her assistance.

"His bottle's in the fridge downstairs and all you need to do is warm it up. There's plenty of food prepared, and you may take a plate up when supper's served. Just get the caterer to help you with that, Louise. You're familiar with everything here, so please enjoy yourself. We gave Anne this time off, but Mrs. Trammel down the street will soon be here, so she will be assisting you, and lunch with you. But everything should be fine. And thank you very much!" I added gratefully.

Louise Walsh was sixteen and lived two houses down from us. Her mother was a nurse and her dad, a doctor. I knew that any emergency would be settled quickly if the need arose. Both of her parents had the day off, so that made it less challenging, especially for me. But I had every faith in Mrs. Trammel. Louise's parents were a secondary plan if necessary.

Ethel looked extraordinarily beautiful. Her face was radiant. I'd always admired Ethel's gorgeous, black hair. However she wore it, every style was wonderfully becoming on her. But on this particularly very special day, her long-flowing hair had beautiful curls, and her tiara, crafted with a lovely, violet-purple-colored orchid-flowered comb that Tom had specially purchased for their wedding, perfectly held it in place. The lacy, rose-flowered veil gently fell a little past her shoulders.

Her gown, elegantly fashioned, was decorated with tiny beads, glittering like white diamonds, that caught every breathless motion of movement. Three-quarter-length sleeves were decorated with identical sparkling beads, and the dress fell in a lovely fluency just above her knees.

The bodice, designed with beautifully fine French Chantilly lace, was underlaid with a breathlessly enchanting organza atop the soft, silky taffeta material. Its sheer and lightweight georgette, like the chiffon and organza, finished the gown in its charmingly delicate simplicity; the resplendent essence holding an enchanting fairytale-like intrigue, whilst portraying a dreamy romance, setting it off to advantage.

The whole appearance of the materials was rich and stunning, with just the perfect flair embodying the effective aura of this wonderfully gorgeous, and delicately lustrous wedding dress. Like a melody writ upon its divinely stunning creation, it couldn't have been more lovely or entrancingly perfect, on my dear Ethel!

"I adore long gowns," she said, "but this I can wear for other special occasions later on."

"I think it's just gorgeous on you, Ethel!" I spoke. "Now, please excuse me a moment. I'll be right back." I went to my bedroom and opened my jewelry box. Retrieving a tiny package, I quickly hurried back.

"This is for you," I said. "I hope you'll like it," as I handed the box to Ethel. A dainty pendant was nestled in a lovely violet-lined insert that held a beautiful lavender-colored rose.

Ethel carefully lifted the pendant out of the box and drew in her breath. "Oh, so lovely," she said, hugging me. "Thank you, Maggie."

"It's my pleasure," I said. "I hope you'll always wear it in honor of our friendship." She held it against her throat, and I helped clasp it in the back. When I stood aback, tears misted in my eyes. "Take a look in the mirror, Ethel," I softly said. "Such impeccable, joyful beauty!" I lovingly exclaimed.

Staring at her reflection, she lightly fingered the rose. It set the dress off to advantage, beautifully accentuating the gown. Even the comb Tom had given to her complemented it perfectly. "Joyful! Oh, it is! Just like you! Thank you so much, Maggie," she said again.

"Just enjoy it, Ethel! I love doing this for you!"

Ethel slipped on her white-heeled sandals, and we were about to proceed downstairs, when she abruptly stopped and said, "You know what?" she suddenly exclaimed.

"No! What?"

"I'm soon going to be a Mrs., like you!"

I couldn't help but laugh at Ethel's unique way of expressing herself. "Indeed, you are!" I spoke. "We'd better hurry now." Drawing the curtain aside, I peered out the window where Ethel's room gave a wide-sweeping overview of the garden. "Everyone is surely waiting. Well, my friend, are you ready to become a Mrs. now?" I asked, my eyes dancing.

"Mmm hmm," she said, smiling. "I am!"

Harry was going to pick Anne up here and she was going to dress at his place so that it would be less chaotic. Suzanne Wilcox would ensure that Anne, likewise, was properly assisted.

Anne chose to wear a beautiful, blue dress, just above the knees, that fit her attractive figure in breathless pleasure. The boat neckline was very pretty and suited her fair shoulders and lovely, white skin. The fabric of the dress was made from a blend of polyester, cotton, and silk, lending a delicately, lovely sheen to the whole appearance. I loved the slightly puffed, three-quarter length sleeves, adding a touch of flair. The straight-cut skirt accentuated Anne's slim figure to advantage. It was exquisite on her!

Suzanne helped Anne fasten the string of pearls her mother had recently given to her, as well as giving Anne a hand with her hair. Suzanne loved hairdressing, and although she didn't do much of that anymore, she was delighted to curl Anne's lovely, brunette hair in beautiful ringlets that gracefully fell a few inches past her shoulders. A blue butterfly comb was tucked exquisitely at the side of her bangs, adding to the simplicity of her natural beauty.

"You're gorgeous!" Mrs. Wilcox praised, when Anne had finished putting on her makeup. "Not only that, but you look like a model! My, but how enchanting that dress is on you!" She paused, then complimented, "I think that you and Mr. Gerali make the most beautiful couple I've ever seen!"

Blushing, Anne was near tears when Harry lightly knocked on the door. "Anne, dear, are you almost ready? We need to leave shortly."

Suzanne answered the door, but wouldn't allow Harry to see her, gently shooing him into the hall. "She's almost ready, Harry. We only need but a moment more, please."

"Sure, Mrs. Wilcox. I'll be waiting downstairs, but fifteen minutes is all we have to spare!" Chuckling, he turned to descend the staircase and Suzanne reentered the spare bedroom.

"Your Mr. Harry is looking most handsome," she said in honeyed tones, "and you, dear Anne, with your Irish soul, and pretty, green eyes, look like a princess right out of a fairytale story!" Suddenly, she noticed her stockinged feet and asked in dismay, "But where are your shoes, Miss Anne? You can't go to the wedding without any!" Anne softly laughed and said, "Right here, Mrs. Wilcox, in my bag." Suzanne breathed a sigh of relief as Anne reached in to take them out. She opened the box, and slowly drew them out.

"Why, how lovely!" Suzanne exclaimed. "But I thought you'd wear something fancier, Miss Anne?" A trace of disappointment was etched in her words.

"Oh, they're fancy enough," Anne assured, "and I'd thought that at first, too, when the salesclerk assured me that they were absolutely the finishing touch to my attire, and not to discard so easily what may seem the obvious, initial impression. And she certainly was right on that! Once I step into them, why a special sort of magic seems to happen!"

The shoes may have appeared ordinary to a fault, as Mrs. Wilcox had suggested, but as Anne slipped into her black-satin, high-heeled pumps, the effect was truly enchanting. They even had a tiny, black bow at the toe of each shoe.

"I'm ready now," she softly said, "and I want to thank you for your help and this delightful time with you, Mrs. Wilcox!"

"The shoes are truly special, Anne, and I can see it now! Forgive me, Anne. I misspoke. And it was my honor and joy to be of aid to you as well!" she said.

"No worries," Anne smiled, patting her shoulder. "None at all!"

When Anne descended the stairs, Harry appeared in the foyer looking up, admiring his date. "You are breathlessly beautiful!" he said, kissing her when she stepped onto the main floor. He gently placed a pink and red wrist carnation corsage on her wrist, a bit shy in his cook's presence. "Now, we must hurry!" he gently said. "If only I had a carriage, Anne."

Turning to Mrs. Wilcox, he called, "Thank you!" She smiled as the tears rolled uncontrollably down her cheeks.

"How I remember these times I had with my Jack," she said to herself as they left. "Such wondrous, beautiful, precious moments!"

Once they stepped out of Harry's home and into the fresh air, he said, with a smile, "I'm happy we're finally alone, Anne. But it was worth the wait! Let's try to relax on the drive, shall we?" he said, his eyes twinkling. He turned the key, and the engine came to life, purring quietly as a contented kitten.

"I'm happy, too," Anne shared, as the car slowly turned off his driveway onto the highway, "and I love especially being so near to you!" she shyly said. Seeing the beauty of the trees along the way, Anne added, "I'm enjoying the ride with you already!" Giggling, Anne turned to face him and teased, "And I think it's more perfect a ride than any carriage, and just as lovely!"

"That's exactly how I feel, Anne! Exactly! Why, if we were in a carriage with horses and we hit a pothole, I wouldn't want your beautiful dress getting sprayed with muddy water, especially with the recent rains we've just had!"

Laughing, Anne smiled, and giggled. "Well, I think that this 'carriage' is just delightful, Harry! It rides smooth as glass and the tires won't be splattering any muddy water on either of us! Truly, it is wonderful!"

The ceremony evoked its own special enchantment. As they said their vows, Tom lovingly looked into Ethel's eyes. "I do not ask for you to obey me or to be superior. I ask only to love you and to share this love with you forever as my wife. Will you accept my love, my dearest Ethel?"

Ethel's eyes held the same love as she lovingly said, "I do, my dearest Tom. And I also ask only for your love, not to be above or beneath you, but to cherish you forever. Will you accept my love, my dearest Tom?"

"I do, forever and forever!" he said, tears filling his eyes.

Pastor Hokan then said, "As you now exchange the rings, I am honored to pronounce you as husband and wife. And Tom," he smiled as he slipped Ethel's wedding ring on her finger, "You may now kiss your wife!" What a lovely sentiment, I told myself. Ethel was now Tom's wife!

We enjoyed the gala celebration and taking pictures of this lovely couple. The ladies presented them with the beautiful quilt they promised the evening Ethel had fallen ill. It had intricately detailed flowers of many colors and varieties in each square, that took my breath away!

When the meal was over, Ethel and Tom came to say goodbye, departing minutes later for the city to begin their honeymoon. Perfect joy shone in their eyes, that I could hardly contain my feelings. And I was more than assured that the purity of their hearts for God and each other, would be strengthened, where this joy would never tarnish, but lovingly shine through the years.

"We'll see you in the morning," I said, hugging Ethel. "We shall look forward to Austria with you and Tom!" Tom hugged me and Dan, and then I whispered quickly to Ethel, "And I especially look forward to spending some special time with you, Mrs. Wafer!"

Ethel's heart held emotion as she whispered back, "Me, too, Maggie! I can hardly wait! But Tom is waiting, and I must go. We'll see you tomorrow!"

My heart held so much emotion, too, that I could hardly think. I was so happy for Ethel and Tom, but a part of my life would share her again as I had been so privileged to have her delightful companionship through these years. And regardless of how far or near the Wafers would be from us, Ethel would always live in my heart. Like Dan, I was thrilled that she and Tom were coming back to live close by on our estate after their honeymoon in Austria. Nothing could be more wonderful, I smiled to myself!

Anne and Harry seemed to be especially enjoying themselves, and that question came back to my mind, Could it be? Anne was a devoted and dedicated worker in our home, and I suddenly didn't know what I'd ever do without her if she and Harry decided to marry.

Well, I soothed my worry, God had given us Anne when Ethel couldn't work, so He surely would have another plan for someone equally wonderful as them! And it would fill my heart with immense joy to see Harry happy and Anne happy together with him. They were truly a lovely couple and suddenly, I prayed that desire and hope beyond anything else for them!

I looked to the future with the anticipation of the greenhouse, and all the wonderful gifts Ethel's presence would still fill in my life. She would always hold this very special place within my heart, where I'd never forget our private talks before Dan and I had wed, and all the talks that had followed.

Ethel was a friend who was more like a close sister to me, as I was to her, that I had found for life, and all because of a book that had brought me to Daniel Danes' publishing firm that beautiful summer day so long ago.

And I thought how strange life is sometimes, for I'd never forget when Ethel had described Dan to me, admitting how handsome he is. Somehow, deep down within my spirit, I knew she was speaking of my editor, but I never dreamed that I'd marry him! Now, Ethel had her own handsome "doll," and I knew that in him, she would find the same joy that I have with Dan. I could hardly wait until the morning to see this joy within their hearts shining in their eyes as we journeyed back to Austria!

For now, I happily walked into my home to thank Louise Walsh, my sitter, and pay her well. Mrs. Trammel had left shortly before, but I would see to it that she also was well compensated. Perhaps, Anne wouldn't mind baking her a cherry pie, and I could take her shopping for a gift of clothing.

Then, I couldn't wait to rest within the pleasant eve beside my husband, knowing that my children were safe, and my world, as beautiful and perfect as I'd long since dreamed upon the fancy of my heart!

CHAPTER 19

Pieces of God's Heart

Dan was gently shaking me as I opened my eyes, squinting against the bright sunlight.

"It's time to be up, my darling," he lovingly said. "We must hurry."

At first, I had no idea what he was talking about.

"I want to sleep," I drowsily said, trying to pull the covers back over me.

"Maggie, wake up! Anne has breakfast ready, and we barely have time to meet the plane on schedule. Blossom is already eating, and Carlos is fed. I let you rest a little longer after the excitement of yesterday."

I still didn't quite get it. "What excitement?" I said, closing my eyes. "Please let me be."

Dan would have none of it. "Maggie Danes, I'm telling you for the last time. Get up, now!" He pulled the blankets off the bed, and despite the sunshine filtering through the window, I shivered. "What will Ethel think if we miss the flight?"

Instantly, I was wide awake. "Ethel! My goodness, Dan! I'm sorry! Grab my housecoat, will you?"

Dan graciously handed me my housecoat.

"I'll be as quick in the shower as I can," I promised.

"Just five minutes, Maggie. I'm going to check that that's all the time you take!"

I rushed to the bathroom and quickly showered. Just as I was stepping out, Dan appeared. It was a good thing, too, that he was a man of his word, because I felt myself slipping. "Dan!" I cried. He reached for my arm as I began to fall and caught me. "My back," I said. "Oh, it hurts!"

Carefully, he wrapped the big towel about me that I'd set aside on the towel rack, and then Dan helped me to the chair in our room. Drying me off, he helped me into my housecoat afterward.

"Where does it hurt, darling?" he asked.

"My left side. But . . . but I think everything's okay. Nothing but a sprain."

Dan shouted for Anne, and she came running, stopping to knock on our door before he bid her to enter. Her face showed dismay when she saw me. "Oh my!" she exclaimed, "What happened, dear Mrs.?"

"Maggie slipped in the shower," Dan spoke for me. "Would you please get the children's jackets on and then call the taxi for us? And Anne, please wrap up some breakfast for me and Maggie. We'll eat on the way to the airport."

Dan helped me to dress, and I felt a bit better. He turned to me with tears in his eyes and apologized. "I'm so sorry, my dearest. I shouldn't have rushed you so! I think you weren't quite awake, and I should have been much more considerate of you."

"I'm going to be fine, Dan," I assured, "but I may need a day or two for that. And it wasn't your fault. Please . . ." But Dan wouldn't let me finish. He kissed me, then, helped me up, supporting me as we walked through the corridor and down the few steps, then out to the waiting taxi.

But by the time we arrived at the airport, I could barely walk, feeling stiff and sore. "Maybe we could take a later flight today. I'll check with the airline. And Maggie, I'm also going to call up your doctor and see if he will give you a prescription we can fill at the drugstore here, unless he insists on examining you first."

"Oh, no. I'll be fine," I said. But when I got up from the chair at the airport, pain shot through my left shoulder, and I collapsed back onto the chair.

At that moment, Dan noticed Ethel and Tom approaching. Happy to see us, they quickened their steps, but stopped short when they realized something was amiss with me.

"Maggie, oh, dear Maggie," Ethel lovingly cried, kneeling before me. "What has happened?"

"I slipped in the shower when I was about to step out, but Dan caught me. But my shoulder, it hurts something awful. And my back, too," I complained.

Tom's expression was serious, but he gently spoke. "Maggie, if you'll trust me, I've studied medicine and some of the ancient ways. I'd like to examine you. Perhaps, we might have a private room temporarily. I'll check with the airline clerk."

Moments later, Tom rejoined us. "We may use their private lounge – over there," he pointed. "The manager has kindly acceded to my request. It isn't very far, and I think with Dan and me helping you, you shouldn't be in too much pain."

Along with both Tom and Dan's wonderful, caring way, it helped to ease the tension in my shoulder. Ethel walked next to Tom, and we soon reached the lounge.

"Please relax," Tom said. Gently touching my shoulder and along down the left side of my back, Tom's hands moved like water on glass – delicate and smooth. "Just tell me where the pain is and where it's the worst," he said.

"It hurts most just under my shoulder blade and down my back from there. It feels like I twisted everything."

"It's a mild sprain. Ointment and a cold compress at the site will really help. If you'd allow me to apply the initial application, then Dan or Ethel can do that for you over the next five to seven days. A pain reliever will help, too. I wonder if you telephoned your doctor after this occurred?"

"Not yet. I was hoping for Dan to do so just when you arrived."

"By the way, where's your children? And Anne?" Tom suddenly asked.

"They're already waiting at the area to board the plane," Dan answered. "An airline stewardess was called to offer assistance, so Blossom and Carlos are with her and Anne momentarily."

"Well, let's call the doctor and have him telephone in a prescription over here. As for the ointment, I always carry it with me on trips, so if you don't mind, I'd like to quickly confer with the doctor to ensure this is also under his instruction."

The call was put forth and because my doctor was familiar with Tom's medical knowledge, everything was approved. The prescription was immediately filled, and we caught our flight with minutes to spare after Tom applied the ointment.

When we boarded the plane, Anne and the children were seated several rows up from us. I was glad that they were settled, excited for the flight.

I soon fell asleep, leaning my head on Dan's shoulder, shifting into a comfortable position. I heard voices, but the medicine was making me drowsy, and I readily gave in to its satisfying desire. Tom spoke to Ethel, and she relayed his message as they sat across the aisle from us. "Dan," she said, not realizing she hadn't addressed him as her Mr. "Don't let Maggie stay in that position too long because her muscles will tighten and cramp up, increasing the pain. If she's still sleeping after an hour, try to ease her off your shoulder."

Understanding, Dan said, "Thank you!"

The flight was uneventful, and the meals served, delicious. I dozed again after lunch as the hours slipped away, wondering where I was when I awakened.

"Dan," I said, almost frantically, "what are we doing here, and so high up, it seems?" Peering out the window, I stifled a scream. "We're in the air!" I said, in a panic. "How did we get here?"

An attendant came, trying to see what the matter was. "Please don't disturb the passengers," she quietly said.

"Pardon my wife," Dan quickly interposed. "She had a fall this morning and she's been sleeping throughout almost the entire flight. She's just a bit disoriented."

"All right, but please keep it down."

Clinging to Dan, I asked, "Who are all these people?"

Chuckling, Dan said, "We're on our way to Austria, Maggie, remember?"

Furrowing my brow, I suddenly realized where I was. "Oh," I said. "Of course."

"You've had a very long sleep between meals, darling. And how's your back?"

"My back? Is something wrong with it?" I blankly asked.

"Maggie! You're still sleeping. You slipped in the shower this morning. The doctor gave you pills for the pain and Tom smoothed on ointment."

"He did? Oh, yes! It's still sore but feels a bit better. How much longer is our flight?" I asked, fully awake now.

"Not much longer. About an hour. Why don't we just relax until then? I'll be glad to get my feet back on the ground and stretch my legs," Dan said.

Peeking over at Ethel and Tom, I saw they had fallen asleep, too. "It's mighty quiet in here right now," I softly said, with a tease to my words. "Dark and quiet," I repeated, leaning in close, kissing Dan.

"Not dark enough for me," Dan said, stealing a kiss from me. "But it will be when we land. And I can't wait to get into a comfortable bed beside you, my dearest Maggie!"

When we debarked, a taxi took us to our motel where we'd spend the night, then we'd settle in our temporary lodging the following day, where the visiting professors and teachers had a lovely campus. It would be our home over several months. Ethel and Tom, however, would share a cabin by themselves over the next four weeks as they honeymooned, where the campus afforded half a dozen extra housing units for such occasions as visitors to on-staff, like Dan and me. Anne and our children would likewise room in another by themselves. A nanny was an important part of the affair which would permit me and Dan to study and prepare our lessons to the curriculum expected within the classes. But we'd be close by and could have our children with us anytime we chose as well, where this lenient code was appreciative of the young professor couples.

Tom offered to apply the ointment the following morning, and Ethel or Dan would continue that over the course of the next several days. I felt stiff and sore, but my shoulder and back were improving, despite the long hours confined within the occupancy of the plane.

When we were having breakfast together with Ethel and Tom immediately afterwards, she suddenly piped up, crunching up her pretty face, "Maggie, how come it's called, honeymoon, and not, honeystar?" Taken aback, I put down my coffee mug, and curiously intrigued, thought about that for a moment.

"Hmm," I said, "that's a very good question. Well, dear Ethel, perhaps it's because the moon is considered so romantic. Couples like to walk in the evening, holding hands and kissing and gazing up at the moon, especially when it's full. So, I think this might be your answer."

Tom leaned close to Ethel, and said, "I like both, darling! That's quite the mind you have, and I love you all the more for it!" He lightly kissed her on the cheek, and blushing, Ethel bashfully murmured, "Oh, Tom!"

The area here was breathtaking. Beautiful, tall trees surrounding the properties lent satisfactory privacy, and separate driveways were set at a substantial distance between the cabins. The cabins themselves were clean and fresh. I was very grateful that the housekeeping weekly provided clean towels, as well as an outside laundry service. They even kept the fridges stocked! There was also a good supply of dishes, so I didn't have to worry how many dishes were sometimes used in cooking!

The yards were well tended, providing swings, sandboxes, and teeter-totters for children residing with their parents and nannies. We were captivated at the peaceful setting and most appreciative of everything it comprised.

One of the best attractions was that of a Hobby Farm, with wonderfully beautiful, gentle horses, located only a few miles away. We enjoyed many delightful days with the children on the weekends, and they adored the experience. Of course, Carlos was very little, but it was apparent that he loved being with the animals just as much as his cousin, Blossom. Wide-eyed with wonder, we cherished this special gift, and were just as enthralled as they! There was no question that we were abundantly blessed!

As for Dan and me, we'd always held a special heart for animals, and it was truly a gift to share this with our children. Anne sometimes joined us, but she was shy, and while she also loved the horses, her hesitation was apparent. But in time, she lost her shyness, and loved riding high up on a horse having the time of her life! That was truly, not only a special moment, but so good to see!

To some, the publishing industry must seem like an uninteresting occupation. But it was anything but that! Marketing executives, especially, are a vital key at the forefront of everything else that falls into place. A wonderful marketing executive creates the atmosphere that keeps everything running smoothly, like oil or grease, to a vehicle. Or as Ethel said in such lovely sentiment, "A person creating the most beautiful flower in an author to flourish!" Their knowledge was also very important in sharing it with their authors. And even though they weren't the creators of the books, their job can effectively serve authors in various aspects.

Of the many facets within the publishing departments, everyone works together to present each author's manuscript through all the stages, until it's printed, then released to the public.

Dan and I had intricately studied as much as we were able to the year prior in being awarded our certificates in teaching. Dan had greater knowledge than me, because he had taken the year before we married to study in-depth various aspects, such as editing, and everything in-between to the printing process, and engaging formulative strategies successful to campaigns, that may eventually bring an author to a traditional publisher. But traditional publishers had their own agendas that were subject to meeting particular requirements to an author's work being acquired.

Standing in front of the classroom was a new experience to me, as it was for Dan. I've always had a yearning to teach and found that I was good at it! My students also inspired my heart to do my very best for them. We loved our new role, where some of the students would also become instructors, and it was certainly good that God had put diverse treasures within each of us to make our world much more interesting!

The days and weeks flew by, that I could scarcely believe it! The students were intelligent individuals, willing learners, and remarkably dedicated in applying themselves to their lessons. It was truly a joyful blessing to teach what we had not only learned, but within the practical side of work as authors ourselves.

Part of the course included creatively creating an outline for a book. We let them decide whether they wanted to work on a children's book or a novel. We were truly amazed at the stories that came through this exercise, where many of the students eventually published their work. It was a moment of realization how inspiration has the yearning to aspire such wondrous imaginations!

Sometimes, as I mentioned to Dan one evening as we took a stroll around the campus, I wondered what the trees would think if they only knew how valuable they were to this industry!

Dan laughed and kissing me, commented, "My dearest Maggie, that mind of yours is ever turning, imagining all it can! But it's just wonderful and I love you so much the dearer for it!"

"Well, Dan," I replied, "just think about it. A tree is life to the author. Without its paper, whatever would a writer write on and whatever would one's story be bound as a book? And the life that the tree is to the author, is life to every word. It's the breath of the author's mind imprinted on its life. Fascinating, isn't it?"

"Yes, my Maggie! Fascinating, indeed!"

I began to understand how God had given so much to humanity long before we had need of paper. He had thought of everything! And everything was so perfect within His awesome design.

While we were privileged to use computers, technology didn't always meet that standard. We encouraged our students to create sufficient drafts on paper because it was their personal authenticated signature which left no doubt, should their book ever come into question before a court, as to whom the author is. Dan and I always signed or initialed our names with the date and time as the proof to the writer behind the novel or the story we were creating.

I was totally taken with learning and fascinated with both sides, as an author, as well as what was important in editing, proofreading, and so forth. While other areas within the marketing executive's position fascinated me, I preferred to edit and proofread. That was my expertise. But when both Dan and I learned that a special class on movie and filmmaking was available, I immediately told Dan that I had to take it! Laughing with me, he was as excited as I to study this intriguing facet. As our teaching continued throughout the months, we spent much of our time learning in evening classes, the profound field that moviemaking offered.

We seemed to have the natural eye and ability within this industry, that shortly after our return to Canada, Dan and I decided to expand the firm and accommodate the field of moviemaking. Dan loved it as much as I did!

Specializing in this field, while still working as a proofreader and editor in this expertise, we adapted it as a part of a learning facility to our staff, also providing outside of our staff, clients with this vital option that could turn their stories into a mini-series, movie, or feature film that may even hit the silver screen.

To those on staff, we were willing to keep them on our payroll when they decided to study the field of moviemaking, but only if they continued to work hard and successfully finish the courses.

Harry Gerali, our wonderful, new addition to the company, although he'd joined us months ago, was equally intrigued, and the first to sign up. We couldn't have been happier with his decision! He was most enthusiastic and hardworking as he attended our lectures, graduating at the top of his class.

We invited Mr. Gerali to join our platform, and sitting in on some of his lectures, we were truly amazed at the natural and prolifically stunning way he had about him as a professor! We really loved having him share our own pleasure, where he became this astoundingly positive influence, changing lives and changing hearts beyond their wildest dreams! His gentle, patient way reflected his personal character, but we also saw a different side of him as he stepped into various roles in his teaching, losing himself in the love of character-acting personas that were profoundly prolific, and a real joy to see! Depicting different tones in their speech and body language, the students were challenged from Harry's profound and natural way in teaching, the realm within that core that was fundamental to the realism and fluency to any scene as though it was second nature. Thus, taking words off the page and creating their life-like characters, we saw this astutely wonderful flair for acting that we all loved in him!

That evening, I remembered my prayer to God in wanting to give something special to Harry for all the blessings he'd so graciously given to me and Dan, especially after I'd been laid up with the spider incident.

"Dan," I thoughtfully chose my words, "I have an idea what we may do for Harry. He's been so loyal and sweet and kind, and the loveliest employee. I think that a change would do him well. How about we offer him a paid trip to Austria with us on our next term?

"Perhaps, you would talk to the Director, and he might even give him a platform to teach a term? What do you think?"

"Oh, darling!" he exhorted, kissing me. "This is truly a wonderful idea! I'll call first thing in the morning and see what the Director says. Harry will truly be a terrific asset to the university, and they always are looking for guest speakers. Harry more than fits the criteria."

"Thank you, Dan," I said. "I'm going to be praying for this to be so, because I couldn't think of a greater blessing we could give to our dear friend, Harry!"

Dan put in the call and the Director was delighted. "I just need his resume faxed, Mr. Danes," he said, "and we can take it from there. Give me a few days after that. We'll be having our next board meeting then and I'm sure they'll be as eager as I am to welcome Mr. Gerali as a guest colleague."

"We sure do appreciate this favor," Dan said.

"Favor? No! No! It'll be our pleasure! Goodbye now and we'll talk soon."

Other staff members joined the course, providing the necessary tools to engage themselves as apprentice producers and filmmakers, and many who studied with us from around the world. I had my eye on one or two of them, who could transition beautifully in teaching in Harry's absence when the time came. Dan did, too! When the call was confirmed, we were thrilled!

We invited Harry over for supper the following afternoon. Ethel scurried about the kitchen, worried that she might forget something.

"You're just fine," I encouraged. "We're not visiting with the king, but our dear friend and employee, Harry!"

"Oh my, yes," she said, "but he is special, is he not?"

"Yes!" I assured her.

"So, I must have everything just right . . . king or no king, this 'special' in him deserves the very best I can give!"

I'd never quite thought of it that way, but Ethel was right. In fact, I decided that everyone, whoever they were, deserved our very best because it was part of God's good pleasure for us to do so in His Name and live by the Golden Rule!

Our company, originally founded by Dan and then co-founded by Dan and me as we advanced with the movie-making curriculum, became a prestigiously recognized facility that we were proud of, sparking new minds to go further than they ever dared believe, creating beauty from the words on pages that came to life on both the stage and the screen!

Carlie Mills, who had acted as our go-between with our letters prior to our marriage, was equally excited. Dan forgave her misunderstanding, knowing that she was, otherwise, an excellent employee. She came to love the movie business so much; she eventually left the company to become an on-screen actress! For these young minds, it was the thrill of a lifetime for many!

I knew that Harry was content where he was, but when we told him the news of going to Austria with us and having a teaching position over the first term, he didn't know what to say at first.

"Oh, this is terrific!" he finally said, as tears filled his eyes. "It will be my great honor to teach abroad and learn myself. Thank you for this immense privilege!"

The day came when Harry asked to speak privately with me shortly before we were to leave for Austria. "I wanted to tell you that I've proposed to Anne and she and I were wondering, Maggie, since your garden is so beautiful and pretty with the roses, do you think that you and Mr. Danes would mind if we married beneath the bower? I want to take Anne as my wife before we travel abroad, and just so you know, I've also asked her to share the platform with me sometimes. She has her degree and has always loved the movie and film industry. She just needed a change and loves children, and so she has been very grateful to share your beautiful home and to be a part of your family, especially your darling children."

I hardly knew what to say, I was so excited for them. "Oh, yes, Harry! We would be honored to host your ceremony in our lovely garden! And I'm very taken that Anne has this special joy like you! I just might sit in on your platform together in Austria!" I teased.

"Anytime!" he warmly invited, his eyes dancing to that anticipation. "Now I must tell Anne this wonderful news, Maggie, and we thank you with all our hearts!"

"The pleasure is all ours!" I smiled, hugging him.

Eventually, I laid down my editing pen and taught fulltime, as students from around the world came to study this thrilling and intricate field. Dan taught part-time, while remaining focused on his work in management within the company. Might I also add that we were happy with the decision that Dan had made years earlier in firing Carletta and her husband, Albert Durif. While they weren't enemies, as in an army or any espionage story, they were enemies that were necessary to foil just the same. Their devious upsets, plotting against my beloved and me, had become intolerant as their boldness mounted in recklessly slighted rebuff of heightened arrogance, all in the name of Jealousy, which had gone on long enough. I couldn't imagine, and didn't dare to even think, what more they were capable of in their insidious ploys. We couldn't afford to have even a hair's breadth of a whisper of mistrust within the company. Months later, we happened to pick up the local newspaper and were astounded to read that they'd been found guilty of stealing thousands of dollars from a major corporation and jailed.

Here, *Pieces of God's Heart* would be much like a patchwork quilt, where the pieces came together within the wonder of it all. And in the palm of His hand, He would ever keep us, angels guarding our every move, fitting the good and the bad of our lives in perfect place, working behind the scenes, and ever before us.

With faith guiding us, peace filtered in my heart as I rested beside my dearest Dan upon my pillow this night, assured that God was looking after us, one day at a time. The daily Presence that He gave to us in Himself, would ever lead our hearts aright, for it is here that we taught our children to love and respect God, and to be a channel of His blessing to everyone around them. No gift more precious or beautiful, would sustain each of our hearts as we love and learn and follow the One Who is the true life – the Breath of all we are. In this light, it really made me think about just how sacred that sustaining breath is, and how we need to use it to honor Him to every breath that's ours within His very heart for us!

CHAPTER 20

An Unexpected Gift

We could hardly wait to fly back home to Canada to celebrate Christmas with Ethel and Tom! I missed them terribly at times and I couldn't wait to share my heart with her again! Harry and Anne were sad to leave Austria, as we were, but also very glad to be back home in Canada. Although he was offered a full-time position overseas, as she was, they both decided to remain in Canada and continue working for us.

"Our meadow . . . we could not bear to leave it so long again," he said, and I understood his heart perfectly. "Anne and I love the solace and the beauty and peace it effuses, not only over the land, but especially in our hearts. It's as much a part of her, as it is me, and that is partly what has drawn us so close together, even before we were married."

I understood their hearts perfectly. There was nothing like the familiar that one so dearly loved and could call one's own. Here, the meadow would forever be an imprint of glorious joy that would captivate our souls together.

I think that Anne was ready to teach fulltime again, and when Dan and I asked her if she'd like to instruct alongside Harry at our firm, her face lit up and she profusely expressed what she was feeling.

"Oh, yes, I would, indeed! But what about housekeeping and caring for your children?" she asked.

"Our dear nanny, Amanda, wants to spend a year in Canada after our term in June is completed, and when we invited her, she was thrilled! So, everything's arranged, and you need not worry about housekeeping and children!"

Before they flew back to Canada, Anne and I went shopping together, and sometimes, with Dan and the children. It was evident how much she loved to browse the shops and spend hours alone with her husband, as well!

We were so happy for this gifted couple who loved the Lord and gave their hearts in such wondrously special ways to us! I knew that Harry had found his soulmate in Anne, and she in him. Their wedding day in our garden had been a dream come true. "It was more perfect than our meadow to marry," Harry confided, "but we have both, and are thankful for your garden paradise and ours within the meadow."

We wanted to give Anne and Harry three extra weeks off to be with their families before they'd join us again in Austria until the finish of the year in June. But when this school term was completed, they would not be flying abroad again. I knew that we'd miss them, but we also wanted them to live their lives in the joy of their own choosing. We were very thankful to have them on this final semester with us. We talked it over, and Dan and I decided that Amanda could take over in the final week, and they could fly back a week early since his requirement with the university would terminate a week before ours ended. That would ensure they had more time at home, especially their first Christmas together.

Anne's eyes misted with tears, hugging me, then Dan. "This is so kind of you," she said. "Thank you so much! Harry will be just as thrilled as I am, although we would have enjoyed wandering Austria's beauty, but to be home again, dearest Maggie, there won't be anything like it more wonderful or beautiful!"

Smiling, I took her hand, and said, "Oh, how I know that feeling, dearest Anne! I can't wait to see the winter wonderland within your meadow, either! Every new season celebrates its own special adornment of beauty, without a doubt!"

When Amanda learned that Anne and Harry were soon departing, she graciously offered to care for our children. I knew that our children would be delighted! Amanda was as sweet as she was pretty, and she adored them, as much as they adored her! While we could have managed, having the help while preparing and correcting exams made our tasks so much easier without constant interruptions. We were very grateful for her help. The children welcomed her back, filled with love and admiration for her, just as we were! Amanda had so enjoyed filling in for Anne, as well, on the days she taught alongside with her husband, Harry. We were so blessed! Yet, I couldn't help but wonder if she might have a hidden secret, too, as had Ethel and Anne. I supposed only time would tell, and the good Lord would reveal it if it should be truly so!

The mountains in the distance were breathtaking, and we loved to walk the streets. From our campus, we had a perfect view of the hills. I'd never been one for mountains, but being here, I began to appreciate their beauty in a different light, which was as unique and diverse as our own home in Canada, where we lived in the prairie province of Manitoba. It certainly was flatland compared to Austria's spectacular mountains!

With the changing season, the entire beauty, bathed in tints of the glorious autumn, gradually faded as the winter took hold and snow abounded in abundance. The children were ecstatic when we took them tobogganing, crying out with glee. What joy this was! Dan even challenged me to slide down a hill with him, and I couldn't resist the temptation! I certainly understood my children's thrill of adventure, for it was the same for me! Dan laughed all the while as our sleigh flew over the snow down a gentle hill and I hung on for dear life, exclaiming the joy that was inside of me as I laughed along with him.

One of the other special adventures was participating in a ride in a carriage, drawn by two beautiful horses at the nearby Hobby Farm, especially in the evening when the Victorian lanterns that lined the cobblestone street, took us along paths through wooded forests with towering, snow-laden trees. What a thrill it was! I loved every moment of it with my Dan all to myself while Amanda stayed back at the residence and did fun things together with our children. It eased the tension of our work, taking on a whole new world. The view was fabulous, and I enjoyed cuddling and kissing with my husband as the rhymical trotting of the horses brought us to a distant past. Yet, here in Europe, it was still an every day, idyllic way of life:

dreamy, romantic, and breathtakingly gorgeous! Such precious memories that would never leave our hearts.

Amanda loved the outdoors and helped the children build snowmen, took them for walks where the barren trees looked like haunted, ghostly stick figures except for the snow upon their scrawny boughs, and showed them how to make snow angels, much to their glee! She never tired of providing entertainment for them, like dressing up in different costumes, changing her voice to the characters as she read from the classic fairytale books. She baked sugar cookies with them, too, as they adored her more each day. We couldn't have been happier doing our work, knowing our children were so cared and loved for in her loving presence.

Ethel and I had traipsed all over when we'd originally returned to Austria for the new school year. While it was her and Tom's honeymoon, it was extraordinarily special to share the gift of their presence during the month they'd stayed. Here, I missed Ethel's sweet ways, but I understood that her heart belonged completely to Tom now, and they needed to begin the journey of their lives, as their love of flowers began to grow within the greenhouse, and the dreams their hearts shared together. Dan had hired a couple of skilled carpenters, and by the time the Wafers returned to Canada, everything was completed.

Ethel's letters were full of joy and new anticipation as they filled the greenhouse with the love of their hearts. And I truly believe that the flowers flourished because of this love, for it was the foundation of a serenely, tranquil setting. I long since knew that flowers didn't respond well to disruptive chaos.

Shortly before Christmas, I realized that I was expecting our second child. I was so happy, and when I shared my heart's secret with Dan, he was overjoyed. Blossom was becoming such a sweet little lady, and her smile was wide with pleasure.

"Mommy," she said, "what will you call her?"

Startled, my heart nearly skipped a beat. "I don't know whether God will give us a boy or a girl yet, darling," I gently said.

Puckering her face, she thought, then said, "I know a sister is what I'm wanting this time, Mommy. And I think the angels will bring me a sister."

"We'll see," I said, smiling.

"Oh, just like Ethel told me last time. Well, I see, too! It's going to be a girl. God's special 'light' to me."

Carlos could be a handful at times, and I wondered what he'd think of our new baby. He would be one in the summer. By the time the baby arrived, he'd be almost two. I could hardly wait for him to peer into my arms and his eyes grow large the first time he'd come to lay eyes on his new sister or brother.

That evening, a few minutes after Dan and I had retired for the night, I suddenly sat straight up in bed. "Dan!" I gently shook him. He sleepily turned to face me, rubbing his eyes. "Are you awake?" I asked.

"I think so, Maggie. Is there something wrong?"

"No!" I quickly assured him. "I just realized something! Well, actually, two somethings, as a matter-of-fact!" I amended.

"Go on," he said.

"I think you wanted another baby . . . the way you looked into my eyes shortly after Carlos had been born. Do you remember?"

"Surprisingly, yes Maggie, I do remember, and I do want another child, as we'll have in the months ahead! But what does that have anything to do with it?"

"Everything!" I chuckled. "Today, Blossom's words suddenly reminded me of the dream I had not too long after I felt you wanted another baby with me."

"How?" he asked.

"Well, she was so insistent that this baby will be a girl. And in my dream, I saw one boy and two girls happily enjoying themselves on swings!"

"I see," he considered.

"I think that Blossom is right, darling, and that that dream confirms it because I believe it's from God. A girl! Won't that be wonderful?" I smiled, kissing him.

"It certainly will be wonderful, indeed, Maggie! But for now, my sweet darling, do you suppose this tired dad might get some sleep?"

"Oh, humbug!" I said, throwing my pillow at him.

"That's not fair, Maggie!" he warned. "You have somewhat of an advantage over me tonight, but don't forget that I can throw, too, you know!"

"I'd like to see that!" I challenged.

"Perhaps, another day . . . I think I'll surprise you on that. Now, please, may I get some sleep?" he pleaded, looking into my eyes. "I worked hard today, after all!"

I lovingly kissed him and sweetly whispered, "Anything for you, my darling! Anything at all!"

We arrived back home on a beautiful, calm evening with large snowflakes gently falling, catching the lights as we turned onto our street. The lights were alit on the porch and down the avenue of trees. It was so pretty and such a welcoming sight. Then the door flew open, and Ethel came running down the stairs with Tom behind her. Her arms were outstretched as she neared the car, and she opened my door. Ethel was beside herself with joy to see us. "Oh, how I missed you, Maggie!" she exclaimed. "It's so good to see you again!"

As soon as I was out of the car, she gave me a big hug. Tom's greeting was equally warm in his own way.

"Don't worry about a thing, Mr. Danes," he cheerily said, turning to Dan and shaking his hand. "I'll help with the children and then retrieve your luggage."

Laughing, Dan said, "I'm afraid it seems to be a lot more than when we left, Tom!"

Blossom sleepily cuddled in Tom's arms as he lifted her out of the backseat. Dan carried in Carlos. They put them to bed, where our children were unaware that they were home again.

"I fixed us a light lunch," Ethel said. "How was your flight home?"

"Good, but tiring. I sure appreciate the trouble of these refreshments, Ethel."

"Oh, no trouble at all, my dear Maggie, and a pleasure! I think I'll have to pinch myself when I see you come down those stairs in the morning. Tom and I thought we'd spend the night and fix you a nice breakfast. With Anne and Harry away on their own holiday to visit her folks in the city for Christmas, we want to fill in. I guess they plan on spending New Year's with Harry's parents here."

"But it's Christmas Eve tomorrow and we want you and Tom to have some special time to yourselves," I protested. "By the way,

Amanda, from Austria, is coming to Canada for a year because we're taking a year off after our term in June is completed. But enough of that for now! I'm so happy to be back home and see you, Ethel!" I smiled, as tears welled in my eyes.

"Oh, that's terrific! As for tomorrow, Tom and I have our time, don't you worry! Just want to fix you breakfast and then on Christmas Day, we spend it with you." A worried look creased her face. "We do, don't we, Maggie?"

Laughing, I assured her, "Yes, we do!"

We enjoyed the lovely lunch Ethel had prepared for us and soon said goodnight.

"I feel so weary right now," I said to Dan, as we pushed back our chairs. "A good night's rest is what I need."

Hugging me, Ethel held me close until Tom gently pulled her away. "There's plenty of time for that tomorrow," he lovingly said. "You know, my darling, I could use a little of that myself tonight!"

Blushing, Ethel conceded, mum as a mouse. Smiling, she reached to gather the dirty dishes off the table, while Tom came alongside her, removing the food.

It would take me some getting used to seeing Ethel as a married woman, I said in my thoughts. But I was so delighted for her! Tom was everything of a gentleman and I knew his heart would always be in hers. Yawning, I made my way the stairs and undressed, then I pulled my nightgown over my head, and got into bed beside Dan. Leaning over, he kissed me, and I fell into a peaceful sleep moments later.

When I came downstairs the following morning, the fresh aroma of perked coffee filtered through the house. I peered into the living room and noted that Tom had already put up a beautiful spruce tree, decorated with lights and lovely ornaments. I was sure that Ethel had had her hand in it, too, I smiled to myself. The hearth was burning, taking the chill of the morning away. It was such a cozy feeling.

I quietly pushed the kitchen door open. Ethel and Tom had their backs to me, and their hands were busy putting food on empty platters.

"It smells divine!" I commented. For a few moments, the scene remained unchanged. Then, Ethel nearly dropped the plate she had just picked up. Tom steadied it back on the counter, as she welcomed me with a teary smile and hug.

"Maggie!" she cried. "It's really you!" She ran into my arms, hugging me close for a long moment.

Tom winked at me, and I grinned. "Yes, Ethel, it's really me. Good morning, Tom!" I greeted.

"Good morning, Maggie!"

I offered to help carry some of the food to the table, but Ethel would have none of it. "You had a long trip, and we insist on pampering you this morning. And we also want to invite you and the children for dinner. Oh, and there's lots of food prepared for your supper. We thought you might want to have the evening to yourselves tonight."

"Thank you!" I said. "I'll appreciate that. But tomorrow, on Christmas Day, we want you and Tom to spend the day with us and you shall be our special guests just like we planned, okay?" I said as I looked deep into her eyes.

"Okay!" she answered, smiling. "But I can still help and bring some of the food, Maggie."

I knew it was pointless to argue, so I simply replied, "That will be very thoughtful of you, Ethel, and most appreciated."

After breakfast, I took Ethel aside. "I'm wondering if I might ask a favor, Ethel?"

"Oh, sure! Whatever I can do to help, I'm happy to."

"Well, I have a lot of presents to wrap. Would you mind helping me with that?"

"I don't see why not."

"Good! Do you think that Tom and Dan could take care of the dishes for us?"

Giggling, Ethel's smile sparkled in her eyes. "Why certainly! That's a right perfect idea, Maggie!"

The children were excited, but quite tired from the long flight and slept most of the afternoon. I feared they may be awake all night, but it wasn't very long after supper before they were yawning, wanting to go to bed.

Laden with the presents we'd purchased from Austria; I was so grateful for Ethel's help with the gifts. She seemed to have a special knack in getting the packages wrapped faster than I'd ever seen anyone do it. Before long, all the packages were accounted for and slipped beneath the lovely tree. When Tom and Ethel left for their own cottage, Dan assisted me in wrapping up their gifts. I was so tired, I wanted to go straight to bed, but Dan insisted that I sit with him in the living room.

The evening was dark, and the lights on the tree, dazzling. Putting his arm about me, the crackling fire in the hearth was truly welcoming.

It had always been a tradition in my family to open our gifts on Christmas Eve. But this year was different. We had both Ethel and Tom, and we wanted to share those special moments with them, too. We'd purchased Anne and Harry's gifts before their flight so that they wouldn't have to wait until after they returned, and we were back in Austria. The children would have been given a few of their gifts tonight, but for the fact that they were too tired to stay up that late. They would unwrap them on Christmas Day. Dan and I opened a few of our gifts from each other, but we'd save the rest for Christmas Day that also included Ethel and Tom, and of course, our children.

At seven o'clock the next morning, I heard a slight sound at the front door. "It must be Ethel and Tom," I said to Dan, as I gently shook him awake. Getting out of bed, I slowly drew the curtain aside. It was still quite dark outside, but two figures suddenly vanished. "Mmm," I said. I was rather concerned and made Dan check to be sure. He quietly tiptoed down the stairs, and peered, unseen, into the corridor. The figures reappeared, and relief settled over his face as he turned back to our bedroom.

"It's okay," he whispered to me. "It's Ethel and Tom." Relieved, we went back to bed, sleeping until 8:30 a.m.

My granddaughter, Emily, Blossom's daughter, was not prone to interrupting me. This story took a long time in reading. At eight years of age, she was highly intelligent and already an avid reader. But this story was much more complicated, and it gave us a way to spend time together, holding close to the love I had come to find in her from the moment she was born.

Emily sleepily rubbed her tired eyes, looking up into my eyes. "Grandmother," she asked, "this sure is some story of *A Lost Love*, isn't it?"

"Yes, Emily, it sure is!" I exclaimed.

"But how does it end?" she pondered, creasing her brow, noting the few pages still unread.

"I shouldn't tell you," I smiled, "but since you asked, I must! There's no one here to mind me telling you, not that your grandfather, Daniel, would object any, so I have only one word to describe the answer to your question: 'How does it end?' Happily!" I replied.

"But Grandmother, that's no answer," she said.

"Why not?" I asked.

"Because it doesn't tell me anything about it, that's why not!" she boldly declared.

"That's true, my darling. But it's all the answer you're going to receive for tonight!"

"Suppose I ask Grandfather?" she quietly considered, deep in thought.

"Dear child. You may suppose all you like, but I think it's best kept between you and me. Now," I continued, "shall we leave the rest for tomorrow? You're getting very tired, and I should soon like to go to bed, too!" I said, with a smile.

"Sure, Grandmother. Goodnight. Thank you for reading to me again."

"Goodnight, sweet Emily," I said, closing the book, marking the page with the bookmark. She gave me a warm hug and we bid goodnight. I couldn't resist chuckling, knowing that Emily was merely pouting a little and wouldn't have the gumption any to suppose with her grandfather about the ending of our story! For her, tomorrow would come soon enough, and she'd be distracted until the evening arrived when we would finish the book together. I arose, my heart filled with joyful thanksgiving as she disappeared around the corner and up the stairway.

My daughter, Blossom, Dan's niece, who is Emily's mother, had become this special gift to me as she had to him. His sister, Julia, who had died several years before, was so sure that Dan's love and mine would meet together through a lifelong marriage, which it eventually did.

Blossom came to love me as her mother and her uncle, Daniel Danes, as a father, and I had found purposed strength within this love, which was unshakable because of all that the cross wholly offers. Living for God, we were daily nurtured in His Word and brought our children up to live in righteous standing. While none of us is perfect on this earth, we are redeemed through the cross of His Son, Jesus.

Blossom grew into a lovely, young woman, who used her special talents to help others.

"I love to teach," she told us, "and share of all the goodness that God has waiting for each of our lives if we'll only allow Him to."

She married a musician and their voices lifted in a beautiful blend of harmony as they shared their gifts within the church and on special occasions wherever they were called to serve. As a music teacher in the local school, her husband, Joel, not only taught in the classroom, but loved to perform on stage. Blossom performed with him, including some of the students as they shared their hearts in song through concerts and even plays!

When Emily was born, Blossom and Joel decided that they wanted to dedicate her to the Lord. I think that's what partly made this little girl so special to our hearts. From this beginning, we saw this young couple surrender their lives to everything they did in honoring God. Emily began to take an early interest in reading, sharing with her parents that one day she would stand before the world and write a beautiful story for God.

When Blossom told me this, I was overwhelmed with joy. "She's especially taken a heart to you, Mom," Blossom smiled. "You've been such a wonderful mother to me. My mom would be so proud of how you and my uncle, Dan, have brought me up."

Holding my beloved daughter close to me, I said, "I've loved you since you were a little girl, my Blossom. And I told your mother that I would never replace her. She will always be your true mom. But I am honored for the privilege and great joy that has been brought to me because of marrying your darling uncle!"

"From how you write, Mom," Blossom said, "my mother really knew that God had brought you to my uncle, who was her brother, and that your love was meant to be found in marriage."

"Yes, she did. And I love your uncle terribly much. When he left unexpectedly, I felt so lost and hurt and abandoned, but God needed to prune my stubbornness and yield my heart to Him in this. I

271

sometimes wonder how many tree branches that took for Him to prune in my life? No less, how many trees!" I added, giggling.

Laughing, we cried through our tears of joy. Then teasing me, Blossom softly said, "Did you ever count the branches that God pruned?"

"Oh, not a one!" I answered, as my heart softly laughed. "I'm afraid it would have been much too much to count! You know how stubborn I can get at times, even though it's few and far between!"

"Oh, stubbornness can be a good thing," Blossom defended me. "Just look at my life. Sometimes, I wonder how my husband ever puts up with me!"

"Well, your daughter is a fine example, Blossom," I commented. "Emily is so laid back, yet she has strengths that I feel will become invaluable to her future as a writer. Her patience is amazing, and her quiescent beauty, unmatched. What a lovely granddaughter you have given to Dan and me!"

That night, Emily was excited for the ending of our story. As the light flickered in the lantern, we made ourselves comfortable on the chesterfield. Dan had already retired for the evening.

"Are you ready?" I asked.

"Oh, yes, Grandmother! Please do start!"

"Well," I began, "let's see. Where did we leave off now?"

Worried, Emily asked, "You didn't forget the page, did you? Where is the bookmark?"

"No. I don't think so," I returned. "Oh, there it is! Here we go!"

Emily snuggled close to me, and the words began to fall like dewdrops on the flowers in the early dawn, where reliving our lives brought joy so overwhelmingly unspeakable, that at times I found that I could barely read for all the wonderful, *Unexpected Gifts* that God continued to bring my way, like a summer shower, filling my life with song!

CHAPTER 21

Christmas Blessings

The fire burned low, but Tom was up early to put more wood in the hearth, the page began. It was Christmas Day. By the time I made my way downstairs, I was surprised that Ethel was not in the kitchen. She had promised to get the dinner preparations ready. Concerned, I discovered him in the living room, adding wood to the hearth.

"Good morning, Tom," I warmly greeted him. "Merry Christmas! Do you happen to know where Ethel is keeping herself?"

Laughing, he said, "Good morning, Maggie, and Merry Christmas to you, too! Ethel decided to do some of the preparations at our cottage. But I know she's waiting eagerly to be with you. She has something incredibly special to share with you. We both do."

I'd long since wondered where Ethel gets her energy from. "Your wife is a marvel," I said. "Such energy!"

Laughing, Tom grinned. "I sometimes think that God gave her a double dose because of the wonderful spirit she has for others," he said. "She's really something, isn't she, Maggie?" he asked, his eyes a twinkle.

Laughing with him, I said, "Oh, Tom, she surely is!" Turning back to my original thought, I posed the question, "When do you suppose she'll come?" I asked. "I hoped to spend some time helping out in the kitchen with her this morning."

"Not too long, Maggie."

"Well, I hope not. I have so much to tell her. You know," I said, "I think I'll just slip on my coat and boots and walk over. Perhaps, I can be of some use to her over at your cottage. You don't think she'd mind?" I abruptly asked, reaching for my hat as I waited for Tom's reply.

Laughing softly, Tom grinned. "For you, dear Maggie? Not at all! I can assure you that she'll welcome your presence!"

"Thank you!" I appreciated, smiling. "Well, would you tell Dan for me please, Tom? We'll try not to be too long. And Dan will need to get the children up and fed."

"Sure, Maggie. I'll be happy to."

I opened the door and nearly fell. The wind whipped it so hard, I was temporarily blinded and had to literally force the door shut again. I reached my hand to pull my hat tighter. The wind was so strong, I thought it might rip it right off from beneath the hood of my coat! "It certainly is gusty this morning," I said to myself, voicing my opinion out loud. "Can't the wind even rest on Christmas?" I asked, still speaking out loud.

A beautifully soft feminine voice startled me. "I don't think it cares one bit about that, Maggie!" My parents were walking toward me, and I was so stunned, I couldn't even move for a moment. I hadn't even noticed their car in the driveway.

"What a lovely surprise!" I finally managed.

"It's wonderful to see you, Maggie," my mother said, hugging me. "Where were you headed off to so early on this blustery morning, my dearest daughter?"

"Oh," I said, chuckling. "Our employees, a young couple, live just on the other side of the avenue of trees, and I wanted to check to see what I could do to help her with our dinner preparations."

My dad smiled and spoke for the first time. "Well, if it's all the same to you, Maggie, I'll stay here, and Mom and you can go see the couple."

"Oh, just Ethel is home. Her husband, Tom, is here with Dan. Mom," I said, as we turned toward the Wafers' cottage, "why, this is such a wonderful surprise. How come you didn't tell us you were coming from the city?"

"But I did!" she said, astonishment reflected in her eyes. "Didn't you get my letter?"

"No! Dan and I and the children just arrived back from Austria the day before Christmas Eve. I didn't see any letter."

"Hmm. Well, we were planning on staying a few days. We hardly see you anymore, Maggie, and your dad and I miss you and your lovely family."

"We've very glad to have you here!" I said, taking her arm. We arrived a couple of minutes later at the Wafers and delight sparkled in Ethel's eyes when she opened the door to us.

"Oh, this is such a lovely surprise . . . a double blessing, I'd say," she happily expressed. "Not just my dear Maggie, but my dear Maggie's mother, too!" Amused, we giggled, and Ethel continued, "Oh, my Mrs.' mother!" she exclaimed. "You and Maggie make yourselves comfortable, and welcome to my home!" Flitting about her kitchen, she continued, "This is indeed an honor, ma'am, especially on Christmas!"

Ethel offered for us to sit. "I just took out a batch of cinnamon buns about fifteen minutes ago, and they should be cooled by now. Maggie, if you'd help me with the cream cheese icing …" she began.

"Oh, of course, Ethel!" Winking at my mom, I teased, "You know, Mom, sometimes the boss is bossed, but it's all in good fun!"

My mother burst out laughing. "I see!" she said. When the architectural plans were drawn, we had made sure that the design included a spacious kitchen and substantial dining room for Ethel and Tom. Scurrying into the kitchen, in a few minutes, we had a plate ready for the table.

We enjoyed Ethel's marvelous cinnamon buns and the hot, steaming mugs of coffee she placed on her table. "I didn't realize I was hungry," my mom said. "My husband, Luke, and I had a quick bite before leaving from the city, and I suppose that is a while ago," she said. Taking a bite from Ethel's bun, she exclaimed moments later, "Oh, these are prize-winning buns, to be sure!" she praised.

Ethel's shyness shone through as she slowly sipped her coffee. "They are, aren't they?" she finally said. "My husband, Tom, says they're the best he's ever eaten."

"I agree with that," I said. "Mom, I'll never forget the afternoon Ethel and I were introduced to each other long before Dan and I married. I didn't know back then that Dan was also my editor, although this particular incident occurred a few weeks later, I believe."

When I had finished telling my mother the story, she boisterously laughed. "That was really something, ladies. Sometimes, God uses a poor writer to take a second job to find her husband, especially a 'doll' like Dan! Well, dear daughter," she said, looking into my eyes, "I'd say it was a right lovely afternoon that day that the Lord brought Dan into your life forever. A man of such wonderful honor. He even gave you Ethel," she finished, peering into her eyes with joy reflected in her smile.

"He surely did," I smiled, 'though Ethel couldn't find the words within her heart that she was likewise feeling, as tears misted in her lovely eyes with a love that said it all.

The children were ecstatic to see their grandparents and we were thrilled to host my parents. That was one of the most beautiful Christmases that Dan and I had ever spent with my family and close friends, Ethel and Tom Wafer. We celebrated the New Year with them, too, and we were all invited to Anne and Harry's the day before the New Year.

Incidentally, when our school term in Austria ended in June, Amanda not only stayed with us that year, but she also decided to immigrate and become a Canadian citizen, eventually marrying Harry's best friend, Landon Grey, whom so far, we'd only met a few times. He seemed a nice gentleman to me.

I finally also met Dan's lovely parents the day after New Year's. I loved them immediately and it felt like we'd known each other all our lives. They stayed two weeks with us, and I cried at their departure. We wanted to travel to Nova Scotia the following summer to spend time with them at their residence, as well as with Dan's twin brother, Justin, and his wife Lil and their son, George. His younger brother, Cole, insisted that we board with him for part of our trip, which we immensely looked forward to in the months ahead.

Oh, and Ethel's special secret was truly special.

"Could you and Dan please take a brief walk with me and Tom tonight?" Ethel whispered, when we were alone in the kitchen getting everything ready for the table.

"Yes!" I assured.

Later that evening, my parents graciously offered to read stories to the children while me and Dan and the Wafers slipped our coats, hats, mitts, and boots on. When Dan opened the door, the moon was hanging overhead, suspended by an invisible hand, full and bright and beautiful. The wind had quieted from the morning's rage, and the stars hung like millions of jewels, sparkling in dazzling array. It seemed to me that the wind had been given a talking to, being that it was Christmas Day, and the perfect stillness within its tranquility of the whole aura was aesthetically and entrancingly resplendent! The glory of the night was enchanting in every way.

"What a glorious night!" I wistfully enthralled.

We wandered along the avenue of trees with the lanterns glowing in the eve. Then we made our way to the far end of the garden, crossing over the threshold of the alcove that welcomed anyone so privileged to be in this lovely niche that Dan had carefully helped plan with the architect a few years before I met him.

Tom had started a fire in the outside stone hearth, and we huddled on chairs that he'd brought over earlier in the day. Placing blankets on the seats, we soon were enjoying a glowing fire.

As the Wafers looked to us, I knew that something extraordinary was soon to be revealed. Taking Ethel's mitted hands, Tom's eyes shone with such beauty of perfect love, it took my breath away.

For one terrifying moment, I was afraid that they were going to announce that they were leaving our employ, and our lives, forever. But Tom's gentle words began to soothe my troubled heart as I began to understand the implication.

"My darling and I have something very special to tell you," he began, "where we shall all be together again."

"Yes," Ethel softly said. "Our greenhouse is doing so well," she smiled, "that Tom and I want to go back to Austria with you and start a greenhouse there. We've been in contact with several people, and they are willing to invest in our project. And you know what else?" she shyly said, looking lovingly into my eyes.

"No," I said. "What else, dear Ethel?"

"Tom and I are going to be teaching at the university with you! Teaching horticulture studies. Isn't that just wonderful?" she cried, as tears filled her lovely, black eyes, shining with joy.

Pausing, they both looked to us with kind anticipation. Then, I couldn't contain myself any longer. "Oh, Ethel! Tom! How simply marvelous!" Then a thought I didn't want to express spoke with tender question from my heart. "But Tom, to teach with Ethel . . ." I couldn't finish the sentence.

He smiled, then assured, "I have my degree, too, Mrs. Maggie!"

I had no words as tears filled my eyes and Ethel continued the break in conversation.

"But we are also considering who will be your nanny for this upcoming term?" Ethel asked, furrowing her brow. "I'd love to continue serving you and Dan, but that won't be possible with my teaching."

"Oh, Ethel! you needn't worry any about that anymore, but that is so kind of you, and I appreciate your consideration. I'm sure that Amanda will be able to graciously take your position over. She adores children and Dan and I have been very blessed to have had her wonderful help last term. Most importantly, my dearest Ethel, you'll be a professor once again, as you should be! Oh, I am truly inspired and thrilled by this wonderful news!" Pausing, I added, "But have you considered where you'll be staying?"

"Yes!" Tom warmly smiled. "As you may remember when Harry and Anne taught abroad, the horticultural department for the university has a special apartment complex for visiting professors. I'm so excited about the teaching positions, especially with Ethel sharing the platform with me, as well as introducing a brand-new greenhouse to the campus."

"But that's not all," Ethel shyly said, reaching for her husband's hand. "We have saved the best for last. That's a funny way to say it, isn't it, Maggie?" she said, crimping her brow. "But I know what it means!" she smiled. As she looked into my eyes, she softly shared, "Tom and I are expecting our first baby at the beginning of September."

"Ohhh!" I said, totally taken aback. "Why, this is such terrific news! Dan and I are just thrilled for you!" I said, my heart dancing.

"We are, indeed!" Dan said. "We're just thrilled about everything!"

We returned to Austria and Ethel and Tom's greenhouse flourished. They were well liked and respected, and we were delighted to have them with us. Amanda loved them, too, and brought over many delicious meals as we worked, both for us and for Ethel and Tom, which we so appreciated!

As they labored, experimenting in their work, on a lovely April afternoon, just prior to our return trip home in May, the Wafers won first place for their hybrid daffodil in their first showing. Its flawless beauty, and gorgeous yellow-mauve petals, softly fringed with an accentuated ruffled edging, appeared ever-so-slightly and gently dipped in a beautifully deep violet, captivating the title: *Midnight Violet Moon.* It was absolutely beautiful, capturing an irresistibly charming loveliness all its own!

While the lady's slipper would always be my favorite flower, I adored the intense tangerine-mauve daffodil they'd also entered into the show with its double frill, through crossbreeding, too! It was such a rare accomplishment, that Dan and I were taken aback at the skill and talent within their imaginations that brought new life into intervaried ways within their craft. They called this hybrid, *Sunset Glow.*

Any success that was created by the Wafers and was endorsed through the Austrian college, received a percentage of the purse, which was high in stakes, since they were supporting the Wafers' greenhouse financially. The balance, still very substantial, was allotted to Ethel and Tom. Dan and I only shared the purses on the Canadian end because it's we who are supporting their efforts in Canada.

As God continued to inspire their hearts, throughout the years, the Wafers' work excelled in almost every showing, winning coveted prizes, taking first place, that was unprecedented. They created and learned, and worked, bringing gifts of joyful bounty to yearning hearts, far and near, within the flowers we all adored, and where our greenhouse held the breath of our Creator to every petal in their love.

Such joy was like a bit of Heaven that brought deep emotions to many of those privileged to figuratively "taste" of their beauty firsthand in this incredible way. While Dan and I knew that the real Heaven awaiting those who have given their lives to Christ was so much more, such joy emanating to the wealth of these tangible gifts was truly an unforgettable experience to behold within such rapturous pleasure!

When the Wafers met success with crossbreeding the lady's slipper, I was captivated by the beauty of their indelibleness, especially since their creation was founded on the Canadian soil of their efforts. That such an attempt of several, met success, we were ecstatic to be a part of it right in our own greenhouse, making history! But there was one I particularly favored. The pink tone of this blossom lavishly deepened to a deep rose hue, and the inside was speckled with a profusion of lovely mauve, which was an immense accomplishment. Its graceful blend arose in breathless wonder, where the enchanting fairytale stories of old seemed to come alive in an almost realistic aura in its own making. This exquisite blossom was named: *Blushing Star*.

When we arrived back home in May, spring was in full bloom. The scents of the blossoms filled the air with enticing fragrance, drifting upon the winds, and delighting the heart with joy! We were planning to delay our school term back in Austria because our baby was due in August, as well as Ethel's shortly after, near the beginning of September. Anne came to help Ethel when she could, but her teaching took up most of her time. That's when I thought of Suzanne Wilcox, and she was most gracious to be a blessing to the Wafers. Harry's sister, Cindy, offered to clean the house twice a week after school, and as it turned out, she was a dandy cook, and prepared many lovely suppers for them, also! The Lord brought my sister, Amy, to help Dan and me out. We expected to fly back to Austria after Christmas.

I gave birth to a beautiful daughter, Victoria Anne, on a gorgeous August afternoon, the seventeenth, and Blossom was so delighted. "God's light has come to us again, Mommy," she said, holding her baby sister, who was in fact, her cousin. "Just as I asked, didn't He?"

Laughing, I said, "Yes, He did, my darling."

Later that night, I smiled to myself. Just as Dan had said, with my Norwegian ancestry and his gorgeous Japanese and Spanish, our children were truly beautiful in our "we!"

Sophia Elizabeth, Ethel and Tom's beautiful girl, was born on September the seventh; the windiest day I'd ever seen!

Our girls eventually became close as sisters, and we were grateful for all the blessings God faithfully provided from the time that Dan and I had originally met. And I realized that *A Lost Love* can be found if the heart is willing to surrender to God's Love, allowing Him to work behind the scenes, bringing all of the pieces beautifully together in perfect harmony.

While we cry for the one we seem to have lost, God hasn't lost them any, and if His plan is right in it, He'll bring the picture together, much like the pieces fitted within a puzzle within that love, because He is Lord over everything. Perhaps, that's partly why I've never favored the broken pieces of a puzzle, for broken pieces exude pain where oftentimes they shouldn't, and in those times, we can neither understand nor see the whole portrait as God does. But like life, when we move forward to do everything we can and then allow God to do what only He can do, the picture becomes clearer to every piece fitted within His will and plan for our lives to live in that wholeness freely offered, whether His answer is yes, no, or wait.

Our story is never-ending in the telling. Now my granddaughter, Emily, is growing strong in the things of the Lord, reading, and giving her heart to, what I believe, she shall one day shake the world with her words, through her books, yet to be writ upon the pages of time.

Sitting by the hearth, here my sweet Emily listens to our story. Of her grandparents, a man and a woman dedicated to God's calling, and loving the children He blessed into their lives, that my husband Daniel Danes and I, have come to cherish more than anything else in the world.

And it was here that I had felt compelled one lovely afternoon while Dan's absence still filled my heart with pain long before we wed, to share God's Word with Him. Although this may seem an unlikely passage, when God brought me to the verse in Nehemiah 6:3 KJV, in that moment as I read these words, I felt fully healed from all the hurt I'd experienced apart from Dan, for it says: "And I sent messengers unto them, saying, I *am* doing a great work, so that I cannot come down: why should the work cease, whilst I leave it, and come down to you?" The heavy burden fell away, and I recognized this important moment in the freedom that had now come to me. Quickly, I took up my pen and paper and offered these words to Dan in a note. I've never looked back in that devastating pain as I found new life and hope within God's heart to mine, and trusted Him Alone for my future.

Dearest Dan,

This letter to you is based on the Scripture from Nehemiah 6:3 KJV. Please take a few minutes to read through this, as the Lord has graciously shown me that my heart hasn't been right with yours.

I have no right to intrude on your heart, my dearest Dan, and I ask you to please forgive me. It's not my place.

I will continue to follow God's path to wherever He leads me . . . I will keep on doing His will and never let go, because He is my Lord and Savior, and He knows what's best for me.

Always, I shall hold the heart of your wonderfully dedicated devotion to our God Most High, for you have taught and blessed me more than I ever could have asked. You have clearly shown to me that good men, such as yourself, really do exist in holding to the pure honor and integrity of all I hold dearest to my soul, not only to myself as the person I am, but as a believer. God knew how much I needed someone like you to show His very heart in this to me! For this, there shall never be words enough to thank you! Sharing devotions with you, Dan, has been the most wonderful of all my gifts from you that I have ever received, and which I treasure deeply! I so thank you for it all!

Always,
Maggie

Irrefutably, this is a story of *A Lost Love* that God took within the palm of His hand and molded for His Purpose. And to it, He is still molding and making something beautiful from the ashes of my pain to the joy I came to have within a man named Daniel Blake Danes. For this man came to me as a gift in my work, where together, we are filling young and old lives with the joys of writing and publishing their stories, just like ours. A journey that took us through rough terrain along the way before we were married, that ultimately led us to the feet of Jesus, and the cross that eventually made us whole in His perfect Love.

And my Daniel, he is most precious to my heart, and I shall forever love and adore him, for he is the gift that God brought to me in such an amazing way! To this day, I've never had another dream like the one God sent to prepare me for my future husband! And I know that his lovely sister, Julia, must be smiling up in Heaven, for she loved me enough to bless my heart in giving me her beautiful daughter, Blossom, who Dan and I have raised on her behalf for the Lord. But most significantly, she knew the love gathered in Dan's heart with mine, and mine in his. Now, my beloved sister-in-law, Julia, is a grandmother as much as me! Emily will never know her beautiful grandmother, but I will tell her all I know about her loving legacy, for she is the entrancingly exquisite image of Julia in every way. While our love had become lost for a time, I sometimes wonder what Julia would think if she could only see us now! Three children! Two daughters and one son. Precious treasures, every one! To each one, these wonderfully beautiful gifts are a sacred trust from God to us. We must not let Him down. And that reminds me . . .

My Dearest, beloved Dan, the story ended, I had wondered about the Agency telling me you were a widower. Shortly after our wedding, I had the courage to ask Ethel about the photograph, even though Dan's brother, Justin, was at our wedding. Looking stunned, she finally said, "Oh, no, Maggie! Not our Mr. That was his twin brother – Justin. His first wife, Olivia, fell ill shortly after they married, and died a few months later. I should have also realized that Justin's eyes are not the same as Dan's, but when you showed me the photograph, I couldn't think in my anguish for you.

"His youngest brother, Cole, had an identical mishap in his marriage. He vowed to never marry again and never has. I'm afraid that the Agency made a dire error in telling you that Dan was a widower."

I was very relieved to know that Dan had never been a widower, but I was most sorry that his twin brother had lost his beloved Olivia, yet found the courage and strength to love again with Lil.

It was unfortunate that Cole felt totally different about remarrying. Although it wasn't until the evening when we wed before I met both of his brothers, Justin and Lil and their son, George, as well as Cole Danes, I think that sometimes, that's why I found him more of a loner through the years, although we both dearly love him. He is always polite and warm, and I cherish Cole as my brother-in-law. But at times, I also felt he was a bruised and broken man, whom both Dan and I would have loved to see happy again with another bride. But alas, some hearts no less can withstand the testing of more than one true love, and for this, my heart sometimes grieved even now with my husband to the tremendous loss Cole could not see beyond to trusting in faith to marrying again. Like his brothers, Dan and Justin, Cole was such a special man. Handsome, caring, and loving, but still afflicted in the tremendous loss of his wife, May.

Please forgive me, my Dearest darling, I penned the final thought, for not trusting fully in your love for me when Justin, your twin brother, wrote that note to his wife, Lil. I'm so happy that it is all it was, and I have come to love your family as my own, even a brothers-in-law that I mistook for you within that photograph many years ago. You are mine forever, Dan, and I love you with all my heart. There'll never be anyone but you for me . . .

Years back, Dan had written a lovely poem in my honor. I'd never known until that moment when I felt so alone just before he returned and we wed, that he often wrote poetry to express his feelings, and I would cherish it to my heart forever. He knew how much I adored his roses, and I think that inspired him to take up his pen and create this beautiful work of enchanting beauty. It fit the book perfectly.

June's Gift

Roses of summer,
June's glorious joys.
Wild or tame,
To dispel all our woes.

Fragrance as soft
As the kiss of the wind,
To carry love's song far and near,
'Round each bend.

Lilt of the birds
So sweetly is heard.
Songs of the rivers
Each passage to ford.

Sunrise and sunset,
Daytime and night.
Whispers of moonbeams,
Glory of light.

Like the cloak of eve's twilight,
When man's work is done.
Cherishing moments, such glory of might,
Like sand on the seashore, of many or one.

Beauty to gather
The hearts all as one,
June's precious roses in warmth of the sun,
Each day ever waiting,
Sweet memories to keep.

You are the love of my life, he wrote, and the
rose of my soul forever.

Lovingly, Dan

Lovingly closing the big, black book with its thick pages, and yellowed with age, I arose and placed it back on the shelf in the Drawing Room. When I turned back, Emily had momentarily slipped away. I was about to quench the flame in the lantern when she suddenly reappeared, quiet as a whisper, shyly standing in front of me with her notebook.

"Grandmother," she sweetly said, "I love you more than all the world!"

"I love you more than all the world, too, Emily," I said, hugging her.

"When I get enough words in my mind, I'll write that book," she firmly said.

"I know you will," I softly returned. "Perhaps, you have already started?" I asked.

"A little," she answered, "and I want you to be the first to read it," she smiled.

"That's going to be my pleasure!" I said. "I don't suppose I can have a peek in it?"

"Sure, Grandmother." Emily bashfully handed me her notebook.

"I'll begin reading this tomorrow, if that's all right?" I posed.

"Okay," she said.

"Then perhaps, we should say goodnight and have a good sleep. Are you ready for dreaming wondrous dreams?"

Giggling, Emily hugged me and said, "If I can!"

I extinguished the lantern and we walked together to her bedroom. Pausing, she suddenly turned around and hugged me again, as tight as she could. "I'm glad to spend this time with you on Mom's holidays," she said. Then her eyes brightened as she softly said in contemplation, "Such a lovely story you and Grandfather have," she expressed. "I hope to get a man who loves God, like you, some day!"

Tears misted in my eyes. "I believe you will, my dearest," I said, kissing her goodnight. "And he will be more wonderful than you could ever imagine, where you shall have your own special prince to always love and cherish you! I'll pray that it be so! Now, it's time for night and those wondrous dreams," I encouraged. "Tomorrow is another day of blessings awaiting."

"Goodnight, Grandmother. I love you so, so much!" Emily said.

That got me thinking as I dwelt on the verse from John 12:46 KJV before I slipped into bed beside Dan. It read: "I am come a light into the world, that whosoever believeth on Me should not abide in darkness." The words lifted on my soul like a butterfly as it offered peace in the darkness of the night, and I soon fell into a perfect rest of pleasant dreams.

The next morning as the sunrise glowed upon the horizon in bursts of aesthetic brilliance and beauty, and while I could hardly wait to turn the pages of my granddaughter, Emily's notebook, that verse continued to speak to me. It was then that I decided that my own story needed a new ending, or at the least, a few more words to add.

Lost in thought as I sat at my desk pondering, I was taken to the time when Dan and I had barely first met, and how I wondered why someone I hardly knew would consider me worthy to be called his Dearest. Even today, I realize that God had His hand on our lives back then. Smiling to myself, I'd always adore Dan's unexpectedly lavish heart that came to me in time within his tenderest extravagant love, just as Julia had seen between us, too! And how I loved being his Dearest!

In the very first letter I received from him, he put something into my heart that no one else had ever given to me before in such a beautifully sincere fashion, and that is honor and integrity within his heart and walk with God.

> "You didn't know it then," he divulged, "but when you shared that you wrote, not only with your heart, but with God's guidance, you imprinted such an immeasurably pure, defining, and deeply profound impression on me, I knew that you already belonged in a very special place within my heart, too. And Maggie," he added, "the country girl in you far surpassed any university degree, as it still does today!"

His words caught me unawares, and as I remembered back, I could only lift my voice in praise to God for bringing everything good through this wonderful man I'd come to find and love in Dan. For it was there, within his extraordinary presence, that I began to see beyond my past pain, like the thorns of a rose; pressing forward to all that God had waiting for me as I trusted my future to Him.

In that moment of reflection, I knew the truth of my heart as Dan had shared a similar feeling, assuring me that I was the one he'd yearned for all his life, too; my everything in him. The words now easily came to my heart. Wistfully, I took up my pen, and allowed God to speak His words through me.

> To all the dreams of our hearts, I reflected, the loveliest dreams will always yield to God's. While my heart had been so torn and broken in Dan's absence, there was but one truth that would matter the most, and that was living in the supreme will of the God Who, not only created the world and everything above and beneath it, but the One who created the man I so love. And if God had never brought Daniel Danes back to my heart, then I realized that He had a better plan, which I quite stubbornly, at moments, didn't want to see nor understand. Yet, through it all, as my heart did not change for Dan, I continued to know deep inside of me that he was the one God had chosen for me as his future bride. In him, honor stood tall.
>
> In those times as I struggled to relinquish these feelings, being in God's will was still paramount in my life to living in the abundant life God had predestined long before I was even born. Just as the roses beautifully flourished as they stubbornly clung on the vines despite the thorns, their perfume still carried on the air, yielding to the Creator in it all.
>
> Even there - and here - I surrendered my will to His in my turmoil. And I realized that God needed to know He could trust me with the man He longed to provide in blessing. As I stayed fixed on my heart in loving Dan, countless blessings would come to thrive and bloom, just like the roses breathlessly exclaiming their splendor to fragrance the lives of many!

As I continued to look to God and believe with all my heart, I knew that in Dan, that beauty and pure joy in the gift of this honor stood rock solid, and it always would. That was a priceless gift worth more than anything else, where our love eventually came to walk side by side, cherished blessings in that honor in our marriage, ordained by God. Nothing gets better than that!

Thorns and all . . . that's my story never-ending. The love that came to Daniel Danes and I have blessed our lives to the honor of God's Name more wonderful than I could ever have imagined!

A thick, yellow, and worn, black covered book. Pages read throughout the generations; today, and to come. Julia knew what my heart had come to find all along. Here, *A Lost Love*, struggling against the fears and upsets of my world, had come to find its way back to the truth. And no matter where that truth of our sacred love may still take us in life, yielding to God's will shall never be far from our hearts!

Oh! I concluded as my pen effortlessly moved across the page, I asked Dan to forgive me for my fiery words when I didn't understand, nor have the full picture. I should've been far more gracious, just like that photograph and note that was meant for Justin and Lil. I was just so afraid of losing Dan at times. But he always held a lovely beauty of an understanding heart in this, and as was his fashion of word in such times as these, Dan lovingly bent his face to mine and kissing me, exclaimed with tenderest passion, "Love and kisses forever, my darling!" Within his passion, I found my heart filled to the joy in his in the covenant of our marriage within all the beauty of our love.

And I also came to realize that it was there, upon the far-reaching branches of a tree, where the fruit grows. When I let go of holding onto that tree trunk, per se, and envisioned the fruit swaying gently to the perfect harmony of the breeze, my soul was renewed afresh as I wholly gave my heart to the one I loved in Dan, and the fire in me was finally stilled. As we daily plucked the fruit of that tree in our love in serving God and each other, everything within me worshipped and praised God for working in my life and blessing me with this wonderful man of His choosing, just as Julia had always known!

I also couldn't help but think about how God carries us, especially in our times of distress and uncertainty, and the beautiful treasures that are hidden inside each of our souls. Dan's exquisitely unique perspective in creating poetry was a gift I would cherish all my days. He didn't always seem to have need of any "titles," so I just smiled, and held his love to every word upon the page as my tears came, soft and sweet, like that fruit upon the vine.

Eve of the garden,
Queen of her household,
Loving woman,
Kindness to ever unfold.

Earnest and endearing,
As bright as the sun,
Gets your life illuminated.
Never lets me down, looming, always appreciates.

Open-hearted, wonderful soul,
Radiant and brave, loves with her all.
Gentlest heart, lenient is she,
Unerring as she can be.

Sensible, she speaks her mind and heart,
Truly, she's a piece of art.
Adamant, not one to falter,
Woman no one can alter.

CHAPTER 22

Journeys of the Heart

The day was warm and beautiful, and I especially loved the eve, enjoying my family in the mansion that had come to be mine when I'd married Dan. From the very first time that I'd been blessed to enter his home, I had felt an amazing peace and joy that never left my heart. When Dan asked me to take a walk with him later that evening, I knew that something specific was pressing on his mind.

"I was so wrong to leave you and Blossom, and Ethel, and everything so dear to me, Maggie," he began. "I felt like I might never come out of the pain in the loss I was feeling without Julia. I tried to convince myself that if I went away for a very long time, everything would come to order. But it didn't, as you know. You were furious with me for good reason," he smiled, looking into my eyes, "and I felt like I didn't belong here or anywhere, but you put everything into perfect perspective for me.

"I know you've regretted your fiery words, but they were necessary to awakening what was truly valued in my life and the people who truly cared about me. I suppose that's why I couldn't be angry with you or feel any anger inside when you told me exactly how you felt and how things were. It tested my heart in fully understanding just how much you truly loved me, Maggie.

"And do you want to know something? I accidentally overheard part of the conversation you had with Julia the day before she died. From the moment we met, I knew all along that I loved you, darling, and that I'd never felt like this before in my life. I saw how special you are and that you are really something. My heart was always with you, and my concern for you grew immeasurably over the months to the love I held inside of me for you as I saw just how very amazing you are. But with Julia's illness, I didn't know how, or if, it was the right time to express my heart and to tell you, because I wanted it to be so special.

"After I'd picked you up and dropped you off at your boarding house the day before she died, I had this deep impression to go back and tell my sister of my love for you. Visiting hours were over by the time I returned to the hospital, and I asked the attending doctor for permission to speak with her, knowing how little time she had left. Patting me on the back, he simply said, 'I see no problem with that. Go right ahead and take as much time as you need.'

"Julia was sitting up in bed and almost seemed to be expecting me. 'I knew you were coming back,' she softly spoke. 'The angels are almost ready to take me home to Heaven, Dan, and I asked God to answer my deepest heart's prayer, if it is true that you and Maggie love each other, and shall soon marry. His Presence overtook my heart and it was then when I felt at peace in a way I never quite have before, nor can explain. I was waiting and praying for this very moment;' she paused, as tears glistened in her eyes, 'with you!' she finished.

"I was so completely moved by her words, that I couldn't speak right away, and I believe that it was exactly when she had prayed that prayer that I suddenly sensed the importance of going back and talking with her one last time, just like we used to.

"When Julia saw me, she lovingly threw out her arms, and we hugged for a long moment. 'I love you, Julia,' I said. She smiled, and her words were sweet and soft as she said, 'And I love you, Daniel Danes!'

"I sat down beside her, but I didn't know quite how to start. Tears welled in my eyes and I bit my bottom lip. Then, it all came to me, and I felt compelled to share everything with her from the moment we'd met in the garage. She seemed to suddenly have strength, rapturously listening with shining eyes that danced with joy when I told her all that my heart was feeling and held for you. She clasped my hands, and we cried together in the joy of this love, and it shall always be a very special memory."

Tears misted in Dan's eyes and for a moment, he couldn't go on. "Julia was ecstatic," he continued, "and she said she was now at peace and could die knowing that her daughter would have a home filled with love in us. She was so thrilled in knowing that her heart's prayer for us to marry was coming true. I know that it was some storm in sharing our hearts, Maggie, that finally brought to us our marriage! But if not for that, I might have been lost forever." He wept in my arms, and I held him close, tears stinging my eyes, weeping with him.

"I'm so very glad you shared your love for me with Julia that night, my darling," I gently said, "and that you're sharing it now! I'll always cherish the gift you so lovingly gave to me in working in Julia's boutique, side by side, with her, and getting to know, and truly love, my future sister-in-law back then. It means the world to me!"

Looking into my eyes, Dan hesitated, then shyly confessed, "I found that poem you wrote, my beloved Maggie, as I waited for you at your boarding house while you were busy with a telephone call that long-ago afternoon. I didn't mean to, but I got too close, and accidentally hit my shin painfully hard against the corner of your coffee table. Just then, a paper suddenly fluttered to the floor with the movement. Bending to pick it up, the title caught my eye, and I was immediately intrigued. I apologize, but I believe it was meant to be, and important to understanding your anguish in your love for me.

My eyes twinkled as I teased, "Well, Dan, I never had any secrets from you, except for how very much I longed for your love, but I'm sorry for that pain you got." I paused, then said, "It's funny, but I vividly recall that morning, too. I had taken the poem from my nightstand to read through one more time, but your unexpected visit surprised me, and I laid the paper down to answer the door. Not ever dreaming it would be you, I never even thought of that until this moment. I'm really sorry, Dan," but he wouldn't let me finish. He lovingly wrapped me in his arms, tenderly kissing me.

Smiling, he said, "I was *A Lost Rose* for a time, just as you penned, and I'm so glad that God fit all the pieces of the puzzle of our lives in perfect place the evening we were married. And believe me, I had that pain for days, but it was worth it to know the truth and forever have this love with you!"

"I truly had no secrets, Dan, and I never meant for you to read the poem. I should have torn it up, and thrown it away, and I thought I had, . . ." but the rest of the words wouldn't come.

Seeing my hurt expression as tears fell unbidden from my eyes, he comforted, "Without every piece being placed into God's hands that night, wherever would our love be today? Maggie, I'm terribly sorry for all the trouble and pain I've caused you in the past, but don't you see? God used it to turn every thorn into something extraordinarily beautiful, like the roses enticing fragrance, for His Glory, because when we appreciate its beauty, we don't consider the thorns upon its vine!" Wiping my tears, he lovingly kissed me. "I love you more than you shall ever know, my darling!"

"I stood up to you as a man, not my editor, Dan, in the anguish of my love for you, and you could have fired me right then, but you didn't. I'll ever be grateful to you for that. I love you so, so much my dearest," I said, "and nothing will ever keep me from this love I hold within my heart for you."

"I'm so thankful that you did, Maggie," he tenderly said, his eyes misting as he held me. "That took a lot of courage and in it, I began to see how very genuine your love was for me, and it confirmed the truth of my heart in my love for you."

That moment has faithfully brought us together to where we are today; where God's truth was found. It was just as Dan had said. "When I saw the word, Forgiven, written across the poem, I knew that you were the one I wanted to marry more than ever, because you had a heart to truly follow after God."

For all the hopeless, yearning emotions that I'd put into that poem, I was very thankful that God had given me the power to change my heart in forgiving my beloved before he ever would find, and inadvertently read it. I had to agree with him. It was meant for him to read, if only to know I loved him enough to forgive, just as God forgave me everything.

Now, I better understand how very much Dan had always loved me, and just how very difficult it must have been for him to hold this to himself as his sister was dying. He was truly very special, I said in my thoughts, and he was mine after all that despite my fiery temper, and times of misunderstanding. Only God could work such beauty out of the ashes of the broken pieces of a heart.

In that time, however, I came to also better realize that God is certainly busy as He teaches me, even though I sometimes need to come to grips that He must always have the final say when the battle rages strong inside of me. Much like an untamed wave spewing plumes in billowing, roaring thunder high upon the ocean for a time, or as a raging fire bursting into flame that burns at times like a rebel, its recourse must bow to God's omnipotent sovereignty, I smiled to myself! For in conclusion to that end, I'm willing to hear the whole truth and accept all it embraces toward the will of my Heavenly Father's heart. And I believe that's why the loss became our greatest strength. *A Lost Love* met at the cross, where, forever and always, His love heals our pain and brings joy to fragrance our souls, spilling in abundant blessing like a song upon the wind!

I surmise that God will be busy pruning more branches in me, too, as Blossom and I shared that day. Well, as my loving Heavenly Father, I welcome His path and His plan far more than any steps or decisions I shall make! I told Blossom that I'd rather be pruned and trimmed to be a flower beautifully fragranced for others to see Christ in me, than to wither on the vine and vanish like the wind, without the care of my Good Shepherd.

In introspect, truly, His was a plan worth waiting for, and much, much more beautiful than either Daniel Danes or I could have planned all on our own, because he allowed God to transform his life, even as I understood, and willingly allowed God to transform . . . my thought and pen momentarily paused, . . . *mine*!, I emphasized.

A love lost . . . and found . . . on all that the cross of love and forgiveness offers to the resurrection of our souls! And I wouldn't want to be anywhere else without a noble heart that follows after the path of righteousness in God.

As I reflected on this verse, I so loved that King David of Israel wrote, that says, "But the noble make noble plans, and by noble deeds they stand," - Isaiah 32:8 TNIV, it held so much meaning to my own life in many ways.

But I also saw the diligent depth of character and the worth of every moment that Ethel and Tom lent to their work, that truly were noble plans laid at their feet by the Creator, God Himself, without any doubt in my mind about it!

We saw again and again that anything worthwhile takes an incredible amount of strength, patience, and diligent tenacity when we are, not only sure in what we know our calling is, but in doing it with great pleasure! Like Harry's love for his meadow, him and Anne, it was identical, and in the work they enjoyed in teaching students!

Equivalently, Dan and I, we always share the faith that the words we use to ultimately glorify God through the pages of our books, and our lectures, will come to change many hearts for Him. We choose to honor our readers because we choose this immense privilege to honor God in everything we do and say to make a better world. Sometimes, however, our world is terribly uprooted when troubles come, just as King David realized where the end of people's lives will be who reject God, wherein his whole perspective changed. And ours can, too, I thankfully noted, when we have the Creator of the universe living in our hearts and lives!

Together, Dan and I loved and cherished the covenant of our marriage, where God would always hold His heart within our lives. 'Though our downs were few and far between, it was this love that was so tested before our marriage that brought this strength, and what had seemed *A Lost Love* forever, that came to be that love that would endure within the Rock of Christ, just like the mighty, boisterous waves crashing against a rock, never wavering: solid, fervent, and true.

To postscript, Ethel and Tom successfully produced a hybrid to that orchid they had presented to me on the day of their wedding. The lavender-mauve blush, steeped in delicate, subtle shades of plum-cherry corals, muted, yet highlighted in its own strength of beauty, and tinged with a hint of burnt orange at the top of the blossom, was both flattering and truly awe-inspiring. Its elusive features were incomparably exceptional and breathtaking, and totally, extravagantly outstanding, and inexplicably gorgeous! The Wafers gave it the perfect name of *Exquisite Rapture*.

While my heart would always favor the indelible simplicity of the lady's slipper, to each masterpiece in defining distinction, I wondered what more God had waiting in their hearts for Him to teach the world of His amazingly wonderful creation!

There was, however, one other surprise that I could have never imagined. Just after we'd returned to Canada from our latest season of teaching in Austria, I recalled a particular afternoon when I'd slipped into one of Ethel's lectures and listened with raptured joy.

Her English had noticeably improved, and I suspected that her husband, Tom Wafer, had something to do with that, as well as her role as a professor again in the classroom. Her expression was bright and animated and her way of instruction, most impressive, which immediately held my interest so that I could scarcely take my eyes off of her. I took a moment, however, to glance at the students nearby, and saw the identical focus in their faces. It was more than obvious to me that she was wholly enjoying herself, and I almost giggled out loud, amused and proud, for all the times we'd shared together in her "Mr.'s" mansion, never once dreaming that my Ethel held the hidden talent in also being a professor! Goodness, I thought to myself, perhaps it was a good thing I didn't know it at the time, or I might have been very uncomfortable and self-conscious, working as the housekeeper with such a learned, and intelligent woman!

Her husband joined her shortly on the platform, and together, they tangibly showcased the original flowers, and then, the successful crossbreeding. The difference was astounding! Of course, God's original would always be perfect in itself, but having the skill to recreate from His original, was truly amazing, and something else, altogether!

A very grave and astounding thought occurred to me in that moment. Just think, I said to myself, that God, Creator of everything, allowed that window for our minds to recreate a part of that perfect beauty from His original idea! That was truly mindboggling! I think it gave Him immense pleasure in knowing how much we loved everything He'd created for our enjoyment and more; enough to yearn for greater potential of excellence from the masterpieces of His hands!

I loved Tom's quiet way that also captured my heart. As they detailed the process, they openly acknowledged their success because of God's guidance and ideas that had brought them this immense favor.

"Whatever we accomplish," Tom was saying, "it is still God's original idea from the creation that He spoke into existence with the power of His words. We will never have, per se, an original idea, because everything we say and do will always come from the core root of what God has already created for us. But He's so loving and gracious, that He gives us, both His wisdom, and these talents, to sharpen that skill as we labor in love to use them for others, and the glory of His Name Most High."

"As someone once said to a farmer," Ethel began, "'Look what God has done with your field! Why, the corn is so perfect – all the rows straight as an arrow!' the man marveled.

"'Well,' the wise farmer said to him, 'that's true! But you should have seen it when God had the field all by Himself!'"

Everyone laughed, and Ethel continued, "I am just paraphrasing that quote, but isn't it true? While God's creation is absolute and perfect, He still expects us to use every talent and every skill in bringing, and drawing, more out of the original, because He infused diversity of potential within those very things, like the flowers. He didn't have to do that, but He did, knowing that we would be strengthened and be amazed and awed and marvel at His omnipotence, so that no one can deny He still stamps every spectrum of it with the fingerprint of His love."

All attention was intently focused on Ethel and Tom as they held their students to a higher authority, committed to teaching the depth of the true origin of authenticity in their work, and the work their students would eventually follow in the footsteps of God Almighty.

"Now," Tom said, "here's the process that we use, and although it has its own diversities as well, the concept is similar within the process of every flower we choose under God's divine guidance."

As Ethel and Tom took turns explaining the process, we listened with rapt attention, along with the students.

"First, we pray and ask God to open our minds to the ideas infused within the colors we select for the flower we've already chosen, and how we can work that into a feasible product within breeding from the original," Ethel began to explain.

"Once we have the ideas," Tom continued, "we lay a blueprint down so we can refer to it from both the original and the new field of concept that we've come up with. And so forth. And of course, as necessary, we make changes of variation to the hues and patterns of the blossom which we are endeavoring to create from crossbreeding."

Sitting there, I was totally blown away. Like shining jewels in the night, I gave praise to God for the passion Ethel and Tom shared in their work, and the love they held in cherished joy together. As they continued to humbly acknowledge Him as their source, no wonder God was blessing them so!

I was drawn back to that humble beginning when I'd first met Ethel, a shy, but delightful, young woman, and then Tom, who held the same spirit of joy as her. In them both, I'd seen this extraordinary and remarkable woman and man daily surrender their lives to Christ, living out each day in that wonderful place of peace and contentment. Rare was the day when they allowed the cares of the world to defeat them. I was truly humbled to share my life in theirs as closest friends, and the journey God had led along that bended path in His love for us.

My thoughts drifted back to the present, and I was suddenly a trifle startled when I felt a gentle hand on my shoulder. I was so intent on the lecture that I hadn't even been aware that the vacant chair beside me was no longer unoccupied. Turning to see who was seated next to me, I was completely surprised when my eyes looked into Dan's! I reached for his hand as tears welled in both our eyes.

"They're the best, aren't they, darling?" he softly whispered.

My heart was so full of emotion, but I needed to verbalize my feelings. "Yes, darling, they truly are!" I answered. Then, I couldn't stop the tears as Dan held me close with his arm lovingly about my shoulder.

As the lecture ended, the students arose, and applauded. Then, Ethel stepped off the platform, Tom beside her, and ran toward us, her arms wide open. Hugging us close, Ethel lovingly said, "My dearest Maggie and Dan. When I saw you both enter the classroom, my heart was breathless to this joy in your presence! Tom and I are truly honored that you came to be a part of this afternoon with us, and we want to thank you for believing in our work, and making our dreams come true!"

Tom hugged me, too, and shook Dan's hand. "We couldn't have done it without you," he said, "and having you here, is truly an honor, as Ethel said!"

The classroom quieted and we found ourselves alone after the students had departed. But it wasn't long before joyful voices filled the room again and we found ourselves surrounded.

"This fruit is just a little something to show our appreciation for your wonderful teaching," Brent, a handsome young man, said, handing a huge basket to Ethel and Tom. "We all pitched in!"

"Thank you!" they said in unison.

A young woman, Margaret, came from behind Brent, holding an identical basket. "We wanted to be sure there's enough to go around for everyone!" she smiled teasingly with a twinkle in her eyes. Brent put his hand in hers, and she smiled.

We were invited to join the students, celebrating their joy. But the greatest part would always be in knowing that, sometimes, when God plants a seed that's kept hidden for a time, as it was both with Ethel and Tom, when His time is right, our dreams will come alive and soar!

It also taught me to see deeper seeds of potential to greatness prospectively in others' souls, because I could never have imagined that Ethel and Tom both had their degrees in the horticultural field, even though it was right in front of me all along. That stunning revelation the evening Ethel shared this news with us in our garden and then later, Tom, revolutionized my thinking.

Seeing the Wafers' greenhouse in their dreams originally come through Dan and me, was one of the best things we ever did! They eventually toured the world with their daughter, Sophia, and while my heart missed my beloved Ethel in these times of separation, I was so thrilled for her and Tom, that I couldn't find much loneliness or sadness too long as I had when she journeyed to Hawaii before her marriage to him. That helped to ease the greater portion of pain as Dan and I continued our own work and raising our children.

When the Wafers returned home to Canada in the autumn after an extended tour, financed through Austria's university while on a six-month sabbatical, we were ecstatic!

"My dearest Maggie," she lovingly said, hugging me close. "Tom and I have crossbred a beautiful flower that we're sure you and Dan will both adore. Can you come to our cottage straight away?" she excitedly asked, taking my hand, her black eyes sparkling.

"Yes!" I said.

After we entered the kitchen, they momentarily disappeared as Dan and I patiently waited. When Ethel and Tom returned, my eyes widened in pleasured joy, and I found myself speechless in the moment. Then, my heart burst with song, and I enthusiastically exclaimed, drawing out the word, "Ohhh! It's just beautiful!"

With breathless emotion, my eyes took in the beauty as Ethel gently handed me the planter containing a stunning, and very healthy-looking and vibrant lady's slipper. Everything about the flower was perfectly balanced in hues of blended perfection that I'd never seen before, and I knew there never before had been such a magnificent blossom as this one was.

The lady's slipper petals were beautifully white, except for a dash of sparkling emerald distinguished on the bottom which flowed into the mouth portion, or slipper, which sported entrancingly fluent, violet tones blended with several deftly fine, overshadowed hues eclipsed of slightly varying depths, much like an artist's paintbrush, graced in lavender, mauve, and purple. The inner slipper was bathed in a background of burgundy-lilac against delicate, crimson spots. It was absolutely exquisite!

"Have you given this lady's slipper a special name yet?" I inquisitively asked, after admiring the flawless details, peering deep into Ethel's eyes.

"I have!" she breathlessly exclaimed. Tears misted her eyes, and for a moment, she could not speak, her emotion was so overwhelming, that I didn't quite understand. But she couldn't have surprised me more than she did when she told me the name of the flower.

Taking my hand in hers, Ethel softly cried as tears overtook her. "I've wanted to crossbreed a very special flower just for you, dear Maggie, from the moment I met you that day when you came to work for my Mr., because I knew that you were someone who was going to be extraordinarily special to my heart.

"And when I asked you if Dan would kindly consider building Tom and me this greenhouse, I finally found my heart's longing in knowing that this dream would come true for me and hold a very special name – yours – and so I named it, *Maggie's Joy*, in your honor! I know it's simple, but it says it all, don't you think?" she asked, anticipation gleaming in her beautiful eyes.

"It does, and it couldn't be a better or lovelier name for such a special and amazing flower!" I cried, tears streaming down my face unashamedly. "Oh, Ethel!" I exclaimed. "Why, it's . . . it's just breathless and exquisite like you! How can I ever thank you for such a beautiful honor?"

"You have already, my dearest Maggie . . . many times over. I know how very much you've always adored the lady's slipper, but it took me some time to appreciate exactly how to create the vibrant colors you so love. Tom didn't even know that I was working on this project until a few days ago. I was perfecting it just so special for you! So, you see, my dearest friend, I've waited a very long time to give you this pleasure!"

"You are my pleasure," I softly returned, "and there's no better friend I'll ever have than I've always had and have right now - here - in this precious, tender moment together with you, or shall ever have, my dearest Ethel!"

Hugging my best friend, Ethel Wafer, I knew that this honor was truly of a priceless gift of extravagant love poured over me from within the grace of her heart, just as the beautiful gift of this lady's slipper would always be to my heart each day I was blessed within her wondrous presence.

Maggie's Joy won numerous awards, too many to count, making it the most diversely prolific, unique, and enchantingly beautiful lady's slipper thus far ever to be bred. The purses they brought in were also the highest ever offered in such unprecedented measure within the horticultural field, but it was Ethel's heart that had long since captured mine in friendship's locket, so much more as closest sisters, that would ever be the most precious beauty in gift to me of all!

Apart from Dan's and my close friendship with Ethel and Tom, I couldn't have been more blessed with all that God had given to me,

302

especially my dearest Dan. I loved spending my heart in time with him to every turning day, knowing his humble heart, and the amazing man he is. To the beautiful worth of his stunning spirit, where God dwells in the honor and integrity of the special gift he would ever be for Him and for me, my soul was filled with the immeasurable gift of Dan's wondrous presence in his perfect love, and the joy of our children who had come as angels in disguise.

Carlos was a happy, handsome child who came to love our walks within the nature we had long since adored. In time, I was certain that our baby girl, Victoria, would follow in his footsteps. Carlos had the sweetest giggle, which always made us smile, and we found that his appreciation of it was truly inspiring. He loved to play amongst the flowers in the big, beautiful garden his daddy had originally designed years back with the architect, and then with Tom.

Together, with his cousin, Blossom, they enjoyed biding lofty days within the turning seasons, playing amongst the beautiful garden that we all enjoyed, and traipsing along the avenue of trees.

I shouldn't so easily have blown caution to the wind! Not for a moment, when I'd shared my secret with Carlos, did I ever suspect that he'd tell Anne and Harry's two-year-old son, Henry! Excitedly clapping his hands and sweetly giggling, Henry couldn't keep it to himself, disclosing to his parents my yearning to dance amongst the flowers in their meadow!

"That's fine by me and Anne," Harry laughed when he stopped by my office before taking the platform to teach. "Dance all you like to your heart's pleasure!"

"Oh, Harry, no . . ." I blushed. "I . . . I couldn't, really."

"Oh, you could really, and I'm expecting that you do so soon!"

"Okay," I cheerily replied, "but what about the poor flowers being trampled on?"

"They'll spring back. Their roots will still be there, so anything, such as bent and broken blossoms, there's no concern for worry. I'm counting on you to have this special joy, my friend! I know it will be worth this gift I give to you!"

"Alright, then, I shall! Maybe I'll consider that tomorrow. Tonight, I promised Dan I'd watch a movie on television with him, so I'll do it tomorrow!"

"Sounds great!"

I was very excited to dance amongst the meadow flowers! I could hardly wait! Dan said that he'd keep me company, and he even thought that the children should join us. "I'll keep an eye on them!" he laughed good naturedly.

Unbeknownst to me, Dan apparently had a secret with Ethel that I could never have expected. Perhaps, in the end, it was a good thing, for it came to be one of my grandest gifts ever! That gave me a lovely idea. Overwhelmed by everything I held in Dan, I let my heart be free upon my soul as the words began to flow, extravagantly spilling onto the paper. It was something I should have done long before to right my distraught feelings when I'd felt so alone and created *A Lost Rose* back then. When it was finished, I drank in the rich nectar of the words, mesmerized by the beauty unfurled, like a flower, in my love for him. That evening as I shared my poem with Dan, tears misted his eyes, as he lovingly whispered, "My darling! It's so beautiful! A masterpiece! And I shall cherish it always. Thank you, Maggie!" As he held me close in our love, Dan would always be this enchanting *Wild Rose* to me, where the *Journeys of the Heart* were more beautiful than I ever could have imagined with this beloved man!

My Wild Rose

In my heart there sings a song,
A melody that's sweet and strong.
For here my fragrant Rose doth live,
Beloved One, my heart, to give.

And through the valleys deep and long,
This love doth deepen, rich and strong.
For in my heart is writ in prayer,
My Wild Rose in you so fair!

And I shall ever love you true,
Like raindrops on the sunlit dew.
Bliss Treasure of my heart to stay;
Beholden joy to every day!

God's gift in you came unaware,
A blessing wrapped in love and care.
And as we live for Him each day,
I've found my heart in you to stay!

Upon the mountains we shall stand,
A view of wonder, rich and grand.
Where there the rarest flowers live;
To you, my love, I solely give.

The fragrance of the rose in you,
Cannot compare to love so true.
But here my heart shall ever love,
God's gift in you from Heav'n above!

I came to see how very profound it is that God is with us every time and every moment, and I am blessed beyond measure to hold so pure a love in my beloved, each and every day! While I'd felt so lost and alone at times before our marriage, I never again mourned for Dan's love, for it was right here, with me, where it would stay forever, poignantly honeysweet and pure, along *The Journeys of the Heart*!

CHAPTER 23

A Book Upon Our Shelf

Ethel was thrilled when I shared Harry's lavish offer with her, and she said she'd like to come along to keep an eye on the children. "I think that Dan might not notice, him watching you, and the children may decide to wander off. Especially, near the creek. It's not deep, but I think it would be safer if I tagged along. What do you think, dear Maggie?"

"I think that's a perfect idea! I just don't want too many people watching me, though, but you, dear Ethel, I won't mind at all!"

The evening was beautiful and still with barely a wisp of a wind. I timidly, at first, ventured into the field where hundreds of glorious colors of beautiful flowers seemed to beckon me, filling my soul with immense joy as I slowly turned and pondered the glory of the creation within my midst. Pausing about halfway into the meadow, I felt wholly cherished and loved as I worshiped God; grateful for the pleasure as the emotion of my soul rose; completely acutely akin to every perfect petal. I felt oblivious in these moments to those around me, and never more aware of God's Holy Presence.

Then, my heart became free, and I stretched my arms wide, dancing and twirling and whirling to my heart's content, serenading across the vast meadow and its immense beauty. The wind suddenly picked up, carrying me to greater joy as it blew my hair, and I felt the warmth of the waning sun upon my naked arms. I closed my eyes, breathing in the fragrances drifting on the air, that were fresh and lovely in every way.

When I opened my eyes, Dan was at my side, tenderly taking my hand, where we danced together upon the beauty of the eve. The music of the wind lisped as it sang amongst the trees, and no better music had my heart ever known! We twirled and whirled about in purest exclamation of joy as we laughed together for the pleasure, all ours.

Then, unexpectedly, Dan lifted me high in his arms, and I cried in gleeful wonder to the breathless thrill as my soul touched each corded note of exquisite emotion, and I stretched my arms to the melody of my heart. My skirt swirled to the spontaneous movements in fluent motion until my shoes touched the meadow floor in time again.

When Dan put me down, I hugged him close, passionately kissing him. Then, I looked across the plain and saw my children running towards us. First Blossom, then Carlos and Victoria. I ran toward them, scooping them into my arms, as Dan followed alongside me, holding my hand. A lovelier portrait I had never seen!

Hugging them close, we laughed and cried to the joy the meadow had proffered on this beautiful night. Looking into the sky, the stars were glittering against the deepening sunset tinged in mauves and blues and oranges, and the moon was peeking through the clouds, splashing its golden glow, like a stream, upon us. It was enchantingly poetic, charmingly sweet, and wonderfully gorgeous; priceless in my heart to each, unspoken word!

As soon as we were out of the meadow, Ethel clasped her hands to her heart and excitedly exclaimed, "Oh, it was so beautiful! Just like a magical scroll!" She paused, then astonished me by adding, "And Harry got it all on film and said for you to take a look tomorrow."

I was speechless! "Harry . . . he filmed me?" I could hardly believe it!

"Yes, darling!" Dan affirmed. "He really did!"

"But . . ."

"He didn't want you to be nervous and asked my permission. He said it would be a wonderful memory and keepsake."

"Well, I don't mind, really. Just as long as he doesn't decide to show the world!" I exclaimed, shivering at the thought, trying to take it all in.

"You were just beautiful, dear Maggie!" Ethel said. "Wasn't she, children?"

Nodding, they giggled. "So pretty, Mommy!" Carlos said.

"Uh huh!" Blossom echoed. "So pretty!"

Victoria merely smiled and it made me laugh.

"Well, it's time to go back home now, my children," I said. "The meadow has gone to sleep and so must we!"

I didn't dare ask Ethel where dear Harry had disappeared to, but I reckoned he wanted to hurry home, and view the film without delay. I honestly couldn't blame him for that! I was becoming quite curious myself about it! Well, I smiled, taking Dan's hand, I didn't mind the pleasure of that just so long as the whole world didn't see it, as I'd already pointed out to Ethel!

Harry called earlier than usual the next morning. "Maggie, please," he said, excitement rising in his voice. "You and Mr. Danes, if you can, must come as soon as you are ready, to view the film from last night! We'd like you to also join us for breakfast," he added.

I looked at the kitchen clock. It was barely past seven-thirty in the morning. "Alright! We'll be right over!"

Anne greeted us warmly when Dan and I arrived a few minutes later. "I have a good breakfast waiting on the stove for you while Harry gets the film set to view," she said. "And" she mysteriously smiled, "I know that you'll feel the same way that me and Harry do about it! There's something so special and magical about the meadow, and you made it come alive to that passion of wondrous persuasion!"

Harry stepped into the foyer and said hello, taking our coats and hanging them up. "As soon as we've eaten, we can see the film," he smiled.

The breakfast was lovely, but I found it hard to eat because my curiosity was overwhelming. Nervous about seeing myself on film, I hoped it would reflect the very essence of everything that I was feeling in those wondrous moments.

Half an hour later, we finished breakfast, and Harry ushered us into his spacious office. Anne cleared the table and joined us just before he was ready to roll the film.

I was mesmerized and stunned when I initially saw myself gingerly stepping into the meadow, pausing halfway, and then stretching my arms to the joy it offered. As the film played out, it was truly remarkable! Not because it was me who was in it, but because of the spirit of joy it carried in my heart, expressed so beautifully and carefree to what my soul was feeling.

When Dan lifted me in his arms, it was like I was back in the scene, enjoying every enchanting moment with my husband, as a ballerina enthralled in a meadow!

As my children ran toward us, and I scooped them into my arms, the joy of my heart overflowed, and I found tears streaming down my face.

When Anne turned the lights back on, I quickly tried to get my emotions under control, but it was useless.

"What do you think?" Harry was asking.

"It's simply beautiful!" Dan said. Turning to me, he put his arm about me. "Darling, are you alright?" He tenderly wiped away my tears as my heart settled once again.

"Oh, it's so wonderful and exquisite and beautiful! It's like a prayer to God as I worshipped Him! I can't ever thank you enough, Harry, for blessing me with such a priceless gift!"

"The pleasure is mine, Maggie!" He looked toward Anne, and she nodded, smiling. "I have something to share with you. I know that you don't want the world to share this portrait of the meadow that I filmed, but I have a producer friend, Ian Grey, and he wants to use it in a special story about sharing the gifts of joy through nature on the silver screen. Would you mind if I had him preview it?"

Without even thinking it over, I knew my answer. Tears misted my eyes as I softly replied, "For whatever joy in blessing this may come to be, I don't mind at all, Harry!"

"Thank you, Maggie. That's all I needed to know! Well, I suppose it's time to head off to work now. I see that we'll be a little late and . . ."

"Late is fine," Dan smiled. "It's for a very good reason, and I think it's wonderful that my wife agrees with you! There is no need to rush today!"

"I'll let you know what my producer friend says as soon as I hear back from him," Harry said, "but it might take a while."

"We understand," Dan said. And we left it at that.

I'd completely forgotten about the film until one Friday afternoon, a few months later, just after we'd returned home from work, the doorbell chimed. Not expecting anyone, I peeked out the window to see who had come. When I saw it was Harry, I immediately opened the door. A stranger was with him, and I welcomed them in.

"Hello, Maggie," Harry warmly said. "This is Mr. Ian Grey. My producer friend."

"It's a pleasure to meet you," I said, as he returned the greeting. "What may I do for you?"

"Well, it's what I may do for you as well," Mr. Grey answered, smiling. I believe that Harry has already mentioned that he thought I'd be interested in the film with you in the meadow."

"Yes, Mr. Grey. I remember."

"Well, it's just magnificent! It portrays a beautiful story of a woman and her husband, then their children, I assume?" he paused to ask.

"Oh, yes! They are!" I answered.

"It's beautiful! Every moment, breathtaking and perfect! When your husband lifted you high in the air and the fireflies came on the scene with their entrancing, bobbing lanterns filling the meadow, they were like tiny, shimmering flashes of jeweled bliss amidst the wonder of your grace and beauty. This is what truly makes this scene, not only so extraordinarily beautiful in lending an aura of quaint portrait, and exceptionally valuable, but of a rare authenticity. It portrays pure magic within every detail of the joy you were experiencing! God even provided the 'special effects,' per se, with the fireflies dancing in their own accord of pleasure!

"Now," he smiled, "I have a contract and a cheque to cover your portion of the payment if you will kindly sign it and in so doing, grant my company permission to use this film for its intended purpose clearly noted."

He handed me a paper and I read it. Everything appeared in order. "Well, I trust you because I know Mr. Gerali very well. Now, a pen . . ."

Taking a pen from his vest pocket, he handed it to me. I signed the document, and he warmly thanked me.

"This may seem rather unusual from most standards, but before this is aired, you will be given the opportunity to see the whole piece and you will then have the option to withdraw. But for now, here's a cheque, and it's yours to keep, even if you decide to withdraw it later."

I didn't dare look at it, and placed it on the kitchen counter, thanking him. Harry and Mr. Grey turned to leave, when he suddenly stopped, and commented, "I wanted to meet the lovely woman in the film and I'm glad I have! You're a special person, I can see, and Harry is blessed to have you as a friend. Such authenticity is rare, as I've already stated, in the film industry and this is not only a treasure, but a trust, I'm deeply grateful for. And" he finished, "I assure you that this film will be used only for the intended purpose and of highest excellence, in offering audiences a positive and uplifting alternative to what God intends our lives to be, rather than the mockery and muck that is overwhelming the viewing audiences we see for a large part in today's society."

Understanding, I smiled. "I'm very pleased to give the world this pleasure, and to know that it will be taken care of in your capable and honorable hands, Mr. Grey! Thank you for the blessing you have given here to us!"

"You really have a wonderful soul," Mr. Grey complimented. "And you know something, Mrs. Danes? I always wanted to create words in a storybook, to enrich lives with the gifts God has given to me, in making others happy and joyful. My work is like that storybook, I suppose," he smiled. "But I've always wanted and yearned and desired to be the one who appreciates even the tiniest, wonderfully, and extraordinary blessings that this world may give to us. I don't want to see even a single person's tears. I think of my work as painting beautifully unique portraits of joy, just like an author. But I've sometimes found myself asking the questions: Can I do that, and do I have the courage? And in my own strength, I know that I don't. But in God's strength, He enables me to do things I never dreamed possible!

"I understand how difficult it must be for you to give the world this most special and sacred gift from your heart. Let me assure you,

Mrs. Danes, I once felt the same way. However, I've come to see that it's about what I can do through Christ, rather than what I can't do without Him. I'll always choose to better the world as I simply strive to do His will and leave the rest with Him! I do thank you so very much for this in every way!"

"It's my pleasure!" I said, as I smiled through my tears.

We said goodbye and I watched Harry and Mr. Grey drive off. Then, I remembered about the cheque and slowly unfolded it. I nearly fainted! It was a huge payment for something I'd so enjoyed and hadn't even been aware of being filmed! It made me feel a little guilty until I realized that Mr. Grey was surely getting a larger stake than this.

I was so happy that Harry and Anne had received a similar payment as Ian had indicated when he handed me the cheque. "It's share and share alike," he had said. "Harry's meadowland and your talent! Really, Mrs. Danes, you're a very natural talent at that!"

Blushing at his compliment, I merely smiled, and said, "Thank you!"

When I later mentioned it to Harry, he chuckled and assured, "God has His unexpected blessings, Maggie, and Ian has a deep appreciation for quality, especially where it concerns God's creation. He is very touched by this amazing piece! In fact, I think that he would like to have all the seasons of our meadow filmed. I hope you don't mind," he paused, "but we returned one day to your mansion, not knowing that no one was around, and he took a peek at your garden. He intends to have your permission to film that, too. He also told me that if everything goes well and as he plans, there will be more money coming into me and Anne, as well as you and Dan. What do you think?"

"Oh, I love the idea! I think it will be wonderful when it's all finished, Harry! And I see no reason why we can't help Mr. Grey with his dream. I'm sure that, had Noel known, he'd be thrilled that his mansion, and the land he loved so well, is going to have a place of positive influence beyond anything we could have ever imagined!"

"I'm so excited about this endeavor, too!" Harry exclaimed. "But, I'm not quite sure what Ian has in mind, although I've known him for some years, and he's a very intuitive genius. He doesn't do anything halfway; never has, and if I may so, I believe that it will be immensely breathtaking when his film is completed, and beyond anything we can truly envision, as you say!"

As he looked into my eyes, I knew how moved Harry was, and all I could think of in the moment was to express my deep emotions as I returned, "Oh, Harry! I look forward to this in a way where I have no words, except to believe that it will truly be an incredibly extraordinary gift of joy, fresh and lovely, for all the world to see!"

"Those are my sentiments, too, Maggie," Harry said, as tears glistened in his eyes. "And we plan on hosting Ian during his filming with his crew, so it will be quite the adventure, I must say! Now, I must get back home to Anne, Maggie, but I also want to thank you and Dan for participating in this wonderful project with us, and thanks for letting me stop by to update you on Ian's plans."

"You're welcome anytime, Harry, and thank you for detailing this for us. It's an experience like none other, and we shall enjoy it every step of the journey, and later in sharing it with our students. Please greet Anne, and we'll see you again tomorrow!" Harry turned to leave when an idea struck me. "Harry! Please wait a moment! I would like to offer our home to the crew during their filming with complimentary meals as well. We have plenty of room and it would be so nice for us, and I'm sure they would appreciate staying on location for the duration of the filming. Perhaps, you would so kindly pass this on to Mr. Grey for me, please?" I asked.

"That is most generous and kind, Maggie! Thank you! I'll speak to Ian and let you know!"

We said goodbye and after Harry had left our home, I considered everything that had transpired in that desire for me to pour my soul in worship to the beauty of his and Anne's meadow. God's creation. His love covered so much in joy to us! The piece that Mr. Grey had already put together with special effects, was truly beautiful and I felt honored to have been blessed with the privilege in one day sharing my joyful experience in the meadow with the world! And sometimes, I decided, secrets were good to share, like this one, but I surely hoped that Harry wouldn't film me again, unsuspecting! Perhaps, I'd need a gentle talk with him as well as both Carlos and Henry! Hmm, I mused in my thoughts, it might not be a bad idea to include my beloved Dan there, too! After all, he'd given Harry

314

permission on my behalf without asking me, and I supposed that was just fine, since I'd done the same to him about agreeing to being in Ethel and Tom's wedding together with Dan on his behalf without asking him, so fair was fair!

One particular aspect I loved in the film was where the camera momentarily caught Dan's beautiful eyes, so blue as the ocean, and no one seemed to know the secret of where he got them! I teasingly suggested that perhaps, there's a throw-back in his Japanese or Spanish genealogy, or he may just need to ask God about it himself!

"Come here, my darling!" Dan said, pulling me lovingly close to him. "I think you're the greatest, Maggie!" he said. "As to my blue eyes, I am assured, my darling Maggie, that it is the loveliest proof from God that I am fearfully and wonderfully made, just as King David declared in Psalm 139:14b KJV."

"Yes," I softly whispered, tenderly kissing him. "And I shall always love your blue eyes and adore you forever!"

As it happened, Ian Grey came again after much talking and negotiating by telephone. He decided to exclusively film all the other seasons of the meadow, also asking permission to film our avenue of trees, and the mansion, and notably, our garden.

It took time waiting on the seasons, but when the film was put together and ready for public viewing on the silver screen about ten months later, together, with the talent of special effects, it was a masterpiece of breathless wonder in an original format that filled my soul with joy! And to think that it all began with my yearning inspiration to dance amongst Harry's meadow flowers! I could never have begun to fathom where that deep desire would come to lead me one day. A little in God's hands, I suddenly recalled, is a whole lot of little He can make into much!

Ian would come to each season to film a host of this glory in the sunrises and the sunsets, breathless upon the land, as well as simple walks with Dan and me in our garden and along the avenue of trees. Anne and Harry and Henry were included in different varying aspects within their meadow, including walks across the footbridge over the creek beyond the meadow, the first spring flowers, and the blaze of color proffered across the meadow in summer's profound beauty.

There was so much added to the spectrum of Ian's talent, that one would need to see the film personally, rather than for me to describe its every intricate detail that Ian portrayed so beautifully within his film, and the fluency captured therein. But suffice it to say that even the beauty of an individual maple leaf up close or a birch tree, made for a thrilling appreciation to the fingerprint of God upon everything He created in that pleasure. Truly, as Harry had considered, Ian Grey's film was everything breathless, and more!

Being that we taught the movie business in our company, it was a precious tool where students learned that sometimes, the best gifts are right under our feet, treasures of joy awaiting, and we must never despise small beginnings, nor the obvious! We often perceive treasure as being hidden away, but oftentimes, God places it right before us – the extraordinary amongst the ordinary, and what often is put off or aside, as insignificant, when in reality, it may hold tremendous value of unthinkable worth. I sometimes believe that that's part of God's humor as well as a part of His nature in seeing how much we appreciate the gifts of His heart, especially in Creation's glory!

"Do you want to know something?" I said, dreamily reflecting, and looking into my beloved's beautiful eyes that night. "I've always wanted to create words, just as God created this beautiful meadow, not only to honor God, but to bring His Light and His Love into my readers hearts in a loving and tangible way. And just as God's 'perfect' within the woods close by is not planted in 'straight' rows, that is His glorious imperfectness 'perfected,' to the whole beauty effected within that joy He has created.

"Unfortunately, we far too often want every word we create to be so 'perfect.' But just like God's forests, or the woods at our doorstep, the words already are 'perfect,' often more times than naught, if we'll only trust enough in ourselves.

"I'm beginning to see just how very much God calls me to this natural beauty of words, like His forest. I have to remind myself that far too many times, however, I tend to 'edit,' or 'weed out,' the very beauty of an original thought or idea. Yet, ever so lovingly, God shows me again and again, that He looks into our hearts, more than in the doing. That's what He cherishes in us best of all. Thereby, the tapestry of words, like a painting, shall always better sustain the beauty of the soul when we enjoy the portrait, just like God's forest! Sometimes, however, we need to stand aback to truly appreciate His gifts around us, within the worth of everything which He has so wonderfully given to us.

"It's my prayer, my darling, that I will always see His forest, and remember that the greatest words ever written from my heart to His, live within that 'imperfectness' within His 'perfect' heart!"

Understanding my sentiments, Dan softly kissed me in the passion of the moment. Breathless with emotion, he said, "I know of no one wiser and humbler who has given that love and joy to countless souls as you, my darling Maggie, and I noted that in your work as an editor every day. You always strove for excellence, yet never diminished that originality within its idea, unless it was totally unworkable. God sees, and He knows your heart exactly as I do," he said, "And one day," he gently emphasized, "you shall know the reward of all your love in Heaven."

Overwhelmed, I leaned against his shoulder. As the tears came, I whispered my thanks to my Heavenly Father for every blessing, great and small, that had come to me. He is the writer in me, the true Author of every word I write. Here, nothing would compare to the peace that filled my heart in these sacred moments with my beloved to the joy of it all!

What a revelation it was that day when I'd taken a walk to spend time with God, and He had shown me how important this value really is – natural woods and forests – as precious as natural words that came from the passion of my soul every day!

Comforting my heart, I knew my Dan understood my every tear as he held me close, loving me in these priceless moments.

But what was dearest to my heart was the sweet memory of Blossom as that little girl, lovingly depicting that *Hope* in her drawing for me, that came to be for us all. It would always resonate to the love I yearned to come to me as Dan's future wife, where Julia had known I belonged within this wondrous place with him, just as my Dan belonged, too, in his grandfather, Noel Danes,' mansion!

I asked Dan to appoint an illustrator to recolor this wonderful picture, making copies, so the original wouldn't eventually become so frayed, as well as faded over time, that it would be lost forever, because it was a huge part of what our lives came to be in the uncertainties we'd both experienced back then. We framed the copy for our bedroom, but the original, I would always keep safely tucked away within my jewelry box.

Years later, one day, I asked Blossom why she chose the word, *Hope*, and not *Love*, in that picture for me. Her answer was truly startling.

"Mom, from my little girl's heart so long ago now, every night I prayed for God to bring my uncle back to us, especially you, because *love* wasn't the question; we already had the answer. It was the *hope* in that love that I longed for, because I knew that God had already brought you to my uncle and my mom, especially after she died, and I wanted so much for you to be my mother, just as I knew my own mother wanted, too.

"I know it was very hard on you and Ethel when I cried and couldn't be consoled at times, but sometimes, it was that cry of my heart more than the loss of my mom, because I needed a mother, and I needed you to be her to me in every way. I loved you so much, and I didn't want to lose you."

I understood how she felt and gave her a framed copy of that portrait of love as a special keepsake in the heart's special memory we'd shared in time past.

As tears trickled down my cheeks, I held my beloved daughter, Julia's beautiful girl, and softly whispered, "Oh!" I exclaimed. "I never knew, and I love you even more for sharing this with me! I wanted so much to have you as my daughter, too, because I loved you so!" Wiping tears of joy from my eyes, I added, "Yes, my darling, Blossom, that hope surely sustained us. And to this day, that beautiful drawing is my most prized possession I've ever received, and you'll never know just what that meant to me that day, or how very much I needed it when I felt so lost and alone."

In that sacred moment, I realized that together, Dan and I, Blossom, Carlos, our daughter, Victoria, Julia, and most certainly the lovely couples we held in friendship with Ethel and Tom Wafer, and their daughter, Sophia, including Anne and Harry Gerali, and their son, Henry, we'd cherish the very heart of God to every blessing that had come that day so long ago in that dreary garage! For it was here that God had sent my beloved to me and all things good, in spite of the thorns that took us through a maze of prickly pain, to our way back from that love that had been lost for a time.

And it was there, where, the overwhelming beauty of its fragrance lovingly drew our hearts together as we yielded to God's perfect plan, and in the *hope* of a little girl's heart. Here, with pen in hand, I considered the finale of the ending script of the story narrative, pausing as I temporarily pondered how God had so wondrously brought us back within the journey of our love.

One evening as Dan and I sat alone together beneath the lush blossoms in our garden, I couldn't help but reflect on everything that had unexpectedly come from us meeting in that garage. Verbalizing my sentiments, I softly shared my thoughts.

"I would never have imagined that we would be where we are today, Dan. Loving you is the greatest gift I have. I want to thank you for being this incredible, amazing man, a man of honor. My life is perfect with you. Thank you, my darling, for making my life so beautiful!"

As Dan leaned in close to kiss me, he gently held me and softly said, "You are my beloved Maggie, and have given me your heart in a love so pure, it has no words to what I'm feeling. My life is wonderfully perfect in yours, and it is *you*," he emphasized, "who have blessed me, and made my life so beautiful! I shall cherish and adore you forever, and you shall ever be my one and only!"

The night deepened, and we admired the sunset profusely painted in colors of coral plums and blues dipped against the transcending inky darkness across the sky. Moments later, a glimmer of orange moved in on the scene, an immense contrast that brightened as the clouds temporarily enshrouded the full moon, glowing in strength upon the gentle stroke of an invisible paintbrush. Leaning against Dan's shoulder, I was perfectly content to the love of our hearts that began this story many years before.

The echoes of the night soon quieted, but for the whip-poor-wills that sang their wondrous, peaceful song nearby. Then, we arose moments later, walking hand in hand, to the mansion that I liked to think that I'd inherited along with Dan from his delightful grandfather, Noel Danes, that would always be this perfect abode where God was welcome, and we lived in the joy of the love that warmed the hearth within. Here, I was so happy that love was our constant stay in God, just as Grandfather Noel had wisely autographed in his book to Dan! Such a tremendous man, I would have been thrilled to meet him, as well as Dan's grandmother, Elizabeth, but the legacy of his book would hold that intrinsic meaning and be passed to our children when we were old and grey! I didn't dare entertain such a thought or dare to mention it to Dan!

That reminds me. I asked Ethel about her taking Mr. West on a tour of Dan's flower garden, when she seemed so shy to visit his beautiful land and mansion when I'd first asked her after we'd met. "Oh," she laughed. "I rather enjoyed giving him a tour of Dan's flower garden every spring, but I'd never personally been to his estate, although he liked to visit Dan every couple of weeks at his mansion."

Well, that certainly answered my question from that time, I mused, smiling. Teasing, I wondered, "I don't suppose there's more to tell?"

Blushing, Ethel sweetly replied, "Not in the least, my dearest Maggie. I mean to say, Not that I'm aware of. But who knows? Why don't you just brave up and ask Dan yourself?" she challenged.

"No mysterious secret, I see!" I said, amused. "Well, then! Perhaps, it's best to leave everything as it already is," I kindly suggested.

"Perhaps, it is," Ethel returned, gaily laughing.

I hugged her close, knowing that my heart was content that Dan had been so blessed and loved as a child. I understood his love for books that totally pleased me, especially in his efforts to build the company he'd originally founded on solid principles of integrity, honor, and excellence. It was all there through these years, and I was privileged to be a part of it, sharing my love and heart in his! I couldn't have been prouder or humbler to all the blessings that had come from this very special, gifted, loving, tender man, not only to me as his wife, but to everyone given the opportunity to be a part of his dreams, where they could also accomplish their own! Without a doubt, it was God's hallmark all along the journey to our book upon the shelf!

The telephone rang just as we stepped inside the spacious foyer. It was Blossom calling . . . our beloved daughter. I smiled as her love carried through across the line, and she warmly invited us over for dinner for twelve o'clock noon the following day.

"I want to spend the whole day with you, Mom!" she happily exclaimed. "With you and my wonderful Uncle Dan!"

Memories still in the making, Julia's love had given me this amazing gift in her family, where the story of our love is never-ending, and I couldn't have asked for anything more, nor anything better! But of all the gifts I found in Julia's family shall ever be her beloved brother, my amazing husband, in this wonderful man I shall forever cherish, my darling Daniel Danes, and her beloved daughter, Blossom, who wholly won my heart, and came as that little girl of cherished blessing in every way!

Immeasurably blessed, I shall always hold the honor of Dan's name, and the Name of the One Most High, who brought this defining journey of my life in Dan in the most unexpected places of all – a garage! It was there that I was led unbeknownst, not only to my editor, but a family who needed me as much as I needed them. In Julia and her daughter, Blossom, how wonderfully God threaded every minutest detail to bringing me the love of my life in Dan, and *A Lost Love* that holds the greatest love of all! And as Dan likes to say, Loving you always, . . . so I would always tell of the same, in Loving him always, forever and ever!

No loftier joy could have come, I reflected. I tenderly kissed my beloved, and gently laid down my pen when the last word of the story was written. Bliss filled my heart and I softly whispered, "My darling," I said, "where the wild roses bloom, that's where I'll always be, loving you in the deepest niche of my soul!"

Lovingly kissing me, with misty-eyed emotion, Dan tenderly answered, "That's just how I feel, too, my darling! Forever, you shall be my one and only perfect wild rose upon the vine, and I shall love and adore you always!"

In those moments, I thought of something: We see miracles as extraordinary and often, far between, but truly, it's just the opposite. And if we look hard enough, we'll find that God regards miracles as ordinary, daily gifts from Him, because that is Who He Is. Amazed to all of God's merciful Goodness, as I concluded the final lines of the script, Dan and I couldn't have been more blessed to every wondrous miracle we'd found along our way!

I closed the book, and we arose from where we were sitting on the bench beneath the beautiful canopy of the trees. The glorious aura of this heavenly garden never looked more lovely as Dan, and I admired the glow of the fiery sunset profusely etched across the horizon. In the enchanting glow of the Victorian lanterns, this delightful intrigue would never grow old.

As my eyes took in the magnificent view, I pondered, voicing my thoughts to my husband. "You know something, Dan, if not for the gift of your grandfather's mansion, we wouldn't be living this beautiful, fairytale-like dream today. You and Ethel - everyone I love so dearly - probably, would never have been a part of my life."

"That's true," he agreed, "but you must also remember, my dearest Maggie, that it was your gift and love for writing that began this journey, and I'm more convinced than ever that it was all a part of God's great plan. We wouldn't have you, either – none of us – so it was you," he emphasized, "who brought our love and the friendships that came, into our lives, as much as we came into yours."

I was stunned! "Oh, Dan," I exclaimed, "I never thought of that before!"

"Well, let's just suffice it to say that God brought us together, where every day I am truly thankful for the blessings we have found through our amazing journey within the story of *A Lost Love*."

That *Book Upon Our Shelf* really was something special, I smiled in my thoughts, and it would forever be a treasured gift of what God will do when our hearts are wholly yielded to Him!

Here, the beautiful perfume of the roses I so loved wafted upon the winds, soft and spicy, to the aesthetic glory of their beauty, and my heart couldn't have found a lovelier joy, loving Dan with all my soul in each and every day!

The stars began to appear and twinkle, and we arose from the bench. The surrounding beauty filled every place of my being with its beauty as Dan kissed me beneath the golden moon, and our love had found its way back. *A Lost Love* that needed time to grow; . . . found. Nothing said it better than that - and nothing ever would. Here, our book would hold to every cherished blessing of God's omnipotent grace, and the love Dan and I had lovingly embraced within its pages.

And that's how that thick, black-covered book, yellowed in time and well-worn, came to have its proper, unique place as *A Book Upon Our Shelf*, to live on in the hearts of those who have shared the gift of our mansion. There, upon the shelf within the enchanting Drawing Room, I'll always hold this sacred joy, for its pages hold a wondrous story. Of redemption, loss, and grief, this joy is found only through the cross, a yielded heart, and the forgiveness, that holds firm in Him. There, this amazing story shall forever claim these promises as truth, and I will always dearly love and adore my beloved Dan! As his grandfather, Noel, had told him, such wondrous books belong in his mansion, the mansion that Dan had always loved from his childhood. And I was more than assured that Noel would say, Amen, to having this fine addition upon the shelf in his beautiful mansion, too!

When we were back inside our home, I handed our book to Dan, and he gently placed the book upon the shelf. Tears welled in my eyes, and I hardly could speak as he wrapped me in his arms as I lovingly said, "God's plan was perfect to every tiny detail, my darling love, even the flaws and cracks in our lives that brought us back to this wonderful love we have."

"Truly, it was, my darling." Holding me close, the joy in my heart couldn't have been more full. Moments later, Dan gently released me. Looking into my eyes, he tenderly kissed me. "There shall never be another rose as beautiful as you. You are my beloved Maggie, and I shall love you forever."

I thought of the enticing fragrance of the wild rose – the most beautiful flower of all to me. "You shall be my *Wild Rose* forever, and I love you so, Dan!" I graciously replied.

"Mmm hmm," he said, kissing me. "Forever . . ."

I suddenly thought of that darling, little girl that so unexpectedly had come to me in Blossom, and the hope she held for our love to become that couple in covenant in marriage. She had become one of my most cherished gifts in blessing, and there were no words to describe what my heart was feeling in this moment to all I held so dear to my heart, especially with her uncle, my beloved Dan.

I thought about Ethel, too, and that I hardly noticed a misspoken word anymore, I smiled to myself. Truly, love gives, and does, so many wonderful things!

One beautiful, warm afternoon, I recalled, I'd decided to ask Amanda about any hidden secrets she might have, sharing first with her, about Ethel and Anne's remarkable degrees I never could have imagined, until they'd revealed that amazing news with me and Dan.

Laughing, her eyes bright and shining, she'd softly said, "Oh, no, Mrs. Maggie! The only hidden secret I have is my love for children. One day, I hope to marry a wise and loving man. A man whose heart wholly loves and adores children as I do. But I assure you, that I haven't any degree to speak of!" Looking into my eyes, she shyly amended, "Well, at least not yet anyway, but I think that loving children is the best life holds, and I do hope to have my own one day."

"Well," I'd gently replied, "Amanda, that is a lovely dream, and every day, I see your beautiful heart, and your love and delight for my children. I know that you will cherish yours no less! Like you say, perhaps, in your future, you shall find an aspiring dream to obtain that unknown degree. But only if you want to! I agree that loving children is the one gift that I shall always hold dearest to my heart and my soul with Dan."

Most of all, however, I thought of my beloved darling and the man I am so privileged and honored to know, for within his highest excellence, the depth of my soul shall cherish him forever to his amazingly stunning soul, and the love that came to me. Here, as petals to fragrance our lives, I shall want for nothing, where Dan shall always be a rose of sacred trust and beauty to me, and my dearest love, and best of all, my greatest friend!

Then, I yielded to Dan's love as my heart sang its own special song, and I couldn't help but echo his joy as I drank in the beauty of his soul with mine as we kissed sweet and long. "Forever . . ." I tenderly said, "and beyond . . ."

THE END

POSTFACE

Please note that any similarities to the hybrid colors of the flowers created in *A Lost Love*, are solely inspired from the author's imagination and are purely coincidental to any known breeding, and bears no knowledge to any hybrids, or hybrid names, physically and successfully, or experimentally, created in this field.

- Eleanor Lee Gustaw

POSTSCRIPT

At the time I was working on the final draft to the manuscript of this novel, my mother, Bernice, went to be with the Lord. I shall ever miss her love for my work, her loving encouragement, and the presence in her sweetness by which she gave it to me.

After reading one of the first drafts, she said, "It's so beautiful! Beautiful! Beautiful! I can see the characters as though I'm in the scenes!"

I shall never forget her joy as she hugged me close, and her smile lit with pleasure to everything I have come to see more and more within this remarkable and extraordinary woman in my mother. She lived her life daily in Christ . . . an example of incredible strength, peace, joy, and honor. I am so honored and privileged to be her daughter!

Because she taught me as a little girl about Jesus, my mother has left an incredible imprint on my heart of what it means to follow God and to personally know His Son, Jesus, in a life-long relationship, and to see His Greatness within all the splendor and power that He is.

It is within this ever-burning passion that I live from a place in the honor of Who He Is, and write my stories, that bears this uniquely distinctive signature to my work in every piece I create. Here, within the niche of my heart, I strive for excellence, laboring in this love to every word that God has blessed within the gifted talent and skill of my craft, and creating scenes of portrait that visually transcends the mind of that portrayal.

To this humble privilege and honor, where He deserves my very best in everything, it's my prayer that *A Lost Love* shall touch the souls of countless readers. To everything within my heart as an author, forever I shall give honor and praise to His Name, for He Alone Is worthy. Amen!

- The Author